Legal Integration of Islam

LEGAL INTEGRATION OF ISLAM

A Transatlantic Comparison

CHRISTIAN JOPPKE

JOHN TORPEY

HARVARD UNIVERSITY PRESS
Cambridge, Massachusetts
London, England
2013

Library of Congress Cataloging-in-Publication Data

Joppke, Christian.
Legal integration of Islam : a transatlantic comparison /
Christian Joppke and John Torpey.
p. cm.
Includes bibliographical references and index.
ISBN 978-0-674-07284-8 (alk. paper)
1. Legal polycentricity—Europe. 2. Legal polycentricity—North America.
3. Islamic law—Europe. 4. Islamic law—North America.
I. Torpey, John, 1959– II. Title.
K236.J67 2013
340.9094—dc23   2012038238

*For our children, who know something
of the complexities of integration*

Contents

Legal Integration of Islam

Introduction

Neutrality, Liberalism, and Islam Integration in Europe and America

THIS BOOK'S earliest incarnation was entitled "State Neutrality and Accommodating Islam in Western Europe and North America" (Joppke and Torpey 2006). It is worth revisiting what we originally set out to do because the final product that lies before you is different, we believe, in not merely idiosyncratic ways.

As students of the nation-state and its transformations in a rapidly changing world, we set out to compare and contrast institutional responses to religious diversity, especially the one religion that for better or worse has received more attention than any other in recent years: Islam. So we are no exception to the bandwagon of macro-sociologists and political comparativists who had previously busied themselves with migration, citizenship, multiculturalism, etc., but who finally arrived at the subject of religion, more precisely of Islam.

What is the added value of this work to the literature on Islam and Muslims in the West, which has exploded in the past few years? Let us try to answer this question by highlighting what we seek to accomplish in the following chapters:

- to offer a dynamic account of institutional responses to Islam in several major Western countries, with a focus on the role of liberalism in this process;

- to show the centrality of the legal process in Islam and Muslim integration;
- to provide a transatlantic comparative perspective.

Liberalism and Changing Forms of Stateness

When we embarked on the project, now over half a decade ago, much of the literature on Islam in the West was about Muslims themselves, their views, actions, organizations, etc. This proclivity was visible at the time in two works with diametrically opposed messages: one that depicted confrontational "claims-making" by Muslim (among other migrant) organizations in Western Europe (Koopmans et al. 2005; see also Statham et al. 2005) and another that found a much less belligerent middle-class leadership among Western European Muslims (Klausen 2005).

The first work with a more institution- and state-focused perspective and from an explicitly comparative angle was Joel Fetzer and Christopher Soper's *Muslims and the State in Britain, France, and Germany* (2005), which used a social movement toolkit of "resource mobilization" and "political opportunity structures" to account for different patterns in the accommodation[1] of Islam across three Western European countries. Though informative and innovative in many ways, this work, in our view, suffers from a too-static view of "church-state regimes," some of which are said to be better suited than others for accommodating Islam. In predictable order, Fetzer and Soper claim that the British are the best of the lot, the French, of course, the worst, and the Germans somewhere in the middle. In our view, this account does not do justice to changes that these church-state regimes underwent as they encountered Islam, and above all it underrates these regimes' overall inclusive and integrative characteristics that are more noteworthy than internal variations in their "goodness" at including Muslims in their societies.

Although a focus on state responses to religious diversity is no longer as new as it may have been just a few years ago,[2] what still strikes us as not so common is to take the accommodation of Islam as a "window into changing forms of stateness," as we announced, somewhat grandly, in our initial project outline (Joppke and Torpey 2006: 2). Our central hypothesis was the following:

> Current conflicts surrounding religious claims by Muslim immigrants and ethnics, such as veiling in public schools, show that the contemporary state has difficulties in privileging the substantive life forms of the majority over

those of ethno-religious minorities. The state is less and less substantive nation-state, expression of a historically particular, bounded collectivity, and more and more procedural post-national state, in which the privileging of one group over another group, even when the former constitutes the majority (i.e., the nation), becomes subject to the charge of discrimination. The major project goal is to examine . . . the *transformation from substantive nation-state to procedural post-national state* . . . by investigating the case of accommodating Islam. . . . A key mechanism of this transformation is the legal system, especially higher courts that protect individual religious liberties and also push for equality in the state's treatment of organized religion.

The centrality of the legal system in integrating Islam is the one continuity that cannot be emphasized too firmly, though its workings are less straightforward and one-directional than originally assumed. But everything else in this statement needed serious rethinking, to say the least. But let us first try to define the main terms. The "procedural post-national state" would be one that is equidistant to majority culture and to minority cultures. More precisely, we sought to array "state neutrality" against "multicultural recognition" as the quintessential liberal state response to religious as much as any cultural diversity (following Joppke 2007b). There is, of course, nothing new or surprising about "neutrality," which is the classic solution to religious conflict in the early modern European state; indeed, neutrality is more or less tantamount to liberalism itself.

Less obvious and more controversial, however, was the idea that neutrality would widen from its original and narrowly religious orientation to a broader "ethical neutrality" (Huster 2002) that would force the liberal state to distance itself from all substantive (not only religious) ways of life, including that of the majority, and to give equal standing to minority cultures. Far from "recognizing" any of those cultures, as in the multicultural prescription, the state would stand equally aloof of all of them. As we still submit, with Stefan Huster (2002: 641), the problem of "recognition" is that "each state declaration of the intrinsic value, say, of homosexual partnership would be an affront to the religious convictions of those that reject this way of life, and vice versa." Instead, to abstain from value judgments and thus to be "neutral" is the adequate way for the liberal state to deal with cultural difference at large.

However, as we see it now, this vision of "ethical neutrality" is more germane to the legal than to the political process, more characteristic of the refined casuistry of constitutional law than the populist temptations of democratic politics. Neutrality's high-water mark was the German Constitutional Court's famous Crucifix decision of 1995 (given due attention by Huster 2002: ch. 3), which told the Bavarian state that it could not exhibit the symbols of Christianity in its classrooms and that forcing non- or other-believing pupils to "learn under the Cross" violated the state's neutrality. But the German high court's decision has since been superseded by the European Court of Human Rights' 2011 decision in *Lautsi v. Italy*, which allowed the Italian state to do just what the German court had denied to the Bavarian state, on the assumption that the crucifix was not an expression of religion (as the German court had argued) but of national culture and identity. Obviously there is no unambiguous legal-constitutional march toward a distancing of states from their national cultures; on the contrary, judged by the European Court of Human Rights' *Lautsi* decision and related policy developments, European states have recently been moving in the exact opposite direction, and maybe reasonably so, as long as the concerns of minority cultures are not simply brushed aside in the process.

There are two problems with an expansive understanding of "neutrality" that inspired our entry into the study of Islam integration. The first is to equate religion with culture. T. S. Eliot once said that "no culture has appeared or developed except together with a religion," but that the relation between the two is "so difficult that I am not sure I grasp it . . . except in flashes" (quoted in Parekh 2000: 350, fn.1). Let us nevertheless try. Though religion and culture are deeply amalgamated in the real world, they are still to be distinguished. Religion, at least in its "post-axial" form,[3] is propositional and involves belief, and hence it is in some sense voluntary and imbued with moral choice that rules out other choices.[4] By contrast, there is much less of choice in matters of culture, at least if anthropologically conceived as a "system of meaning and significance" that "encompasses more or less the whole of human life" (Parekh 2000: 143). In this sense, culture is more about dispositions, ways of being, than about propositions and truth claims. One could even argue that "the big selling point of cultural identity . . . is that cultures are essentially equal," as Walter Benn Michaels (2006: 176) put it rather flippantly. Disagreement with other beliefs is inherent in belief itself, but to reject other cultures in their totality[5] has the smell of bigotry or racism, as it rejects a way of being and thus devalues people simply because of who or what they "are."

A related and more rigorous way of formulating the distinction between religion and culture is to describe religious beliefs as "justificatory structures," providing "guidance about how to live," whereas cultures are merely conventions: "'culture' is a descriptive, ethnographic category not a normative one" (Scheffler 2007: 120). That religion and culture are different is perhaps most compellingly revealed in that most distinctly religious act, "conversion." Olivier Roy deems conversion central to a whole host of "new religious movements" that thrive precisely on distinguishing sharply between religion and culture: "One doesn't convert to a culture, one adopts it gradually, or one leaves it. The suddenness of conversion clearly marks the disjunction between culture and religion" (Roy 2008: 52).

We do not claim to have resolved what a mind much larger than ours could not grasp "except in flashes." All we want to suggest is that in some sense religion and culture are different things—after all, no one ever seriously suggested that both are the same. If that much is agreed, this has implications for state neutrality. Neutrality is a possible, perhaps even required stance with respect to religion, because the decision of whether to believe is only for the individual to decide, unless we violate her fundamental freedoms.[6] In contrast, neutrality is neither possible nor morally required with respect to culture, where one is the way one is by way of historical fact, with no claim that any specific way of life is closer to truth. As all states are historical formations, different here from there, why should they now deny this fact, in a false and politically hypercorrect overgeneralization of neutrality that may be appropriate for dealing with the fact of religion but not of culture? Samuel Scheffler has thus plausibly argued that, as "a country is a contingent historical formation" (2007: 113), the state "cannot avoid coercing citizens into preserving a national culture of some kind" (p. 111).

Interestingly, when the Bavarian and Italian governments were forced to defend the privileged display of Christian insignia in public schools, they argued, however implausible one may find it, that this was the privileging of a tradition, and thus of a culture rather than of a religion, as it might appear at first sight. The government of Bavaria, for instance, responded to the Federal Constitutional Court's outlawing of the crucifix with this new paragraph in its education law: "Considering the historical and cultural formation of Bavaria, a cross has to be posited in every classroom. . . . In case of opposition, a just balance *(gerechter Ausgleich)* has to be found, which respects the will of the majority as far as possible" (Article 7.3 of the amended Bavarian Education Law, quoted in Huster 2002: 243). One may doubt whether it is possible to demote the central symbol of Christianity from religious to merely cultural symbol, and thus to secularize it, which seems to be a contradiction in terms. But if, indeed, the crucifix were a cultural symbol, neutrality would not be an appropriate stance. This is because, as Will Kymlicka (1995) has trenchantly argued, "benign neglect"—that is, "neutrality"—is possible with respect to religion but not culture: "The analogy between religion and culture is mistaken. . . . The state can (and should) replace religious oaths in courts with secular oaths, but it cannot replace the use of English in courts with no language"

(p. 111). Note that Kymlicka thus arrives at a defense of both the (liberal) nationalism of the majority and multiculturalism for the minorities.

The second problem with an expansive reading of state neutrality is more empirical than conceptual: it conveys too passive a view of the liberal state's role in its encounter with Islam and in its responses to Muslim immigration. As Jeremy Waldron pointed out, neutrality presupposes a "contest" between two or more parties and focuses attention on a "third party," an umpire, who is to be "neutral" (1989: 63). This makes for an anodyne, legalistic view of the state, as a court writ large. But the state is also a political state, the embodiment of democracy, which in a modern context entails majority rule. In this respect, the state cannot be blindfolded for the sake of justice: its eyes must be wide open for majority preferences. In fact, many of the responses to Islam by Western states, some of them reviewed in the following pages, from Ontario's suppression of shari'a law to France's prohibition of the burqa, but also most of these states' attempts at nationalizing Islam and furthering the "civic integration" of Muslim immigrants, could only with some difficulty be interpreted in terms of neutrality. Instead, Western states have proactively defended liberalism against a perceived challenge to it, confirming Charles Taylor's (1992) felicitous characterization of liberalism as, also, a "fighting creed."

In light of these conceptual and empirical difficulties, we shifted emphasis from "neutrality" to "liberalism" as the central engagement in the Western encounter with Islam. This is not necessarily a conceptual shift, as both notions closely overlap, have a common intellectual and political history, and denote the same institutional realities. However, the term "neutrality" conveys the image of a blank slate and of being passive and aloof, which is not helpful in understanding the frictions between certain Western ideals and principles and those of Islam (more precisely, its politically articulated and visible versions), of which a good many will appear in the chapters that follow. "Neutrality," as two philosophers argued, is "an instrumental value, rather than a fundamental one" (Goodin and Reeve 1989: 4). Yet this would not be an apt description of "liberalism," especially today. Liberalism has always been marked by a tension between being thinly procedural and being substantively ethical (Gray 2000). Recently, however, it has taken on decidedly ethical, if not repressive and exclusivist, connotations, thus endangering the "liberal" core of liberalism itself. This is a development that cannot be well captured with the bloodless term "neutrality" (see Joppke 2007a, 2013b).

In sum, we had to discard our initial hypothesis that the confrontation with Islam would give rise to the "neutral" state that stands equidistant from the culture both of majority and of minorities. This thesis never made sense, on conceptual grounds alone. Empirically, it was disproved by the tendency of contemporary states to more proactively embrace and protect the majority culture, if mostly in terms of a liberalism that is imposed on all, or at least expected to be shared by all, Muslim minorities included.

Constitutional Politics

As indicated by its title, the main ambition of this work is to demonstrate the importance of the legal process in Western states' engagement with Islam. However, legal decision making is not quite as unsullied by politics as it first appeared to us. Both the centrality of legal integration and the countervailing force of democratic politics are especially visible in Europe. In France, the Conseil d'Etat as well as the entire guild of constitutional lawyers have been the main opponents and obstacles to the political state's religious liberty restriction in the recent law banning the burqa. In Germany, we recount a veritable "long march" of Islam through the courts, which has been amazingly successful, working against a certain trend of the German state (especially in some conservative Länder) of defining itself as parochially "Christian-Occidental."

The accommodation of Islam is a prominent example of "judicialized politics," which its foremost chronicler in Europe defined as follows: "Today judges legislate, parliaments adjudicate, and the boundaries separating law and politics—the legislative and judicial functions—are little more than academic constructions" (Stone Sweet 2000: 130). The reason for the prominent involvement of the judiciary in accommodating Islam is that the latter involves individual rights, especially religious rights and family rights, which enjoy constitutional status in a liberal democracy. Rights, as Ronald Dworkin (1984) put it memorably, are "trumps" that the individual can hold against the wishes of the majority in society. Rights in the strict sense are anti-majoritarian: they constrain the democratic process, and courts have the mandate to check the democratic lawmaker and the administrative state for their compliance with these rights-based constraints.

To the degree that legal actors take the lead in judicialized politics, and that the latter thus becomes properly anti-majoritarian, it is rendering obsolete a key tenet in the nations and nationalism literature: that of the state being "owned" by the nation whose name the state most of the time carries. Legally dominated, judicialized politics tends to dissolve the band between state and nation—the most prominent example being the afore-mentioned German Constitutional Court's banning of the crucifix from Bavarian schools in the mid-1990s.[7]

However, to repeat, it would be naive to assume, as we initially did, that this would lead to the rise of a "procedural post-national state." This is because judicialized politics is still politics. The latter involves other than legal actors, with the political state resisting its disempowerment by "un-elected" judges. So there is always the possibility of backlash, a prominent example of which is the making of the French burqa law in 2010 (see Chapter 2). This political backlash, in turn, affects the legal process. As the German experience suggests (see Chapter 3), different types of legal claims are differently receptive to political pressures. The collective claim to be treated equally to other religions, though not fully realized until the present day, has been a robust constant throughout Germany's intensifying Islam debate; it even gained ground as the campaign for "nationalizing" or "domesticating" Islam grew stronger. By contrast, another type of legal minority claim, which is individual exemptions from general laws that are seen as conflicting with religious precepts, has been more vulnerable to political considerations, and courts now quote integration concerns and the need to fight "parallel societies" as justification for being less forthcoming in granting exemption requests than in the past. In short, legal equality claims are more robust than legal exemption claims (we thus partially confirm Koenig 2010: 155–157).

An interesting recent study of the dynamics of immigrant and ethnic minority rights in Europe dismissed the role of courts in explaining a general trend toward the expansion of these rights "of others" (Koopmans, Michalowski, and Waibel 2012). Comparing broadly conceived "immigrant citizenship rights" (which include "cultural and religious rights" and seven other types of right) in ten Western European countries over the last three decades, the study found instead that other factors (especially the strength of right-wing populism and the size of immigrant electorates) better explain why in most countries most of these rights expanded over the observed time period while in a few others they did not. To demonstrate the irrelevance of courts in this process, the authors point to the fact that the three European countries with the strongest rights provisions (Sweden, Britain, and the Netherlands until 2002) have only weak or no judicial review at all. Instead, these countries became so inclusive of immigrants because of the weakness of the populist right and large shares of immigrant and ethnic minority voters putting pressure on established parties— and if the Netherlands diverged after 2002, this was due to the Pim Fortuyn phenomenon and the meteoric rise of the populist right at that moment.

Not pulling a punch, the authors dismiss most previous works that have emphasized the role of courts in the expansion of immigrant rights as "anecdotal" and based on "arguments-by-example."

Although these findings and the approach utilized for arriving at them are important and value-adding, they do not prove insufficient or wrong how and what we argue in this book. With respect to form, the large-N, multivariate approach does not render obsolete the small-N, in-depth case analysis that we engage in here; the former is not better knowledge but other knowledge, and there is a place for both in the social scientific enterprise. To mention only one shortcoming of the large-N approach, the need to standardize forced Koopmans and his coauthors (2012) to lump together under the category "cultural and religious rights" many a measure that is not a "right" but a "concession" on the part of a fair-minded administration, such as separate "Muslim" sections in cemeteries or Islamic religious programs in public television and radio, to mention only a few. It is then easy game to discount the importance of courts, if many of these things do not involve them in the first.

But more important, with respect to substance, our point, to repeat, is not that courts trump legislatures. That would be plainly wrong, even on the small range of cases and evidence considered in this book. In fact, one might well argue the opposite: that in nearly all national cases considered here, courts in important respects were trumped by legislatures. In France, for instance, a long period of judicially licensed toleration of the Islamic headscarf was ended, first, by the 2004 law prohibiting the headscarf in schools (see Joppke 2009: ch. 2) and, second, by the 2010 burqa law that we discuss in Chapter 2. In Germany, as mentioned, the recent backtracking of courts from exempting Muslims from certain state laws is clearly dictated by politics, and in our discussion of ritual slaughter we will show a German parliament neutralizing by way of a constitutional amendment a court-ordered exemption that was deemed cruel on animals (see Chapter 3). Only in Canada has there not as yet been a case of parliamentary backlash against too strident courts, but then you never know, and perhaps the Bouchard-Taylor Commission on "reasonable accommodation" is a (lame-duck) equivalent (see Chapter 4). In the United States, the entire picture is backward, because here courts restricted religious liberty rights in the early 1990s that were then restored by Congress, so that one also cannot assume an automaticity of "liberal" courts versus "restrictive" legislatures.[8] The picture is complex. Considering again Europe, most Islam decisions by the European Court of Human Rights over the past decade simply ratified the restrictions that some national parliaments and governments had imposed earlier on Islam, the argument being that national governments were better placed than a remote European court to decide on the sensitive state-religion relationship (see Evans 2006; Danchin 2011).

So if we investigate the constitutional politics of Muslim and Islam integration, the outcome is not predetermined. But although courts do not always win, sometimes do not even pick up a fight, or fight on the "wrong" side, the legal-constitutional constraints articulated and mobilized by them are still felt in the very attempt by the political state to circumvent them. Not anything goes, and, stated as a counterfactual, without the (possibility of) intervention by courts things would be worse. But things are not bad, not least due to the legal factor depicted in the following chapters.

Transatlantic Perspective

The third and perhaps most obvious contribution of this work is its transatlantic perspective. Of course, we are not the first to compare Muslim and Islam integration in the United States and Europe. Jocelyn Cesari (2004) first did it, in her valuable overview of Muslim politics, religious practices, and Islamic reform trends on both sides of the Atlantic. By the same token, we bring her empirical picture, by now almost a decade old, more up to date. Moreover, we provide a sharper focus on the legal-institutional dimension of Islam integration (and, conversely, a lesser attention to Muslims themselves, whose beliefs, practices, and organizations fared much more centrally than the legal-institutional dimension in Cesari's work).

We admittedly picked the usual suspects, and yet another look at France and Germany may elicit a bored yawn, at best. Still, we hope the comparison between Western Europe and North America—both the United States and its often-neglected neighbor, Canada—is a value-adding undertaking in the form proposed here.

In particular, the transatlantic comparison allows us to tackle and further elaborate on a striking difference that had already been noticed by Cesari (2004: 2), who contrasted the "conciliatory" approach to Islam in the United States with the "more conflictual and hostile" climate prevailing in Europe. One could sharpen it as a paradox: although it is the United States that has waged a War on Terror, which made it (along with Israel) the most hated country in the Muslim world, the Great Satan in Islamist demonology, American society has up to this point not known any particular problem with integrating Muslim immigrants and, even after 2001, is frequently seen by Muslims as more accommodating than European societies.[9] *Grosso modo,* the same holds true for Canada, despite flickers surrounding multiculturalism.

Aristide Zolberg and Long Litt Woon (1999) argued memorably in their influential United States–Europe comparison that "Spanish" in the United States is like "Islam" in Europe—that is, the main cultural integration problem in the respective societies. This captures an element of truth, but it is incomplete. Zolberg's key point is that European states are Christian states, while only the American state is neutral with respect to religion, and that this is what accounts for the different degrees of friction concerning Islam on either side of the Atlantic. This diagnosis already has difficulties to deal with the case of "laicist" France, which appears more devoutly secular than latently Christian. But its main problem is that it is too static and too negative with respect to Europe. On the one side, it obscures the fact that it is precisely the encounter with Islam that is forcing European states to dissociate themselves from their Christian pedigree, at least to a degree, as a result of which they come to look a bit more like the universalistic states of North America. This process is never complete, and it is marred by political backlash, perhaps even a reasonable embracing of one's historical heritage, but it is still an undeniable, mostly court-driven reality. On the other side, to be "Christian" is not necessarily an obstacle to Islam integration, as a certain reading of the *Lautsi* decision (see Chapter 6; also Joppke 2013a) but also as the case of "Anglican" yet unabashedly "multicultural" and Muslim-friendly Britain suggest (for the latter, see Joppke 2009: 88–89).

Moreover, Chapters 2 and 3, on France and Germany, respectively, suggest that the institutional accommodation of Islam in Europe has been more successful than is suggested by Zolberg and Litt Woon (1999; and by many other American analyses of the European scene, such as Scott 2008 or Nussbaum 2008). In fact, the problem with Muslim integration in Europe is not in the first a failure of institutionally accommodating Islam; instead, the root problem is the sustained socioeconomic exclusion of second- and third-generation postcolonial and guest-worker immigrants, who in their majority happen to be of Muslim origin (see Crul and Mollenkopf 2012). Socioeconomic exclusion, not a failure to accommodate Islam as religion, is why the French *banlieues* exploded in 2005 (see International Crisis Group 2006) and why many Muslim youngsters have tuned in to globally politicized Islam, sadly sometimes including its terrorist variant (see Leiken 2011). Of course, an account of the socioeconomic integration failure of Muslim ethnics in Europe is outside the purview of this book. However, a demonstration of the relative successes of institutional accommodation, especially through the legal route, shows by implication that religious discrimination against Islam cannot be the reason for deficient Muslim integration in Europe.

In sum, the comparison with North America brings into sharp profile the sociodemographic underpinnings of the so-called Islam problem in Europe, which tends to be obscured when looking at Europe alone. The fact that the vast majority of North American immigrants are Christian, and that the small number of Muslims who still arrive are on average better educated and better earning than Americans and Canadians, is more important for explaining the lesser degree of conflict surrounding Islam overseas than an alleged superiority of their institutions or their more welcoming cultures (all of which they are, but for immigrants in general, not just Muslims).

Overview

Precisely because we picked the usual suspects, especially on the European side, we abstain from giving comprehensive surveys on Islam and Muslims in each country. To avoid repetition and competition with the vastly more resourceful Islam-in-the-West industry, we decided to focus on particular aspects, even episodes, of Islam accommodation in each country, which, however, we deem representative of broader patterns and reflective of "where the action is."

In France, home of Western Europe's largest Muslim population by far, the most significant problem associated with its "laicist" regime of excluding religion from an expansively defined public sphere is the risk of restricting religious liberties. This risk is very evident in the burqa law of 2010, whose political creation, against the legal odds, is the topic of Chapter 2. The curious matter of this law is that it happened against the backdrop of a certainly conflict-riddled but overall successful process of Islam accommodation in France, which was not meant to be rolled back by it. On the contrary, however implausibly, the burqa law is fashioned as dealing with a political, not a religious, fact—namely, a sectarian-fundamentalist practice that is not prescribed by Islamic core doctrine and is not condoned by the moderate majority of France's estimated five million Muslims.

As we point out in Chapter 3, despite a certain restrictive trend since the late 1990s, there is less of a problem with religious liberty restrictions in Germany, which upholds an even more protective regime for religious freedoms than one can find in the United States (see the comparison by Eberle 2004). In Germany, the bigger issue is to treat organized Islam on an equal footing with the historically established religions (Roman Catholicism, Protestantism, and Judaism), which enjoy public status within a corporatist church-state regime. But the equality claim is not rebutted in principle but contingently, and on thinning empirical grounds. And, as we show, a rights-focused reinterpretation of corporatist inclusion is about to liberalize this church-state regime, rendering it more flexible and inclusive. This creates the odd prospect of organized Islam, which in Germany is not a moderate affair at all, figuring as a "cooperation partner" of the state in fulfilling important public functions, such as education and regulating the media.

In Chapter 4, we connect the story of Islam in Canada with a larger theme in our transatlantic tour d'horizon, which is the decline of multiculturalism wherever Muslims and Islam are moving to the center of a country's integration debate. Notwithstanding Canada's status as the Mecca of multicultural ideas and policies, the integration of Muslims has generated a major challenge to this mode of incorporating minorities even there. Muslims in Canada have sought to extend the use of shari'a-based adjudication of family law matters, and this has provoked a backlash by both Muslims and non-Muslims concerned especially about the consequences of such institutions for women's rights. Efforts to limn the meaning of "reasonable accommodation" in Quebec and elsewhere have been forced to confront the fact that Muslims' demands have widely been found to be "unreasonable." The flagship of liberal multiculturalism has found itself trimming its sails and tacking more closely toward the reaffirmation of individual rights, to the (mostly exaggerated) degree that the latter had ever been out of the picture. Surely that change only confirms the direction that integration policies have already taken elsewhere in the West.

In Chapter 5, we depict Islam in the United States as "the dog that did not bark." In yet another demonstration of American exceptionalism, the United States is the one country in our transatlantic selection that did not have a major Islam debate with significant legal-political battles. This fact unavoidably makes this chapter less focused on legal issues and more of a spread than the others. The American case is perplexing to Europeans but also to Canadians, because it combines a vigorously "hands-off" posture on the part of the state with regard to religion and a deep constitutional-legal affirmation of the right to be religious in (almost) whatever way one chooses. During the long period when "Islam" was mainly a creed associated with native blacks, the main legal question was whether it constituted a religion at all. One distinctive aspect of the American story is that for a long time it was not clear that the Nation of Islam was really Muslim at all, as opposed to a political ideology. More recently, however, Islam has arrived in the baggage of various immigrant groups and has increasingly come to be seen as a foreign import—especially since 9/11. Yet the more firmly established its credentials as religion, the more clearly it has had to be protected by courts as a legitimate form of activity and expression. There have certainly been outbursts of popular disdain for Islam and for Muslims, but insofar as the practices of Muslims have been adjudicated by courts, Islam is, as three U.S. presidents have by now affirmed, an American religion.

Chapter 6 weaves together the main threads of our transatlantic comparison, and in particular addresses the challenge of Islam for the identity of liberal states. This is surely no small way of ending a small book. We claim that problems surrounding Muslim integration have been central to the current retreat from multiculturalism and turn to a more "muscular" and identity-tinged form of liberalism. However, "muscular liberalism" is perhaps the more serious threat to liberalism than Islam could ever be. An interesting and surprising possibility to escape the dilemma of mutually reinforcing fundamentalisms, Islamic and liberal, is the embracing of a Christian identity, understood as a more relaxed attitude toward national culture and history. At least, so we suggest in reference to a controversial recent European Court of Human Rights decision, *Lautsi v. Italy* (2011).

NOT to feed wrong expectations, we wish to underline that this book is not about Islam but about liberal state responses to Islam. Except for a small digression in Chapter 6, we remain agnostic as to what "Islam" is: threat to liberal societies (as eloquently argued by Caldwell 2009) or commensurable with liberal principles (as equally eloquently argued by March 2009 or Fadel 2008, to name just a few). Liberal institutions are precisely designed to remain indifferent to the creeds or "comprehensive doctrines" (Rawls 1993) to be processed by them. As this book demonstrates, liberal agnosticism is notoriously imperfect. The challenge of Islam has even triggered a powerful trend to abandon it in favor of an ethical, "muscular" liberalism. But to abstain from evaluating religious doctrine has still been the joint regulatory ideal or "ought to" as liberal states on both sides of the Atlantic struggled with accommodating Islam. To stick to this ideal, which is what "neutrality" is all about, is as such a stunning achievement if one considers the society-, even civilization-making powers of religion, Christianity and Islam alike.

By the same token, this small book with a narrow focus must disappoint the more sociologically minded reader who expects to hear the "voices" of Muslims themselves, as they struggled—most often successfully—to bend their minority beliefs and practices to not just other-religious but thoroughly secular societies and institutions.[10] Ideally, one should bring into the picture mutual accommodations and approximations between Islam and liberal host societies, as John Bowen (2010: ch. 8) has masterfully done in his ethnography of French banlieue Islam.[11] Our focus on the legal-institutional dimension certainly falls short of this, in capturing mostly one, the more formal aspect of reality. However limited this reality is, "reality" it is nonetheless. Whether the effort was worthwhile remains for the reader to judge.

WESTERN EUROPE

Selecting two North American and two Western European cases of Islam accommodation allows comparisons at two levels: across two continents and within each of them. At the intercontinental level, what distinguishes Europe from North America is that, in the former, state and church have been competing for supremacy over the centuries. In the process, "the state ... has gradually assumed many of the historic functions performed by the medieval Church," from education to welfare and the creation of a common culture (Whitman 2008: 90). As a result, there is a tendency in Europe for the state "to constitute itself as a kind of updated, secularized Church," while in turn church and religion have lost much of their "moral force" and "political energy" (pp. 95–96). New religions, especially Islam, whose charismatic edges have not similarly been cut and which resist being pushed into a "private" corner, meet "a certain kind of intolerance" in Europe (p. 99). By contrast, in America, which experienced no similar competition between church and state, the state remained minimal and religion never lost its vitality. As the state does not drive religion out of public life, new religions are "likely to experience daily life in the United States as more tolerant" (p. 100).

At the same time, James Q. Whitman (2008) sees both the European and American regimes as joint variants of the demand, which typifies the "Western Christian tradition" generally, that state and church be separated "in *some* way" (p. 90). Unlike more flag-waving American observers (like Nussbaum 2008, 2012), he wisely declines to proclaim one (the American) as the "'correct' standard" to be followed by all countries (p. 98). After all, there is a downside to the American church-state variant, which may be more tolerant of new religions but in which there is a notorious infusion of "religious rhetoric" (p. 86) into politics and even the court-room, in a manner that turns off the European observer (representative for many, see Habermas and Derrida 2005).

Whitman's analysis is a brilliant first stab at a complex matter, com-mendable for refusing to celebrate the American while denigrating the European model of separating church and state. On the negative side, how-ever, Whitman (2008) reads the "northern continental" model of church-state separation in Europe strongly in light of the French case. Germany—where the churches enjoy public status, religion is invited to partake in public space, and the state has never pursued an aggressively secularist line—does not fit easily into this model. A more complete analysis thus demands an intracontinental level of comparison, which, indeed, may be fruitfully carried out in terms of the French and German cases.

In this section, we propose to contrast France and Germany as examples of church-state relations that reveal the limits of "excluding" and of "in-cluding" Islam, respectively. This requires explication. When assessing the accommodation of Islam (as of any new religion that encounters histori-cally established relations between state and religion), one must distinguish between an individual-rights and an organization-level or corporatist track (see Joppke 2009: 17–20).[1] This reflects the fact that religion is practiced by individuals yet is also dependent on collective organization, because rituals must be practiced in common. The two tracks of inclusion have dif-ferent speeds and intensity. The individual track kicks into gear immediately and uncompromisingly, reflecting the strong religious liberty protections that are guaranteed in a liberal-constitutional state. By contrast, the orga-nization track is slow and asymmetrical, reflecting the historical compro-mises that had to be made as the state emancipated itself from the stran-glehold of the church.

The French and German ways of accommodating Islam show interest-ing strengths and weaknesses in both respects. For two decades now, France has experienced multiple *affaires de foulard,* which resulted in sig-nificant religious liberty restrictions. But this period has also seen, with the active help of the French state, the creation of a national umbrella organi-zation, the Conseil Français du Culte Musulman (CFCM). However inef-ficient and internally embattled this troubled federation may be, in principle it puts organized Islam on a par with the historically established religions of France (Christianity and Judaism). This suggests that the main threat posed by the French religion-state regime is that it may restrict religious liberty. At the same time, there is no hesitation about treating Islam as organized religion on a footing equal to that of the historical religions—which, in a way, is easy enough because excluded from public space they both are, the historical and the new religions (see Walter 2006: ch. 6). Certainly, Islam still suffers from a factually unequal status, visible above all in the lack of adequate prayer space and a paucity of Islamic schools. But this is not legal inequality or anything inherent in the logic of the French regime (pp. 178–185).

By contrast, Germany has surely had its *Kopftuchaffäre* (headscarf affair), leading to a religious liberty restriction, but only concerning teachers, privileged *Beamte* (civil servants), with a legal obligation to uphold the state's neutrality vis-à-vis religion. In sharp contrast to the situation in France, a blanket prohibition on religious dress among schoolchildren, not to mention all citizens, would be unthinkable here. At the same time, organized Islam is stubbornly denied the public status of *Körperschaft des öffentlichen Rechts* (public law corporation), which marks it as inferior to the religions historically recognized in Germany. This lack of recognition, as we shall see, is not on principled but factual grounds and ever more difficult to uphold. But it still suggests that the main challenge for the German religion-state regime, which readily binds organized religion into public space, is to integrate Islam on an equal basis to the historical religions, and this despite the fact that individual religious freedoms are more strongly protected than in most other states in the world.

Liberty and equality are the lodestars of liberalism, and they are differently heeded in the French and German modes of accommodating Islam. But this is not to fall back into a static view of church-state regimes as working out in only one direction and as being unaffected by the process of integrating newcomers. On the contrary, as we shall see, these regimes, and the images of the state associated with them, are themselves affected and revised as they encounter Islam. In France, the 2010 burqa law shows *ex negativo* the high legal obstacles to restricting even this most extreme sartorial expression of Islam, which is adopted by only the tiniest minority of Muslims, and on which the last legal word may not yet have been spoken. And the call for a *laïcité positive*, which does not reject religion but embraces it as a substitute for an exhausted republicanism, and which comes from the mouth of no one less than the previous president of the Republic (Sarkozy 2004), betrays a very un-republican move to deploy religion as a source of cohesion in society. In Germany, meanwhile, the old corporatist *Staatskirchenrecht* (state law of the churches) has been challenged by a new rights-focused *Religionsverfassungsrecht* (constitutional law of religion), which calls into question the privileges of the historically established religions from the point of view of equal religious liberty rights. And Germany's own comparatively muted *Kopftuchaffäre* has at least opened up the possibility of a French-style distancing of the state from religion, and hence of a "separating" rather than "open" neutrality.[2] Admittedly, this possibility is overshadowed by a more potent tendency of the "Christian-Occidental State" to reassert itself as a touchstone of law and policy, if mostly at the subfederal Länder level (see Joppke 2009: 62–65).

While each book has to ravel in novelty, the French and German stories still confirm a long-established pattern and insight connected to it. There are only two ways of dealing liberally with religion, either to drive all of them out of public space or to bind them into public space on equal terms. France and Germany still stand for these opposite options of excluding and including, respectively, each equally legitimate from a liberal point of view. However, each solution is also unstable and fraught with conflict and contradictions, of which the following two chapters will try to capture some of the more important.

CHAPTER TWO

Limits of Excluding

The French Burqa Law of 2010

IN JUNE 2009, addressing both houses of French Parliament *(Congrès)* in a historic Versailles venue, French President Nicolas Sarkozy de-nounced the burqa[1]—an Islamic garment covering the entire body and face—as "a sign of subjugation [and] of debasement" that is "not welcome on French territory."[2] One day later, a parliamentary commission led by Communist Party deputy André Gerin was established to "review the practice of wearing the burqa and the niqab by certain Muslim women . . . on the national territory," with the mandate to "better understand the problem and to find ways to fight against this affront to individual liber-ties."[3] What became known as the "Burqa Commission" would notably not recommend a "general and absolute prohibition of the integral veil [*voile intégral*][4] in public space," even though such prohibition had clearly been the driving motivation of its initiators (Assemblée Nationale 2010: 187). Overriding two negative recommendations by the Conseil d'Etat, France's highest administrative court, and in defiance of practically the entire legal guild of France, the National Assembly nevertheless passed a law in July 2010 that prohibits "the dissimulation of the face in public space." Although Belgian legislators quickly followed suit, and countries like the Netherlands and Switzerland are considering such a law, the French were still the first to consider and carry through this hitherto most extreme restriction of Islam in Western lands.

One can read this outcome in various ways. The most obvious response is outrage about the restriction of elementary liberties, not just to practice one's religion freely but also concerning what to wear in the street. What the *New York Times* said about the rather modest, only partial prohibitions that the Burqa Commission had earlier proposed in lieu of a total burqa ban is even more valid for the far more drastic "general and absolute" prohibition that became law half a year later: "French politicians seem willfully blind to the violation of individual liberties," practicing a kind of reverse Talibanism.[5]

A second, perhaps more apposite response is ridicule. How can one not shake one's head about the disproportionate measure of passing a law to reign in an ultramarginal practice by less than one-tenth of a percent of France's Muslim population, and for which a number of administrative restrictions already existed that made French law tougher in this respect than most other jurisdictions in Europe (see Conseil d'Etat 2010: 11–15)? If one of the main instigators of the burqa campaign, André Gerin, ignoring the tiny numbers laid out to his commission by no less than the interior minister himself, deemed French society in the grip of "Talibanization" and drowning in a "marée noire" (oil slick) of dark Muslim veils, this was moral panic, better understood in psycho-pathological than politico-rational terms. When assessing the "collateral damage" done to France in the world by its anti-burqa campaign, it is an understatement to conclude that "We are not understood in the world, not even in Europe."[6]

In this chapter, we propose a third, less obvious, reading of the French anti-burqa campaign: even though a restrictive law was passed, the legal-political debate surrounding its making spells out in fascinating detail the limits of restricting Islam in the liberal state. Indeed, equally legitimate to being astounded or outraged by the law (which we profess to be) is to recognize the significant legal-constitutional hurdles that had to be taken, or rather blithely ignored, in order to get it passed, and which may still prove fatal to it if brought to bear by the European Court of Human Rights. We concede, however, that the story to be told in the following pages cuts both ways: it demonstrates the high legal hurdles that needed to be taken and the chilling ease with which these hurdles could be taken if only the political will existed.

Institutionalization of Islam in France

This third round of French headscarf battles, after the dramatic opening shot in Creil in 1989, and after the law against the ordinary headscarf *(foulard)* (and all ostentatious religious symbols) in public schools in 2004 (for overviews, see Scott 2007; Bowen 2007; Joppke 2009: ch. 2), occurred against the backdrop of a thorough institutionalization, if not nationalization, of Islam in France. The transition from Islam in France to French Islam, which was as much the result of legal integration as of the political will of the state, had long been under way and was, in fact, never questioned by anyone who went after the burqa. Discussing a state-level campaign for "national identity" that was running parallel to the quest for restricting the burqa, Jonathan Laurence (2010: 22) puts both into perspective: "Negative rhetoric and repressive measures that have put Muslim communities on the defensive . . . belie a broader trend toward greater religious freedom and institutional representation."[7]

One also has to consider that none of the Muslim representatives testifying before the Burqa Commission, from shiny media star Tariq Ramadan to the gray suits of the Conseil Français du Culte Musulman (CFCM), had anything positive to say about the integral veil. For Ramadan, the burqa and niqab were nothing less than an "attack on the rights of women," "restriction of their liberty," and "contrary to human dignity."[8] Not unlike the president of the French Republic and the feisty apparatchiks of the Burqa Commission, the president of the CFCM called the integral veil "an extreme practice that we do not wish to see gaining ground on the national territory."[9] And the rector of the influential Paris Grand Mosque, Dalil Boubakeur, traced the niqab back to its original function of sun and desert-wind protection for the nomadic Touregs in the Sahara, adding caustically that this was "evidently not a relevant consideration in France."[10]

The coincidence of the restriction-bent French Burqa Commission and the shocking Swiss referendum prohibiting the construction of new minarets, in late November 2009, might lead one to conclude that both are made of the same cloth, that is, an all-European assault on Islam and Muslims. But that conclusion would be misleading. Certainly, if presented with the opportunity to vote on the matter, the French, like most other Europeans, might well decide as the Swiss did, if not more so.[11] Yet nowhere in Europe outside Switzerland, France included, would it be possible to put such a sensitive issue to a public test. It is instructive to look at French President Sarkozy's carefully worded response to the Swiss vote, published a week later on the front page of France's leading liberal newspaper, *Le Monde*.[12] While respecting the Swiss poll as a desperate scramble for "national identity" in a globalizing world (thus justifying his own campaign for national identity that was running parallel to, or rather undergirded, the Burqa Commission), Sarkozy nonetheless insisted that "one does not respect people if one obliges them to practice their religion in cellars or garages [*dans les caves ou dans des hangars*]."[13]

In other words: no problem with minarets and visible Islam in France. Indeed, when the new mosque of Créteil opened its doors for up to 2,000 believers in December 2008, 200 similar large mosque projects were under construction throughout France. This would add so much prayer space to the already existing 2,000 mosques that some of these, it was feared, would have to close down, considering that only an estimated minority of 20 to 30 percent of France's nearly five million Muslims attend mosque regularly.[14] Compare this concern to the alarm sounded in the 2000 report of the Haut Conseil à l'Intégration (High Council on Integration) that France had "an insufficient number" of Islamic mosques (2000: 36). Also, the days when provincial mayors were raiding mosque construction sites with bulldozers are long history (as reported in Haut Conseil à l'Intégration 2000: 37). According to a leading French and European Islam expert, "At present no town councilor would deny the right to have a mosque and nearly everywhere representatives of Muslim organizations have established relations with local authorities" (Cesari 2005: 1025). The French state has long followed the quasi-multicultural principle of "compensating" Islam for its factual disadvantages vis-à-vis the historical religions of France (Badevant-Gaudemet 2000). Concretely, this means that the French state, also intent on preempting the foreign (especially Saudi Arabian) financing of mosques, routinely circumvents the formal ban on state support for religion under the 1905 Law on the Separation of Churches and State by funding mosque construction through the *culturel* (cultural) rather than *cultuel* (religious) route; moreover, the state hands out building sites through inexpensive long-term loans of publicly owned land (so-called *bails emphéotiques*). Overall, as Sarkozy underlined in his response to the Swiss referendum, the lodestar of the French state's treatment of Islam has been to lift the latter "onto a foundation of equality with the other great religions," a process that he sees as having been completed with the creation of the CFCM during his first spell as interior minister, in 2003.[15]

However, Sarkozy also admonished his "Muslim compatriots" to practice their religion in "humble discretion," because France was a country "where the Christian civilization had left profound traces, [and] where the values of the Republic are an integral part of our national identity." Disrespecting or challenging "this heritage and these values" would "condemn to failure the establishment of Islam in France that is so necessary."[16] Invoking the Christian roots of France, however obvious and beyond question they might be, was a trademark Sarkozy provocation to the republican establishment, enamored as it is of the claptrap of *laïcité*.

What fires this latest round of Europe's protracted debate about Islam is not a questioning of its institutional accommodation, which has mostly occurred by now, and successfully at that, on the premise of formal (not always substantive) equality with the historically established religions. If one considers 1,400 years of often violent confrontation between the Christian and Muslim worlds (see Pagden 2008), this is an astonishing development, and notably not one to register in Muslim societies, where other religions (including the Christian) still face severe discrimination (see Griffith 2008). Instead, this latest round of Europe's Islam debate revolves around a highly visible practice of this religion, ever more separated from a context of immigration, and symbolized by the niqab and burqa. Both are perceived as a provocation and a mocking of the principles and values on which European societies are founded, at least today, above all that of gender equality. The issue is a visibly uncompromising Islam that is not doing its share in the "two-way process" that has by now become the standard interpretation of "integration."[17]

Interestingly, and demonstrative of the intention not to roll back but to complete the "recognition" of Islam in France, a red thread underlying the French debate over the integral veil is to expel the latter from the ambit of religion. "To reject the integral veil is to respect Islam," the forever slick immigration minister Eric Besson testified before the Burqa Commission.[18] Already in his Versailles statement, President Sarkozy had argued that "the problem of the burqa is not a religious problem, but it is a problem of the liberty [and] dignity of women. The burqa is not a religious symbol."[19] This claim was true only in the sense that the integral veil is not a religious prescription that can be found anywhere in the Quran or Sunna, the religious core texts of Islam. In this sense, it was affirmed by the Muslim representatives and Islam specialists testifying before the commission. The burqa and niqab "are not an Islamic prescription," Tariq Ramadan avowed coolly;[20] "the burqa is the most violent symbol of the oppression of women and has nothing to do with the Muslim religion, my religion," exclaimed Sihem Habchi, president of the *banlieue* feminist movement Ni Putes Ni Soumises (Neither Whores Nor Subalterns), not so coolly.[21]

However, to expel the burqa from the ambit of religion is an altogether more radical undertaking than denying its centrality to Islam. In front of the Burqa Commission, the claim that the burqa is nonreligious was made, in rather questionable detail, by the anthropologist Dounia Bouzar.[22] She correctly interpreted the "Salafist discourse" by those who propagate the burqa and niqab as "sectarian." However, its being "sectarian" ipso facto disqualified Salafism in her eyes from being "religious." This is because, argued Bouzar, the thrust of religion as indicated by the Latin root word *religare* is to "assemble" or "gather together" *(accueillir)* and not to "separate."[23] She thus made an idiosyncratic distinction between sect and religion, one that would disqualify the founders of America as lunatic politicos, not members of a religion. Indeed, the distinction between church and sect, but as different forms of religious organization, has been essential to the sociology of religion at least since Weber and Troeltsch. "[We should] treat these factions [*groupuscules*] as if they were not Muslim," Bouzar suggested at the commission's first expert hearing.[24] This strange proposition became a kind of idée fixe throughout the entire anti-burqa campaign.

Some lawmakers realized that the problem with the religious excommunication of the integral veil, if executed by the state, was also that it would force the state to "decide what religion is" and thus draw it into the "war of Gods."[25] The liberal state generally leaves the definition of religion to those who practice religion, though within limits. For altogether different reasons—namely, out of solidarity with coreligionists—a subjective definition of religion was also the stance taken by the official Muslim organizations. After stating that the integral veil was not a "religious prescription," the president of the CFCM added that it was still "a religious practice founded on a minority view" of Islam.[26] The religious disqualification of the integral veil was inconsistent, and—as we shall see—it could not be entirely maintained. It was, at best, a (perhaps hypocritical) strategy of immunizing Islam from wanting to get rough with the burqa. However, the more likely, and widely resented, effect of the whole enterprise was "stigmatizing an entire religion."[27]

The Burqa in France: Chosen and Ultramarginal

What do we know about the burqa-wearing women in France, their background, and their motivations? The interior minister, Brice Hortefeux, relying on French intelligence sources, characterized the donning of the integral veil as a "completely marginal practice among the Muslims of France," amounting to an estimated 1,900 cases in the entire country, 50 percent of them in the greater Paris (Île-de-France) area alone.[28] The majority of veiled women are young: 90 percent of them are under forty years of age, 50 percent are under thirty years. Two-thirds of them are French citizens, half of them of the second or third immigrant generation; no less than one-fourth are converts to Islam. Among the Islamic legal traditions, only the Hanbali School, whose roots lie in the Arabian Peninsula, today favors the integral veil. More concretely, most of the veil's proponents are members of Salafism, which is a largely pietistic, apolitical sect favoring a literalist reading of the Quran and Sunna, and whose adherents seek to "live like the companions of the prophet" during the seventh century in Mecca and Medina. A leading French expert estimated Salafism's total number of followers in France at between just 5,000 and 10,000 persons, dominating at most 20 to 30 of the approximately 2,000 mosques in the country.[29] Among the motivations for donning the integral veil, this expert cited a mixture of "symbolic protest," the quest for "social distinction," and—the dominant explanation in most accounts—"hyper-individualism," achieved not within but against the ethnic origin community (and thus precisely not the expression of *communautarisme* ["communalism"] that the French political elite from left to right sees in and resents about the veil).[30]

This sociological account of burqa-wearing women creates difficulties for the two main arguments for reining in this practice. First, as it apparently is more likely to be chosen by the woman than imposed by her male environment, it is difficult to find in it the affront to female liberties and dignity as which it has predominantly been construed by its critics, from womanizing French President Sarkozy to pious Muslim icon Tariq Ramadan. Perhaps the most famous of all niqab-wearing women in France (recall that the burqa is practically nonexistent there), Faiza Silmi, who was denied French citizenship in July 2008 on account of her niqab, certainly does not appear to be a victim of Muslim male chauvinism. "Don't believe for a minute that I am submissive to my husband," she tells a *Le Monde* journalist, "It is me who pays the bills and deals with the paperwork!"[31] Nevertheless, the Conseil d'Etat denied her application for citizenship on the grounds of "a radical practice of her religion . . . incompatible with the essential values of the French community and notably the principle of the equality of sexes."[32] Conversely, it also has to be conceded that a ready attribution of "choice" as the main motivation for donning the integral veil is skewed by selection bias: those women for whom the veil is not a choice are unlikely ever to reach a microphone.

However, the second, somewhat auxiliary, justification for restricting the burqa—its alleged threat to security—also clashes with the sociological reality. If, indeed, the vast majority of the tiny Salafi sect in France is "pietistic" rather than "political" or "jihadist" in orientation, as its leading French chronicler argues (Amghar 2006), it is very difficult to see in the integral veil any security threat at all. Rather than pursuing the dreaded "entry-ism" in French public institutions (for which the Muslim Brothers had once been infamous, before they became domesticated within the UOIF [Union des Organisations Islamiques de France] and, of course, the CFCM), "the only project of young Salafis is, in my view, to leave France for a Muslim country."[33] For one thing, Faiza Silmi announced that this was precisely what she intended to do after her denial of French citizenship in the summer of 2008.[34]

The marginality of the integral veil in France was impressively (should one say: eerily) demonstrated by seven local mayors who lined up to testify before the Burqa Commission, some from the more ill-famed banlieues. The mayor of Evreux, in the Paris region, which includes two large working-class neighborhoods ("quartiers populaires"), knew of "fewer than ten" integrally veiled women in this city of 85.000: "One cannot say at this point that the burqa is a problem in local life . . . it is not a subject of debate."[35] Even with respect to the ordinary headscarf *(hijab)*, he knew of only one case of a woman insisting on working in a school canteen with a headscarf on, but that was back in 2004, and she had quickly agreed to remove it. "We have not encountered any other difficulty," he noted.[36] Although this mayor evidently had little to report from the local front, he still was firm that "legislation on the burqa question is necessary."[37] The statements by most of his colleagues were very similar. The mayor of Conflans-Sainte-Honorine, in the Île-de-France region, observed "in the past 2 or 3 years, at least 2 or 3 women in integral veil and with gloves, walking 3 meters behind what I believe were their husbands."[38] Even the mayor of Montfermeil, not far from Clichy-sous-Bois, epicenter of the notorious 2005 banlieue unrests, had to concede that the integral veil "is a marginal question" there.[39]

For Burqa Commission president André Gerin, the integral veil was "only the visible part of the iceberg that is fundamentalist *intégrisme*" (Assemblée Nationale 2010: 13). However, it is not likely to be one that could ever rock the boat. In fact, if one considers the sociological marginality of the phenomenon, in terms both of quantity and of quality, it is difficult to make sense of the inflated rhetoric surrounding it, such as the apocalyptic conclusion that "the alternative is clear: it is either the Republic or the burqa."[40]

The Burqa in the Republican Triptych

But what is it that the French consider problematic about the burqa? The one commonality between the present controversy over the burqa and the past debates over the foulard is that integral veil and headscarf are both perceived as threats to "national cohesion" and to "Republican values" (Assemblée Nationale 2010: 87). Restricting it is part of the great French, even European movement of getting serious about "integrating" its (mostly

Muslim) immigrant and ethnic minorities. In France, it is better understood than elsewhere in Europe that such integration does not succeed in the absence of explicitly detailed conditions that newcomers and minorities have to fulfill and that it requires spelling out what it is that immigrants are to be integrated into.

However, the key difference between past and present veil controversies is that prohibiting the burqa cannot be justified in the name of laïcité, the French version of liberal state neutrality. Recall that protecting laïcité had been the leitmotif in the 2004 legislation against ostentatious religious symbols in public schools, which had come out of the deliberations of the Stasi Commission. The 2009 parliamentary resolution establishing the Burqa Commission (or more formally "a commission of inquiry concerning the practice of wearing the burqa and the niqab on the national territory") still presented the incriminated garb as a threat to laïcité, the latter figuring as symbol for national unity: "If *laïcité* is threatened, French society is threatened in its unity and in its capacity to offer a common destiny" (Assemblée Nationale 2009). Yet this alarum was but a reflex of the past that quickly receded.

Why did the rallying cry of laïcité move into the background? For two reasons: first, because of the setting in which the integral veil was to be restricted—namely, in all public places, which does not (or only peripherally) involve the state; second, as discussed above, because of the dominant perception that the burqa is not a religious symbol but rather a political symbol not intrinsically related to Islam.

With respect to the first, which is really the main consideration, the main purpose now was to prohibit the burqa in all public places. The state is mostly absent in this setting; instead, this involves ordinary individuals and their relationships. But laïcité is a principle that obliges the state (in terms of an obligation to be neutral in religious affairs), not individuals. So it cannot be the operating principle governing relationships between individuals in public places. In the 2004 law, a public service provided by the state (education) was the key issue, so that the principle of laïcité applied. And if this principle came rather dubiously to be extended from the providers to the users of public services—that is, to school children—the reason is that children and adolescents in education were deemed in need of "reinforced protection" (Assemblée Nationale 2010: 91).[41] Conversely, "public space" and the relationships between individuals in it are to be afforded "respect for fundamental liberties"[42]—the right of private life, of free movement (*droit d'aller et venir*), of free expression. These guarantees mandate a daunting degree of individual rights protection and highlight the rather extraordinary, if not sinister, project of restricting something as fundamentally private as what to wear in the street.

But there is a second reason why laïcité cannot be invoked for restricting the burqa, one that is connected to the peculiarly nonreligious perception of the garment that was shared by most of those pushing for restrictive legislation, even most experts involved (though not those on the side of the Islamic organizations). Laïcité is a principle for regulating religion. However, if the burqa is taken, however unconvincingly, as extrinsic to Islam and not as religious expression at all, it falls outside the ambit of laïcité.

With laïcité out of the picture, which "Republican values" are put to the test by the burqa, and why? Let us go through the "Republican triptych" one by one.[43] With respect to "liberty," one could argue that the integral veil "clearly negates the freedom of choice of women" (Assemblée Nationale 2010: 95) only if it is being worn as a result of external pressure. However, fewer than twenty of those wearing the burqa in all of France are believed to be minors (p. 99), who are intrinsically vulnerable to such pressure. Moreover, as discussed earlier, the sociological profile of fully veiled Muslim women in France hardly suggests that their clothing is the result of outside pressures. Given these facts, "liberty" favors rather than opposes the donning of the burqa; its very appearance is likely to be an expression of the liberty to dress as one prefers.

What about the second value enumerated in the republican triptych, namely, "equality"? In contrast to the unconvincing claims about liberty, the matter of equality goes to the heart of why the burqa is rejected: it denies gender equality. Remember that the Conseil d'Etat's denial of French citizenship to Faiza Silmi was in reference to her niqab's violation of such equality, this "essential value" of the "French community." As the envisaged legislation against the burqa in public places was built primarily on the equality principle, we will discuss it in a separate section below.

"Solidarity" *(fraternité)* is the third republican value, and it is distinct from the other two in that no legal case and no legislation have ever been attempted to substantiate it. This omission is astonishing in the land of Durkheim, which has forever been obsessed by the "integration" of society. As a noted legal participant throughout the two-decade-long French veiling controversy put it, "solidarity has never been considered a legal principle."[44] But if one perceives the burqa as undermining "national cohesion" and "Republican values" (which signal the ties that bind), it should be tackled first and foremost as an affront to solidarity. However one stands on the liberty- and equality-constraining charges leveled against the burqa, it is incontrovertible that it constitutes "a rupture of the social compact [*pacte social*]" (Assemblée Nationale 2010: 118).

As we will show later, the solidarity concern became the main justification of the 2010 legislation against the burqa. By enabling the veiled woman to see without being seen, the burqa interrupts the elementary reciprocity of seeing and being seen that undergirds everyday life. The burqa signals withdrawal and refusal to communicate, and this in permanence. It is "symbolic violence"[45] inflicted on those exposed to its sight. For French feminist Elisabeth Badinter, it even signifies "all-powerfulness over the other": "The woman thus dressed arrogates to herself the right to see me but refuses to me the right to see her" (quoted in Assemblée Nationale 2010: 118–119). One sees the wildly oscillating perceptions of burqa-wearing women on offer here: hapless victim of archaic religion and male power on one side, sly and arrogant destroyer of the social contract on the other. While the "symbolic violence" charge appears construed, the integral veil's affront to solidarity is difficult to deny. Yet no one can be forced to walk and talk with the others. If it were otherwise, we would no longer live in a liberal society.

The fact of covering one's face, which is peculiar to the integral veil, also invited reflection on the significance of the face in the Occident, which the always philosophically minded French picked up with relish. The Burqa Commission report cited lengthy passages from the works of philosopher Emmanuel Lévinas pondering the face as the "mirror of the soul" and as the locus of the "individualism" and "humanism" that are the mark of Western civilization. According to Lévinas, only the face in its totality, not reducible to its parts (chin, nose, or eyes), has this quality of expressing the soul. Therefore it is rarely covered, except when one's emotions win over— but then it is precisely the mark of civility for others to look away. "The best way to encounter the other," Lévinas writes, "is to not even notice the color of the eyes! If you observe the color of the eyes, you are not in a social relationship with the other" (quoted in Assemblée Nationale 2010: 118). From this follows that covering one's face behind a veil, or leaving only a slit for the eyes to see, robs the individual of her soul or her humanity for others, who cannot but relate to the veiled woman as "an object" (p. 118). This conclusion, which reduces rather than enhances the capacity of the veiled woman, is hard to reconcile with the diametrically opposite charge that the integral veil grants its wearer a kind of "omnipotence" allowing her to rupture the social contract. Irreconcilable as they are, the two opposite charges offer a sense of the irritation evoked in the streets of Paris by the presence of a full-body veil.

The Flawed Legal Bases for a Burqa Ban

There are obviously many ways in which the integral veil is an affront to republican, nay, Western values. The next step in the Burqa Commission's efforts was to reflect on the legal viability of restricting or even fully prohibiting the integral veil. These legal deliberations between lawyers and politicians open up a fascinating window into the reality of "judicialized politics," that is, a politics conducted "through the medium of legal discourse" (Shapiro and Stone Sweet 2002: 187), with lawmakers trying to sort out in constant (often explicit but always internalized) dialogue with lawyers and legal experts how an essentially political project could be made compatible with the top-heavy constraints of an autonomous legal system, in this case especially of constitutional law and international human rights law. "We have to liberate ourselves from the dictates [*décisions*] of justices," exclaimed one exasperated member of the parliamentary Burqa Commission at one point.[46] This is why France, much like any other liberal-constitutional state, can only with great difficulty impose a general ban on the wearing of the burqa that democratic representatives still want to have for populist or morally principled reasons.

In essence, the half-dozen lawyers cited before the Burqa Commission (counting only those appearing under their hat of legal expert) all had the same story to tell, if one disregards smallish nuances. There are three legal-normative principles on which a legislative case against the integral veil could be built: "laïcité," "human dignity," and "public order"; each avenue, however, is insufficient to deliver the desired result. Accordingly, the lawyers, and grudgingly the commission also, concluded that a "general and absolute" prohibition was not a viable project.

Laïcité. If one considers the centrality of laïcité in the adoption of the 2004 law prohibiting ostentatious religious signs in public schools, one is astonished at how quickly and categorically every single legal opinion expressed during the burqa deliberations dismissed it as "inopérant" (Assemblée Nationale 2010: 173). According to the wittiest and most impressive of the testifying lawyers, Denys de Béchillon, a law professor at the provincial Université de Pau in the French Pyrenees, the principle of laïcité "weighs on the state and not on private persons."[47] If that is so obvious and uncontested, one wonders: why didn't anyone mention it in 2003–2004, when the principle of laïcité became creatively reinterpreted as a norm that not just school teachers but also, and above all, schoolchildren were to follow and internalize?

Human Dignity. Consonant with the moral rejection of the integral veil, the justification for building a law against it had to rest on the principle of "human dignity." This principle, though it cannot be found explicitly anywhere in the French Constitution, fuses together all elements of the republican triptych, especially those of liberty and equality, with different emphases—a subjective concept of dignity aligning more closely with liberty, an objective understanding more closely with equality. Kant defined dignity as the condition of being an "end in itself" and not just of "value" relative to some other purpose (such "relative value" of a thing being called its "price"). Only human beings, endowed with the faculty of morality, that is, to decide between right and wrong, have "dignity" and each one of them equally (Kant 1785: 434). This is the classic enlightenment view of the individual as free and equal. However, underneath this philosophical formulation hides a fundamental ambiguity that has become pertinent to a legal-political understanding of the term: is dignity an objective (and thus idealized) image of humanity that may be brought against the individual who violates it against herself, even if no other party is involved; or does dignity merge with freedom of choice and thus become capable of being violated only by a third party?[48]

The ambiguity of "dignity" has implications for its utility in prohibiting the burqa. A subjective reading of dignity, in which it becomes fused with freedom of choice, would amount to a defense of the burqa as expressive of religious liberty. Only an objective reading of dignity allows using it to restrict the burqa. The import of this alternative becomes clear when considering the sociological reality of the burqa phenomenon. The situation would be straightforward if the burqa were simply imposed on the woman and thus against her will—who would argue that this does not violate her dignity? Incidentally, the argument that the headscarf is externally imposed was the main interpretation of the facts when the 2004 headscarf law was crafted. But now the situation was different—to all appearances, the integral veil seemed to be mostly a matter of choice. The phenomenon that the aspiring lawmakers were faced with has been succinctly described as "voluntary servitude," because one was dealing with "adult women who, for the most part, affirm that they wear this dress voluntarily."[49] How could this choice be declared illegitimate "without questioning the capacity for self-determination that modern thinking has posited as a foundation of our democratic system"?[50]

Considering that "voluntary servitude" constituted the on-the-ground reality of the burqa, an objective reading of the concept of dignity offered the only basis on which one could legitimately restrict it. Dignity thus understood was surely consonant with a focus on equality, as the ideal picture of woman as equal to man could be violated by a woman who, through her own choice, put herself under and behind her husband, or God, or both. Such objective dignity was more difficult to reconcile with a focus on freedom, both being contradictory. This fact explains the focus on sex equality in the French burqa battle.

The problem is that an objective understanding of human dignity would push the state toward the questionable pursuit of an ethical project. As far as Minister of Immigration Eric Besson was concerned, this posed no problem: "Public authority is founded on protecting the dignity of the person, if necessary against the person herself."[51] A very Rousseauian instinct for putting the collectivity first to emancipate the individual (some people have to be "forced to be free"), shared by the left and right alike, popped to the surface. For conservative Union pour un Mouvement Populaire (UMP) deputy Françoise Hostalier, "society must protect its members, even if they voluntarily torture themselves, mutilate themselves, or impose on themselves an undignified appearance."[52] On the opposite end of the political spectrum, Pierre Forgues, a member of a radical leftist party, similarly holds that "freedom itself must be organized, and it is up to the legislator to protect the citizen, even against her- or himself."[53] Although a conservative himself, law professor Guy Carcassone retorted to such views that "the legislator would cease being democratic precisely if it superimposes itself over liberty, telling the citizen under the cover of dignity what to do or not to do." A ban of the integral veil in these terms would be a "formidable signal to the virtue leagues to prohibit also pornography, prostitution, or piercing."[54]

There is a second problem with an objective understanding of human dignity. As an objective principle, it must be treated the same, whether in the public or the private sphere; like pregnancy, it cannot come in terms of a "more" or "less." As law professor Anne Levade pointed out, dignity thus defined would call for a "general and absolute prohibition [of the integral veil] in all circumstances," the private sphere included.[55] Decreeing an objective meaning of dignity by way of law would be the end of France as a liberal society, as the French state would be forced to follow people into their bedrooms.

The major hurdle to an objective understanding of dignity, however, is all on the technically legal side, at the national and European levels alike, where a subjective understanding has come to predominate over an objective understanding of human dignity. The main legal ammunition for an objective reading of dignity had been a noted but immediately criticized decision of the Conseil d'Etat, known as *Commune de Morsang-sur-Orge*, of October 1995.[56] The court had argued in this case that the practice of a dwarf being thrown, for public amusement, as a projectile through the spectator ranks of a provincial discotheque (dubbed *lancer de nain*) constituted a violation of this (handicapped) person's human dignity, even though he had consented to the activity (in fact, he did it for a living). Thus, according to the high court, the municipality was acting lawfully when it prohibited the spectacle for the sake of protecting "public morality" as an element of "public order."

Yet the *Morsang-sur-Orge* decision was anomalous, never affirmed or upheld even by the same high court. At the European level, certainly, there is a similar judgment by the European Court of Human Rights (ECtHR) of the same year, 1995, concerning sadomasochistic practices by a group of British homosexuals. However, it likewise stood alone and was never affirmed. In this 1995 decision, the ECtHR upheld the severe punishment of the defendants by a British court as "necessary in a democratic society for the protection of health," even though their sexual practices were consensual and not harmful to third parties, and thus, as the defendants argued, "part of private morality which is not the State's business to regulate."[57] The European court thus left standing Lord Templeman's House of Lords indictment of the practices as in violation of an objective concept of human dignity: "Society is entitled and bound to protect itself against a cult of violence. Pleasure derived from the infliction of pain is an evil thing. Cruelty is uncivilized."[58]

However, in a subsequent decision involving similar sadomasochistic practices by a heterosexual trio in Belgium, the ECtHR reversed its previous stance in favor of a consent-based, subjective understanding of dignity. This later decision upheld a similarly harsh punishment by a Belgian court, but this time on the argument that the "victim" had at some point withdrawn her consent to the pain inflicted on her, which was not honored by the (heavily intoxicated) defendants. As the court argued: "Although individuals could claim the right to engage in sexual practices as freely as possible, the need to respect the wishes of the 'victims' of such practices—whose own right to free choice in expressing their sexuality likewise had to be safeguarded—placed a limit to that freedom. However, no such respect had been shown in the present case."[59]

In general, the lawyers testifying before the Burqa Commission agreed that the legal development in France and at European level had moved in the direction of a subjective understanding of dignity, according to which dignity was identified with freedom of choice. This was also the gist of the Simone Veil Commission's recommendation for including the concept of dignity in the French Constitution, which was to occur without unduly "moralizing" the term: "[Dignity should] remain fundamentally a matter of choice, of liberty, in a word, of autonomy" (Veil Committee 2008: 134).

The rub is that as a subjective concept, dignity kicks in only if a third party violates it; a self-inflicted harm to dignity becomes impossible. "From a legal point of view," argues matter-of-factly Bertrand Mathieu, a professor of law at the Sorbonne, "the principle of dignity is utilized in relationships between self and others, and not in internal relationships within the self."[60] Thus understood, dignity is "a protection of our liberty."[61] But this implies that dignity constitutes a protection of rather than a challenge to the burqa: "The heart of the dignity of the woman is precisely the exercise of her free judgment, of her liberty, including the liberty to wear the burqa if she so intends."[62]

Laudable as it may be, however, this freedom-protecting stance creates the dilemma that religious liberties may be used for the destruction of liberty, which is the core paradox of the entire struggle surrounding Islam in liberal societies. A subjective concept of dignity, which happens to be the legal status quo in the contemporary liberal state, is but one element in the unfolding of this paradox. Just as the outraged lawmakers were yelling to be liberated from the "dictate of justices," Sorbonne law professor Mathieu insisted that he privately also favored an "objective conception of dignity, one that may limit liberty." But he dryly added that this view was "not shared by all" and that it was surely "not [the view] of the European Court of Human Rights." This self-described "mechanic of law" cut to the heart of the matter: "Whether you like it or not, today the legislator is controlled by the judge. I myself regret this disequilibrium in favor of the judge, but it is the reality."[63] Thus, in a powerful demonstration of the workings of judicialized politics, the invocation of the concept of dignity in the French anti-burqa campaign turned out to be a dead end. Thus was buried the most hopeful and heavily invested legal avenue for a wholesale interdiction of the integral veil, because this was the one avenue that resonated most closely with the campaign's moral-cum-political motivation.

Public Order. The last resort for arriving at a general prohibition of the burqa was to construe the latter as a threat to "public order." This, of course, is an established concept in French public law and includes the elements of "security," "tranquility," "public health," and—last and least, though eventually the shooting star—"public morality." Building on the views of the legal anti-headscarf veteran, Rémy Schwartz,[64] one could argue that a general burqa ban in public order terms could be built only on the basis of its "public morality" aspect. Therefore, the Conseil d'Etat's 1995 *Commune de Morsang-sur-Orge* decision kicked back into the picture, as it had introduced human dignity as an element of public order that the state was mandated to protect, looked at under its "public morality" aspect. A general prohibition of the burqa on the basis of public order concerns thus had to merge with one on the basis of human dignity, or rather, the former had to collapse into the latter. But then both must fail on the same ground, namely, the fact that an objective conception of dignity has no traction in the legal system. As one of its leading justices pointed out, the Conseil d'Etat had immediately heeded the loud critique of its *Morsang-sur-Orge* decision as potentially destructive of individual liberties, and the principle of human dignity thus understood has "rarely" ever been mentioned since (Sauvé 2009: 15). In fact, legal restrictions on "public morality" grounds, which had flourished in the early twentieth century, have almost entirely disappeared in French (and other European states') jurisprudence.[65] It is no longer possible, say, for the mayors of beach resorts in Bretagne or Côte d'Azur to require trousers and shirts on Main Street. This development parallels and reflects a general retreat of the state from its prior role as ethical watchdog.

A moralistic notion of public order no longer having much traction, perhaps a security-focused understanding of order might provide a viable basis for outlawing the veil. The rub is that on security grounds, at best a limited and local but not a "general and absolute" prohibition could be built. The audacious scope of the anti-burqa effort is nowhere more apparent than here: public space is in the first instance a "space of liberty,"[66] a space in which "liberty is the principle and restriction, not to mention interdiction, is the exception."[67] This makes restriction in public spaces a rather more difficult matter than restriction in public institutions, which had been the thrust of the (school-focused) 2004 headscarf law. A permanent ban on the burqa on public security grounds could take effect only if there is a "permanent threat" to public order deriving from "a manifestation of religious liberty,"[68] conveying the rather exaggerated "image of France in danger."[69] Where would it end? With respect to a jilbab-style body cover, which might allow one, say, to smuggle weapons or explosives under it, one would have to equally prohibit "rucksack, handbag, *boubou* [a wide African dress], even the *soutane* [worn by Catholic priests]."[70] But the real affront would be a security-based order always to keep one's face uncovered, in order to be at any single moment identifiable to the state.

Among the lawyers, the first to seriously make such a proposition was Parisian law professor Guy Carcassone: "One must not cover [*dissimuler*] one's face, in any public space, without exception."[71] Yet Carcassone justified his position not on security grounds but with a heavy dose of public morality considerations. This would prove to be the approach eventually taken by the lawmakers in 2010. Since the "social code" in France and the West requires that one "reveal one's face" and not "expose one's genitalia," which might well be the opposite in "a thousand years," Carcassone argues, one could prohibit face coverage insofar as its symmetrical opposite, nudity, has already been prohibited, and indeed for the sake of public morality *(bonnes mœrs).*[72] In addition, Carcassonne gives an important twist to his essentially dignity-focused justification for prohibiting the burqa (though it was one that technically paraded under the "public order" umbrella). While he sided with those who rejected the possibility of a self-inflicted violation of dignity, thus confirming it as a subjective (not objective) concept, it was still possible to see the dignity of others violated by the burqa's rupturing of the reciprocity of everyday life. In signifying to the other that "he is not sufficiently dignified, pure, or respectable to allow him to look at you,"[73] the integral veil could be construed as "harm" according to Article 4 of the Declaration of the Rights of Man and Citizen, which states that "Freedom is the power to do anything which does not harm another." This was a rather strained interpretation of an article that was usually held to protect the freedom of expression in public spaces and was thus on its face more protective than restrictive of the burqa.

The first, wildly forward-shooting burqa law proposal by UMP deputy Jean-François Copé, which would cause the Socialist members in the Burqa Commission to noisily abstain from voting over the commission's final report, ran along the lines laid out by Carcassone: "In our societies, the face is part of the body which carries the identity of the individual. To dissimulate one's face from the regard of others is a negation of self, a negation of the other, and a negation of life in society." Article 1 of the Copé proposal, which is in essence identical to the first article of the 2010 burqa law, states: "It is prohibited to dissimulate one's face in all public places and on all public passageways [*les lieux ouverts au public et sur la voie publique*] except in the case of legitimate reasons as laid down by the Conseil d'Etat."[74]

In its rejection of a general ban on the burqa in March 2010, the Conseil d'Etat (2010: 26) stipulated that a general prohibition would have to rest on a "new concept of public order," one in which "public order rests on a minimal foundation of reciprocity and of essential guarantees of life in society." Although this would become the central metalegal reference for the lawmakers' quashing of the integral veil in the summer of 2010, the Conseil d'Etat immediately dismissed the idea as insufficiently "elaborated as legal doctrine" and likely to be rejected by a Conseil Constitutionnel beholden to a "traditional conception of public order," that is, one in terms of security, not public morality (2010: 28). At best, the Conseil d'Etat argued, one could reaffirm what amounts to the "solidarity" part of the republican triptych in terms of a solemn parliamentary resolution, "affirming the constitutive elements of the social contract that grounds our national identity" (p. 28). This, however, would be symbolic only and not have the force of law.

Irrespective of its justification, an order to always uncover one's face still amounted to a Foucauldian dystopia of a totally legible society, a panopticon writ large, a society turned into "a vast zone of video surveillance."[75] As this would have to be a generalized rule, beyond the burqa, what about the motorbike rider who fails to remove her helmet on the sidewalk? What about Santa Claus? What about masked Carnivalists? All these examples were seriously discussed by the Burqa Commission as necessary exemptions. Also note that, back in June 2009, the government had passed an administrative decree prohibiting the wearing of hoodies *(anti-cagoule)*, fashionable among banlieue hipsters. But this ban could be effected only "in the presence of a threat," like a public demonstration, and notably not always and everywhere. A permanent prohibition along such lines, everybody knew, would require legislation, because of the fundamental restriction of liberty involved. But there are daunting constitutional hurdles to such a move: "The actual jurisprudence of the Conseil Constitutionnel does not indicate that citizens are obliged to uncover their faces in permanence, to be everywhere and under all circumstances recognizable, and that any police officer may check their identity."[76] Rémy Schwartz expresses the prevailing legal opinion, which was loud and clear and nearly uncontested during the hearings of the Burqa Commission: "Even if it is true that public order requires the power to identify people, this authority cannot be permanent. One cannot impose on citizens a state of permanent surveillance."[77]

CONSIDERING the legal difficulties involved in achieving a general ban on the integral veil on the threefold grounds of laïcité-dignity-public order, Denis de Béchillon provides a compelling conclusion to the entire debate: "I don't like the burqa, it disgusts me, but I don't believe that we have the tools and the political culture for prohibiting the wearing of such dress on the territory of the Republic."[78]

What Is to Be Done?

Although the Burqa Commission could not agree on a recommendation for a "general and absolute" prohibition, not even on the "least risky" public order basis, it still made no fewer than fifteen policy recommendations.[79] At the top of the list was a symbolic parliamentary "resolution" (a novelty available after a 2008 constitutional reform) that would "reaffirm the Republican values of liberty, equality and solidarity" (notably not laïcité, previously the standard reference in the long-standing French Islam *querelles*). This resolution would "proclaim that all of France says no to the integral veil and demands that this practice be prohibited on the territory of the Republic" (Assemblée Nationale 2010: 210). This was a curiously self-referential "demand," as it could logically address only Parliament itself. The National Assembly still unanimously passed such a resolution in May 2010.

Next to prohibiting the integral veil in public offices and public transport, the most interesting among the not-so-symbolic proposed restrictions was to circumvent by way of immigration and nationality law some of the constitutional constraints that normally protect citizens and legal permanent residents. As the final commission report cunningly muses, one-third of integral veils are worn by non-French citizens, and they could be "captured" this way (Assembleé Nationale 2010: 165). A first measure would be to make the granting of family unification and long-term residence visas dependent on the immigrant's recognition of "equality between men and women as well as the principle of laïcité" (p. 165). Furthermore, a permanent settlement permit (the famous *carte de dix ans*) was to be refused if the applicant "manifested a radical practice of his or her religion that is incompatible with the values of the Republic, especially with the principle of equality between men and women" (p. 165). That was the precise formula used by the Conseil d'Etat when it had denied French citizenship to Faiza Silmi in 2008. These immigration law measures were brought full circle by inserting the exact same condition into nationality law. First announced in Immigration Minister Eric Besson's testimony before the Burqa Commission, all of these measures were instantly put into effect by way of administrative decree, and they are now the law of the land.

The Burqa Commission also issued a few ameliorative proposals that had already been part of the Stasi Commission Report of 2003 but that had never been seriously considered ever since: the introduction of an Islamic holiday, promises to fight discrimination more effectively, a more "just representation of spiritual diversity," etc. To repeat what was the strangest but also the central premise of the anti-burqa crusade: "The integral veil is not a religious sign. However, the fact that it has often been presented as such . . . has contributed to an image of Islam as an archaic religion, incompatible with the values of the Republic, thus feeding prejudices against the Muslims of France. It is therefore important for the Commission to distance itself from such views by . . . reaffirming our solidarity with all Muslims who suffer from discrimination" (Assembleé Nationale 2010: 128). As the integral veil was categorically dissociated from Islam, it was no contradiction to complement the proposed restrictions with positive integration measures.

The Conseil d'Etat's Rejection of a General Burqa Ban

As it still insisted on the "largest and most effective possible [restriction]" of the integral veil, the French government, upon the Burqa Commission's disappointing termination in January 2010, called on the Conseil d'Etat for "juridical solutions" (quoted in Conseil d'Etat 2010: 43). In its report to the prime minister in March 2010, the Conseil d'Etat distinguished the "political and sociological" nature of the Burqa Commission report from the "strictly legal" nature of its own report.[80] This is a misleading distinction, because it ignores the weight of legal-constitutional considerations that had already forced the "political" Burqa Commission to step back from its original project of a "general and absolute" burqa ban. In fact, the Conseil d'Etat *étude* comes to almost identical conclusions as the Burqa Commission, and it differs from the latter mostly in being less wordy.

The only "very solid" basis for prohibiting the integral veil, under the more general auspices of prohibiting all dress that "dissimulates" a person's face, was on "public security" grounds, but this in turn was possible "only in particular circumstances" (Conseil d'Etat 2010: 30). Negatively formulated, "public security does not justify imposing on everyone the obligation to have one's face uncovered during all times and in all places" (p. 32). Concretely, the court suggested exactly what the Burqa Commission had already proposed in terms of "hard" legislation. This was to adopt a partial prohibition, mostly by way of "harmonizing and reinforcing" the many already existing restrictions, "that is applicable only in certain places open to the public where the circumstances or the nature of the places warrant it" (p. 37), while leaving it to the legislators to specify what precisely these "places" and "circumstances" would be.

Shortly before the Conseil d'Etat presented its view to the prime minister, his boss—the president—noisily restated that "for too long already have we accepted the assault on laïcité, on equality between men and women, the discriminations. It's enough. . . . The response must be the complete prohibition of the integral veil."[81] Not much learned on his side, one must conclude, had not the Conseil d'Etat reconfirmed the impossibility of exactly such a totalizing response. "The political will could falter yet again before the law [*droit*]," France's leading newspaper commented.[82] This seemed the *point final* under France's anti-burqa campaign, as one that had failed over the high legal obstacles.

Politics against the Law

The politicians did not give up, however. Although the issue fell dormant after the Burqa Commission's disappointing lack of backbone in January 2010, it was cunningly resurrected three days before the regional elections of March 2010, in an obvious "signal" to the voters of the right-wing National Front: "The integral veil is contrary to the dignity of women," thundered the president of the Republic, "The response is prohibition of the integral veil. The government will introduce a bill conforming to the general principles of our law."[83] The latter part of this statement signaled the legal difficulties that lay ahead.

The rhetoric for this move, which so obviously contradicted the Conseil d'Etat's negative recommendation of March 2010, was supplied by a parallel move toward a total burqa ban in Belgium, whose parliament was the first in Europe to seriously work toward such a law (though it was passed only in April 2011). According to its Belgian protagonists, this was a matter of "risk taking" and of shouldering "political responsibility." Well aware of the French Conseil d'Etat's negative opinion on the matter, a liberal Francophone Belgian deputy expressed his "great respect" for the French court but then declared that it was up to the political world to "take responsibility" against the legal odds.[84] This was, one should note, the last matter on which the Belgian legislature could agree as the country was heading to the abyss, in terms of dissolving into a French-speaking and a Flemish-speaking part; only in the front against Islam could one still "be proud to be Belgian."[85]

"Risk taking" and "political responsibility" also became the dominant rhetoric in the French legislative move toward a burqa law. When he officially announced the project in late April 2010, Prime Minister François Fillon pronounced himself "ready to take juridical risks," much as his Belgian colleagues.[86] In a sane moment, the president conceded that "this is not the sort of thing that will help people to find work." His front man in the legislative burqa campaign was Jean-François Copé, who heavily invested in this largely symbolic affair in his bid for leadership of the UMP.[87] It was a matter of "political courage," and one could not afford "to let go of it," said Copé.[88] The Conseil d'Etat March 2010 opinion was merely a legal "interpretation," "respectable but contestable."[89] Moreover, Copé added smartly, "if the Conseil d'Etat says that the legal foundations are contestable, this means it is not impossible to imagine that they could be constructed."[90]

This was still polite. What now occurred was a veritable political backlash against what was perceived as "juristocracy" (Hirschl 2004), an imperious dictate of the legal system. The anger that had accumulated during the forced constitutional law lessons at the Burqa Commission hearings now erupted into the open, with a vengeance. One UMP delegate declared himself "shocked" by the "bossy tone" of the Conseil d'Etat and admonished its judges to "leave their ivory tower and face reality."[91] Another UMP delegate averred that it was "not the first time" that the Conseil d'Etat had proved to be "seriously wrong," referring to the court's liberal headscarf opinion of 1989 which came to be annulled fifteen years later by the headscarf law of 2004.[92] Calling the legal defense of religious liberties between 1789 and 2004 "error" was a peculiar way of understanding the relationship between politics and law in a liberal-constitutional state. A third UMP delegate declared high-handedly that "Parliament is there to make law, not to follow the views of the Conseil d'Etat" and that the latter was "obliged to recognize that this interdiction rests on legal foundations."[93] The chorus of conservative court-bashers was completed by yet another UMP delegate, who found that "the French don't understand these legalistic disputes and prefer that we pass effective laws." This was the political (or rather populist) heart of the matter: 70 percent of the French public supported a general burqa ban, so imposing one was the easiest way to placate the people in austere economic times.

These rabid views were triggered by the Conseil d'Etat's second rejection of a total prohibition of the burqa in May 2010, issued in the presence of the general secretary of the government. The Conseil d'Etat restated that "a total and general prohibition on the wearing of the integral veil could not find any incontestable juridical foundations" and that it would be "exposed to strong constitutional and statutory uncertainties."[94]

The burqa bill that was brought to Parliament in July 2010 was all in the language of dignity, equality, and high-flown republican principles that had been found wanting from a legal point of view: "The dissimulation of the face in public space is a form of symbolic violence and is dehumanizing," the bill claimed, and even if voluntary, it "violates the dignity of the person."[95]

However, as mentioned earlier, the legal case was built more narrowly on a niche that had been unknowingly prepared by the Conseil d'Etat itself, in its (however skeptical) speculation on the "non-material" dimension of public order. To reiterate the central line: "Public order rests on a minimal foundation of reciprocity and of essential guarantees of life in society" (Conseil d'Etat 2010: 26). Akin to the "solidarity" part of the republican triptych, this dimension of public order had never been "legally theorized." But it clearly existed, as one could see in extant prohibitions of incest, polygamy, or nudity in public. Spelling it out, which the Conseil d'Etat abstained from in its March 2010 *étude,* would entail "affirmation of a right and an equal belonging of everyone to the social body" (p. 27). Only in the land of Durkheim could one imagine a law that makes everyone an organic part of society. Yet this is precisely what the burqa law does.

When the burqa bill was introduced to Parliament in early July 2010, its main justification was the reference to "immaterial" or "social" public order, as Justice Minister Alliot-Marie put it in her opening statement. "The Republic is lived with the face uncovered," she said.[96] Or as Dominique Schnapper, sociologist and former member of the Conseil Constitutionnel, phrased it in almost comical terms, "France is the country where everyone says *'bonjour'*" (quoted in Bowen 2011: 337). The burqa was to be prohibited for the sake of "living together" *(vivre ensemble)* and to reject "separatism" *(repli sur soi).*[97] Jean-Paul Garraud, chair of a new parliamentary commission studying the prohibition of the burqa, cleverly added that the "majority opinion" among jurists was "sensibly evolving" on the issue.[98] In fact, Sorbonne law professor Anne Levade, who had earlier declared, like every single one of her peers, that "neither laicity nor dignity nor public order could ever justify a general and absolute prohibition,"[99] now could be heard saying that the immaterial aspect of public order was "an indispensable counterweight to the excesses of the absolute primacy of individual rights."[100] It is not clear how her earlier and later statements logically cohere. But her "opinion" on the matter had, indeed, "sensibly evolved."

The invocation of immaterial public order concerns made it possible to smuggle back in the dignity discourse that had had to be thrown out earlier for legal reasons. "Dignity" was openly invoked by the justice minister's presentation of the bill to the National Assembly: "The Republic does not accept the compromising of human dignity."[101] So it was not difficult for a Socialist opposition deputy, Jean Glavany, to call the bluff. "You claim not to invoke the principle of dignity," which was apparently not quite true, "but this is finally the only principle that is written into your text," which also was not quite true.[102] But Glavany aptly grasped the essence: "Immaterial public order rests on public morality and respect for the dignity of the human person. The dignity of the human person: here you go again."[103] And this was at significant cost: "The fundamentalist jurists are already rubbing their hands."[104]

This is not to say that the Socialists did not happily participate in the political backlash against constitutional law. While abstaining from the final vote on the burqa bill, which the National Assembly accepted on July 13, 2010, with only one member dissenting, the Socialists took a self-described "responsible attitude" in not submitting the law to the Conseil Constitutionnel, which otherwise is the routine political game between government and opposition. In fact, a leading Socialist later defended the burqa ban as a "victory for the Republic," and he was as happy as his UMP colleagues were that the Conseil d'Etat "does not make law" in France.[105]

So safe did the governing conservative party (UMP) feel that it itself referred the fresh burqa law to the Conseil Constitutionnel for a test of its constitutionality. Although the law was couched overall as a matter of "risk taking," one must assume that the risk of failing before this Conseil Constitutionnel was calculably low. After all, this is a court not made up of professional judges but of political notables. And in its present incarnation, it included former presidents Jacques Chirac and Valéry Giscard d'Estaing, as well as Jean-Louis Debré—all conservative politicians who in the past had taken vocal and often controversial anti-Muslim and anti-immigrant stances and who were unlikely to obstruct a government close to (if not identical with) their own political leanings and affiliations. In a characteristically brief and apodictic decision in October 2010, the Conseil Constitutionnel declared the burqa law "in conformity with the constitution," apparently agreeing with the lawmakers' view of the burqa as "manifestly incompatible with the constitutional principles of liberty and equality."[106] This was a stretch, if not an impossibility, given the prevailing jurisprudence and legal opinion, as laid out in the previous pages.

However, the Conseil Constitutionnel included a surprising and potentially dangerous proviso: the burqa prohibition "shall not restrict the exercise of religious liberty in places of worship that are open to the public." This provision was intended to avoid violation of Article 10 of the 1789 Declaration of the Rights of Man and Citizen, the religious liberty clause. As Patrick Weil pointed out in a brilliant commentary, this exemption "reveals the real—religious—object of the law."[107] Remember that the red thread in the burqa campaign had been that this was "not a religious question" but only "a problem of living together in the Republic."[108] The exemption for places of public worship exposed this claim as false. If, deep down, one did not suspect the prohibited attire of being religious, why should there be an exemption on religious grounds? No religious exemption, after all, existed for the prohibition of incest or public nudity, which the burqa restriction was compared with by the lawmaker. On her way to

Notre Dame cathedral in the center of Paris (which, like all Catholic churches in France, tolerates the burqa), a burqa-wearing woman "could invoke the right to religious liberty that the legislator has deliberately refused to associate with the law, but which the Conseil Constitutionnel has now connected with it," Weil concluded.[109]

Most important, after the Conseil Constitutionnel's recognition of the possible religious significance of the burqa, the prohibition becomes even more vulnerable to an intervention by the ECtHR. In February 2010, the Strasbourg court had branded as a violation of religious liberty, under Article 9 of the European Human Rights Convention, the Turkish government's arrest of members of an Islamic sect who had publicly paraded in their traditional garb near their house of worship.[110] The European court distinguished here between dress restriction in "public institutions," which is legitimate when imposed on public servants who are to "respect neutrality," and dress restrictions "in public places open to all like streets or places," addressed to "simple citizens," which constitute an Article 9 violation. But this is exactly what the French government has undertaken in its burqa law. Of course instantly aware of the European Court's February 2010 ruling in this age of constitutional politics, French lawmakers deemed themselves immune from its reach, retorting that no particular (religious) dress was targeted by the envisaged burqa law (instead all dress that "dissimulates the face") and that the restriction was based not on the religion-centered principle of laïcité but of *ordre public sociétal*.[111] Now that France's own Conseil Constitutionnel, called on to ratify the eventual law, has done so only by bringing back in the religious dimension, the Strasbourg court may not be convinced that the French and Turkish situations are "totally different."[112]

In his indictment of the Conseil Constitutionnel's "confused and contradictory" assent to the burqa law, Patrick Weil expounds how this submission of law to politics was possible: "Mostly composed of former political officeholders, the Conseil Constitionnel has not dared to oppose public opinion and to engage in proper legal reasoning."[113] In sum, the limits of restricting Islam could be transgressed only by denying that the burqa is part of Islam. But this has already been disconfirmed by France's own constitutional court, opening up the possibility of European legal intervention.

IT MAY APPEAR odd to take a law that entails a drastic liberty restriction as demonstration for alleged limits to excluding Islam in a liberal state. Doesn't the French burqa prohibition show the exact opposite?[114] Let us be frank. When the first draft of this chapter was written, in March 2010, all available evidence and legal opinion allowed only one conclusion: that a law banning the burqa was constitutionally impossible. So our first draft would conclude on a triumphant note. We had to darken the tone as the story evolved, which eventually shifted from one of triumphant constitutional liberalism to one of successful political backlash against too much of it. We are still impressed how French lawyers, *more geometrico,* initially debunked each possible legal avenue of instituting a burqa ban, in striking uniformity, without a single exception. And it cannot be said that these lawyers were all unfriendly to the political project they were asked to comment on, quite the contrary. Their considered opinions thus showed constitutional liberalism at work, to protect even those whose ways we may despise (as long as they do not do us harm). But one must be equally impressed how quickly these opinions were pushed aside by a political state acting with determination and a sense of mission (or opportunism, considering the popularity of the cause and electoral arithmetic).

There is a larger point to make here, already made before (in Chapter 1) but worth reiteration. When stressing the legal dimension of Islam integration, our claim is not that the legal trumps the political, only that law is a pivotal resource in the process of integration. Anything else would be naive or worse as law is always the result of politics and thus moldable and not written in stone, even if endowed with constitutional hue. Accordingly, when addressing the "limits to excluding" in this chapter, we take these limits to be resources, most of them legal-constitutional in nature, but no claim is made that they always win the day.

CHAPTER THREE

Limits of Including

The German Reluctance to "Cooperate" with Organized Islam

Iᴏ Fʀᴀɴᴄᴇ is struggling with the limits of excluding Islam, Germany must grapple with the opposite problem of determining what, if any, are the limits of inclusion. The contrasting dilemmas—call it France's problem of freedom versus Germany's problem of equality—are deeply grounded in these countries' divergent solutions to linking state and religion in an age of secularization. France's strict separation of state and religion, whose aim is to keep the state free of religion,[1] bears obvious risks for individual liberties, as the current attempts to restrict the "burqa" demonstrate. Germany's more cooperative approach of linking state and religion, which endows officially recognized religions with public status and functions, has a different problem: that of coping with "religious pluralism" (Walter 2006: ch. 7) and to include organized minority religions that arrived only late and that, in form or content, may be ill adapted to the existing corporatist arrangements—especially Islam.

As the German problem is only incompletely grasped as one involving the denial of religious "rights," it is all the more astonishing that it is being corrected by way of legal mechanisms, namely, by a transformation of the old institution-focused "state church law" *(Staatskirchenrecht)* into a more up-to-date, rights-focused "constitutional law of religion" *(Religionsverfassungsrecht)*, which notionally (though not always in reality) wipes out the historical privileges that the established religions had once enjoyed in the German cooperation regime.[2] A major proponent of Religionsverfassungsrecht draws the contrast thus: "*Religionsverfassungsrecht* advocates a civil-society based, constitutional rights-oriented definition of the relationship of the state to religious associations, whereas *Staatskirchenrecht* sticks to the historically evolved, institutional conception" (Walter 2007: 3).

From a legal point of view, the final frontier in the accommodation of Islam in Germany is to grant Islamic organizations the status of "corporation under public law" *(Körperschaft des öffentlichen Rechts),* according to Article 140 of the Basic Law, and to allow them to teach, at public expense, religion as a required part of the school curriculum, according to Article 7 of the Basic Law. Although public corporation status[3] is not formally required for the right of religious instruction in public schools, the conditions for both are "materially" similar: a religious organization must be considered a "religious community" *(Religionsgemeinschaft)* and deemed capable and willing of "cooperating" with the state in the fulfillment of a public function.[4] Accordingly, the two claims for corporation status and religious instruction, which have been in the center of Islamic mobilization in Germany for the past two decades, are closely connected. And they have routinely been rejected by German governments and courts, though on thinning grounds and less and less assertively.

As a result of the legal evolution from Staatskirchenrecht to Religionsverfassungsrecht, to be traced in the pages that follow, the state rejection is no longer principled (if it ever was) but factual, pointing to formal-organizational requirements that Islam does not (yet) fulfill. As one legal observer notes, there are "no principled objections" to granting Islam corporate status today (Walter 2005: 40). For a prominent critic, the "new practice of merely formal examination [of corporate status] is an astonishing event" (Kirchhof 2005: 128). It is premised on yet also repudiates the structural asymmetry between established and new religions that marks (or mars) the old Staatskirchenrecht.

From Staatskirchenrecht to Religionsverfassungsrecht

To fully appreciate the scale of this legal evolution, it is helpful to recall some of the peculiarities of German "state church law" (Staatskirchenrecht), whose "crux" is the attribution of public corporation status to the churches (see Hesse 1964–1965: 357). Staatskirchenrecht is a part of public law that structures the legal relations between state and churches as "commensurable powers" *(kommensurable Mächte),* which face one another "like two property owners" (Smend 1951: 6). The churches figure here as public powers that share certain commonalities with the state, such as eschewing merely "particular interests" in favor of a concern for the "entire human being"[5] or, more mundanely, of "exercising power over human beings."[6] The public law status of churches assimilates them to the state in that "the churches, like otherwise only the state, are in principle altruistically concerned about the entire human being and the entire society" (Muckel 1995: 313). This echoes the legacy of Christian Europe, in which *sacerdotium* and *imperium,* sacral and secular authority, had coexisted as rival powers since the early Middle Ages. At the same time, Staatskirchenrecht, as secular state law regulating the churches, signals a "departure from the dualist conception of order" (Pirson 1994: 4), though not without the concession of letting the disempowered churches retain the public status that is normally the prerogative of the state.

In an incisive comparison of the "Atlantic divide" in separating church and state, James Q. Whitman pointed to the European commonality, in Catholic and Protestant societies alike, of "states that have been gradually absorbing church functions" (2008: 95), from marriage and family law to education and welfare, even the production of a common identity and culture. In Germany, Staatskirchenrecht is both ratification of and compensation for the churches' inevitable loss of power in the process of secularization. Note that this law regulates not "religion" but rather "churches," historical formations *hic et nunc.* One author thus spoke of the inherent "institutional bias" of Staatskirchenrecht (Morlok 2007: 187). Like all corporatist arrangements, Staatskirchenrecht is tailored to its constitutive actors, which happened to be the Christian churches, and later entrants inevitably had to adjust to the strictures of this arrangement (most notably the requirement of "church"-like compression of all believers of one creed into one hierarchical organization, which is familiar in Christianity but not in all religions, Islam included).

The constitutional core of Staatskirchenrecht is Article 140 of the German Basic Law, which simply incorporates into the new German postwar constitution the five church-related articles of the 1919 Weimar Constitution. These Weimar articles reflect a compromise at the time between right-wing clerics wanting to retain the old *Staatskirche* (state church) and leftist atheists pushing instead for a French-style strict separation between state and churches. The heart of the Weimar church compromise is the churches' retention of public status along with the possibility for other "religious associations" *(Religionsgesellschaften)*[7] to attain that status in the future. The condition that newcoming religions have to fulfill is that "through their constitution and size of membership they pass the durability test

[*Gewähr der Dauer*]."[8] From the start there was disagreement about the meaning of public law status as decreed in Weimar Article 137(5). In the view of a left-wing critic, "the nature of a corporation is that it is recognized by the state as a state-like power [*obrigkeitliche Gewalt*]."[9] For a liberal supporter of public law status, conversely, it did "not express any special dignity"; it was "no sign of a particular excellence"; and because "a state church no longer exists, all other churches [*Nebenkirchen*] are of equal dignity."[10] The two positions have marked the spectrum of views on the scope of churches' public law status ever since, the first limiting it to a designated historical few, the second opening it up as much as possible to newcomers. However, with the ascent of the rights-focused "constitutional law of religion" (Religionsverfassungsrecht), the latter position could not but gain the upper hand.

This was not immediately obvious. After World War II, the Christian churches in Germany, which had survived the Nazi regime morally untainted, were revalorized as "forces of pre-political integration" (Maier 1994: 89), while the moral authority of the state was at its historical nadir. This was the heyday of the "coordination doctrine" *(Koordinationslehre)* in classic state church law (Staatskirchenrecht), according to which there was a "basic parity between state and church" (the German Constitutional Court, quoted in Walter 2006: 190). According to one influential view in this mode, the state does not "grant" but merely "encounters and acknowledges" the churches' public law status, and "in no way is there any subordination of church power to state power" (Peters 1954: 187). It was almost as if state and church were two sovereign powers. To this position a statist countermovement quickly retorted that this would mean "the end of the state" (Quaritsch 1962: 298) and that, after all, "*Staatskirchenrecht* is state law" (Schlaich 1972: 188).

After the quick demise of thinking about Staatskirchenrecht in terms of "coordinating" two coequal powers, a new way of cutting—or rather retaining—a special deal for the established churches was in terms of "cooperation and partnership" with the state (see Korioth 2007). In this view, the churches fill the vacuum of meaning that coincides with the rise of the neutral state, which must abstain from soul making for the sake of individual liberty. The intellectual ammunition for this view was provided in a classic essay by prominent constitutional lawyer Ernst-Wolfgang Böckenförde (1991). Böckenförde incontrovertibly interpreted the "rise of the state as a process of secularization" but then argued that the price of liberty is that the secular state can no longer engage in an ethical, identity-making project. In other words, the secular state cannot do nation building. This would conflict with the idea of human rights that underlies liberty: "The individualism of human rights, fully unfolded, emancipates not only from religion, but in a further step also from the (ethnic) nation as homogenizing force" (Böckenförde 1991: 112). This leads to his famous conclusion: "The liberal, secular state relies on conditions that it cannot itself guarantee. This is the great wager that it has made, for the sake of liberty" (p. 112). The liberal state depends on a liberal culture that it cannot produce by the typical means at its disposal, which is "law and order" (p. 113). Into the void of meaning steps religion but only the religion that is genealogically responsible for and thus commensurate with secularization: Christianity. So Böckenförde asks, "again, with Hegel, whether even the secularized state does not in the last instance depend on the inner motivations and cohesive powers that religious belief gives to its citizens" (p. 113).

The "Böckenförde paradox" (Huster 2007: 124) is usually cited by those who give an exclusive, asymmetric reading to the public law clause that is central to classic Staatskirchenrecht. Religious communities that are granted public law status are "closer" to the state than ordinary religious associations, and they become enlisted in "pursuing the common interest in the public realm" (Muckel 1995: 313). In a particularly effusive formulation, corporation status is even "an institution for spiritually grounding the political community" (Albrecht 1995: 3). The most eloquent defender of this view today is conservative constitutional lawyer Paul Kirchhof. Only the Christian religion, with its tenet that God has become human in the person of Jesus, supports the principles of "personality," "dignity," and "equality" on which "our concrete constitutional order rests" (Kirchhof 1994: 664; Kirchhof 2005: 110). Being "embedded in the Christian-Occidental legal culture," the Basic Law does not allow a "competition of cultures" (Kirchhof 1994: 669). With an eye on Islamic organizations clamoring for public law status, this status is to be denied "if no participation in the culture underlying the Basic Law is to be expected" (p. 668).[11]

Aware that this view is running "against the tide," Kirchhof (2005: 130) ridicules the multiculturalism condoned by Religionsverfassungsrecht: "There are two teams which fight against one another, Christianity and Islam, and the state is the spectator." No, he responds, only the Christian churches are the "humus of this constitutional state." This naturally goes along with a traditionalist reading of Staatskirchenrecht in which state and church figure as two coequal powers, "free neighbors that order their legal relationships" (2005: 112), as Kirchhof writes, citing constitutional jurist Rudolf Smend. The claim that the churches may be "separate from" but are still "parallel to" the state is rendered plausible to him by the fact that qua being public law corporations, churches enjoy certain "sovereign" *(hoheitliche)* prerogatives. Examples are taxing their members, employing civil servants via *Dienstherrenfähigkeit* (which exempts the churches from the strictures of labor law and social security law), and, of course, determining the contents and modalities of religious instruction in public schools. The churches' *Hoheitsgewalt* (sovereign authority) even has a territorial reference, in terms of the *Parochialrecht* that makes mobile members of a religious association join a different parish automatically, by the mere fact of changing residence (Kirchhof 1994: 671).

Indeed, an inclusive, rights-oriented reading of the public law clause, within the ambit of Religionsverfassungsrecht, cannot make plausible why public law should be engaged for the sake of religious liberty: "The classical means to unfold societal liberty is private law" (Korioth 2007: 65). By contrast, the meaning of public corporation status is "the possibility of a deepened partnership between religious communities and the state" (p. 65). In seeking public law status, the religious community "turns to the state"; it asks for privileges that exceed the extensive religious rights already granted to it by Article 4 of the Basic Law. Why should the state not be allowed to be choosy in this respect? Paul Kirchhof (2005: 114) defends the state's selectivity with an evocative metaphor: "[The state] protects academic freedom in general, but it seeks the counsel only of the highly qualified scholar."

It has to be seen that the German church-state regime, enshrined in Article 140 of the Basic Law, sits on top of one of the world's most extensive systems of protecting religious liberties, one that incidentally has been voraciously inclusive of minority religions (as well as of nonreligious worldviews [*Weltanschauungen*]). Its constitutional locus is Article 4 of the Basic Law, whose first paragraph stipulates: "The freedom of belief, of conscience, and the freedom of religious and non-religious [*weltanschaulich*] creed [*Bekenntnis*] are inviolable." A constitutional right without statutory proviso, and in this sense absolute (restricted only by other constitutional principles), this is notably a right not just to adhere to one's belief privately but to exercise it in public and collectively. This is laid out in its second paragraph (Article 4.2): "The unhindered exercise of religion is guaranteed." Religious liberty rights thus have an inherently collective dimension, entailing the freedom to form religious associations, which is prior to and separate from the public law status available in addition through the "institutional" church Article 140 in the Basic Law.[12]

Kirchhof's (2005: 114) justification for the state to be choosy when granting public law status now appears more plausible. Witness that a comparison of "free exercise" freedoms in Germany and the United States concluded that "German law accords wider scope [of protection]" (Eberle

2004: 1025), with no "ebb and flow" that has marred American law (p. 1062). Moreover, Eberle continues, with respect to granting exemptions from "generally applicable neutral laws," German law is much more accommodating to religious minorities than American law, whose tolerance has rarely stretched beyond Christian sects (p. 1085)—no small surprise considering the usual celebration of American liberalism (nay, multiculturalism) over European parochialism in this domain (e.g., Nussbaum 2008: ch. 1).

The benchmark case for Germany's exceptionally strong protection of religious liberties is the Federal Constitutional Court's *Aktion Rumpelkammer* decision of 1968.[13] This case concerned the free collection of old clothing to be resold for charity purposes by the Catholic Country Youth in Bavaria, which led to the collapse of the regional used-clothing industry. For the Constitutional Court, this case did not involve illicit economic competition under the pretext of religious charity, as the lower court had agreed with the—by then—bankrupt plaintiffs, but rather was an "expression of churchly love" *(Ausdruck kirchlicher Liebestätigkeit)*[14]—even though the group in question did not formally qualify as a Religionsgemeinschaft (religious community), and even though it may seem farfetched to call the collection of old clothing an "exercise of religion" according to Article 4(2) of the Basic Law. The court, in fact, established in this rule a quite extensive definition of religious liberty, which applied to ordinary organizations *(Vereine)* and which included the "freedom of religious [*kultisch*] action, proselytizing, and propaganda."[15] As the court explicated, such extensive definition of religious freedom was especially warranted as a "defensive posture against the restrictions of religious practice under the Nazi rule of violence."[16]

Even though no minority religions were on the radar when the *Rumpelkammer* decision was issued in 1968, the court did not forget to add that such expansively defined religious liberties applied not just to "Christian churches" but also to "other religious . . . communities."[17] This followed from the state's "mandate of *weltanschaulich*-religious neutrality" and the "principle of parity of churches and creeds." From the principle of neutrality also followed that what counted as religious practice had to be in accordance with the "self-understanding" of the respective religious community, which in this case happened to consider "charity" a religious action.[18] Much as expansively defined religious freedoms trumped the market in this case, religious freedoms would in future trump criminal law,[19] even the special loyalties that were expected of the state's civil servants *(Beamte)*.[20]

The new "constitutional law of religion" (Religionsverfassungsrecht) may be understood as reinterpreting from the vantage point of the more recent, individualistic religious liberty rights provided for in Article 4 of the Basic Law the older, corporatist prong of the German religion-state regime, which dates back to the Weimar Republic and which from there reaches even further back deeply into European state history. One proponent of Religionsverfassungsrecht explicates the sociological context of this move: "The recent individualization, pluralization, and secularization of society, but also the rise of an individual rights culture suggest an interpretation of the Weimar church articles from the vantage point of the religious liberties guaranteed by Article 4 of the Basic Law" (Morlok 2007: 197). Indeed, if Article 4 is taken to be the lodestar of the German religion-state system, the oddity of an asymmetric, Christian-preference reading of the public corporation clause in Article 140 jumps to the fore.

Most important, to grant public corporation status according to a religion's compatibility with "Christian-Occidental" values, as demanded by Kirchhof (1994, 2005) with the help of the Böckenförde paradox (1991), would force the state into a "selection according to the contents of the particular religion" (Walter 2006: 553). This, however, would violate the liberal state's neutrality mandate, which tells the state to abstain from any substantive evaluation of or stance taking toward religious beliefs.

Second, the awarding of public law status according to a religion's "usefulness" for the state reifies the state as a self-reproducing, unitary actor standing apart from society and abstracts from its democratic form. Paul Kirchhof awkwardly appraises Nazi lawyer Ernst Forsthoff's characterization of the churches' public law status as "documenting the self-interest of the state to maintain and reproduce itself" (Kirchhof 1994: 663). Such reasoning echoes Article 13 of the 1794 Prussian *Allgemeines Landrecht*: "Every church association is obliged to instill in its members a respect for God, obedience of the laws, loyalty [*Treue*] to the state, and morally good attitudes toward the other citizens." Formally speaking, there is little difference between then and now in the attempted "instrumentalization of religion for public order" (Korioth 2007: 46). Yet the Prussian state was a self-declared "Christian state," while the pre-1945 Weimar and post-1945 Bonn-Berlin Republic emphatically was not and is not, respectively. "The 'Christian state,' still present in the Prussian Constitution of 1850, has irretrievably disappeared in history," writes one conservative lawyer, who does not like the fact (Link 2002: 58). There is a ceremonial reference to the "responsibility before God" in the preamble of the Basic Law, but no one has ever argued that this amounts to a preference for monotheism or

Christianity. Hans Michael Heinig and Martin Morlok dryly summarize the dominant legal opinion: "The pivotal cultural importance of Christianity for our constitutional order is historically beyond doubt. However, it has no independent legal force; the Basic Law shows neither a preference for Christian culture nor a legally relevant affinity to a particular religion" (2003: 784).

The famous 1995 *Kruzifix* decision of the Federal Constitutional Court, in which the display of Christian crosses in Bavarian public schools was declared unconstitutional, powerfully denied to the Christian majority, as to any other religious group in society, "the right to have its creed expressed with the help of the state."[21] This followed from "the principle of state neutrality," according to which the state, "even if it cooperates with or supports a particular religious association, must never identify with it."[22] The Christian prime minister was so upset about this rule that he called on the Bavarian people to "disobey" it. But the constitutional impossibility of a preference for Christianity has never been more effectively stated, and, paradoxically, in its reference to the religious liberty clause of the Basic Law, the crucifix decision has become a cornerstone of the new Religionsverfassungsrecht.[23]

Third, and more profanely, the painting of the churches' public corporation status in state-like, quasi-sovereign colors ignores the fact that this is a sui generis variant of public law status. Unlike ordinary corporations under public law, like the federal state, the Länder, municipalities, and most universities, the religious communities granted this status do not thereby become part of the state; instead, they still meet the state "as parts of society" (Walter 2006: 592). From this reading it follows that religious communities with public law status do not thereby partake in public power according to Article 1(3) of the Basic Law,[24] which obliges the three branches of the state to respect the basic rights of the constitution. Instead, qua religious community they remain entitled to these rights as defensive rights against the state.

The Federal Constitutional Court's September 2000 decision granting public law status to Jehovah's Witnesses marks the culmination of a rights-focused reinterpretation of the Basic Law's public corporation clause and of the new Religionsverfassungsrecht trumping the old Staatskirchenrecht. In this decision, the court famously declared that the status of a corporation under public law was a "means to unfold religious liberty," thus reading Article 140 of the Basic Law entirely from the perspective of Article 4.[25] This decision affirmed the plaintiff's claim that public corporation status was an expression of "protecting basic rights through the state" and thus could not entail or presuppose a special "proximity to the state."[26]

Furthermore, it could not be expected that the religious community shows a deeper "loyalty" to the state, as the Federal Administrative Court had demanded in its rejection of public corporation status to Jehovah's Witnesses in 1997.[27] From a rights-focused perspective, "loyalty" was an odd requirement, as "this concept aims at an inner disposition, an attitude, and not an external behavior." Such a requirement would "not only endanger legal security [*Rechtssicherheit*] but also lead to an approximation between religious community and state, which the *Staatskirchenrecht* of the Basic Law neither demands nor condones."[28] It would have been more appropriate to call this stance Religionsverfassungsrecht than stick to the old notion of Staatskirchenrecht. Within the ambit of the former, all that could be expected of the religious community, or of any other individual or group in the state, was "faithfulness to the law" *(Rechtstreue),*[29] which is less than "loyalty."

It is helpful to contrast this benchmark decision with the 1997 Federal Administrative Court ruling concerning Jehovah's Witnesses, whose denial of public corporation status had still affirmed classic positions of institution-focused Staatskirchenrecht.[30] To be granted corporation status was here "not a necessary consequence of religious liberty but a privilege granted by the state."[31] In fact, the administrative court drew a sharp contrast between the rights-focused Article 4 and the institution-focused Article 140 of the Basic Law, in which the public corporation status was grounded. That being so, the entitlement to corporation status had its basis not in "religious liberty" but in "current *Staatskirchenrecht.*" This was Staatskirchenrecht as one knows it: a law of institutions, not of individuals and their entitlements. Considering the "not inconsiderable privileges" connected with corporation status, it was not enough to be merely "faithful to the law" *(rechtstreu);* a deeper "loyalty" to the state was required. Corporation status, after all, entailed the "delegation of sovereign state power" *(Übertragung staatlicher Hoheitsgewalt),*[32] which, as it were, could not be given away for free. Recognition of corporate status was an "offer to cooperate by the state," to be granted only if the religious community's activities "were also in the interest of the state."[33] At the same time, being "rooted in society and thus by nature separate from the state," the religious community "followed its own interests."[34] This required a "minimum of mutual respect."[35] A religious community, which "seeks proximity to the state" and claims "this state's legal means and tools of power for its purposes," could not at the same time "question the bases of the state's existence in a principled way."[36] Indeed, a group that, like Jehovah's Witnesses, called the state "the instrument of Satan" and called on its members not to vote in state elections would unavoidably "weaken the legitimate basis of state power," which is democracy, and it certainly could not become the state's "cooperating partner."[37]

The Federal Constitutional Court's September 2000 rejection of the "loyalty" proviso and its interpretation of public law status as a "means of unfolding religious liberty" wiped out these considerations at a stroke.[38] Only such a position was consistent with the liberal state's neutrality mandate, which prohibits the state from evaluating the contents of a religious creed. The constitutional court cautiously criticized the administrative high court's loyalty requirement: "In asking for loyalty to the state . . . the Federal Administrative Court may have crossed the limits that are drawn to the state with respect to evaluating religious practices and expressions [*Lebensäusserungen*] by the neutrality mandate."[39]

The Constitutional Court's *Zeugen Jehovahs* decision has monumental implications for the corporate recognition of Islam: as not "loyalty" but only "faithfulness to the law" could be expected as a precondition for public law status, a lack of "proximity to the state" or of Occidental cultural pedigree could not be a ground for denying this status. All the state could do was check the formal-organizational but not substantive-creedal prerequisites. This it would do from now on, one is tempted to say, with compensatory vengeance.

One cannot fail to appreciate the state's persistent reluctance against the background of classic Staatskirchenrecht, which was sharply repudiated in the *Zeugen Jehovahs* decision. Though stringent from the point of view of neutrality, there are certain oddities and inconsistencies connected with this decision. As Article 4 of the Basic Law already provided for a religious "comprehensive basic right" *(Gesamtgrundrecht)* (Hillgruber 2001: 1348), which included individual and collective liberties, one could not but interpret the corporation clause of the Basic Law as an expression of a "special relation with the state" or recognition of the "public usefulness" *(gemeinnütziger Charakter)* of a religious community (Hillgruber 2007: 216). Isn't it bizarre to couch in terms of a defensive right against the state—which is what all constitutional liberty rights essentially are—the positive turning to the state, which is what the public law status clause in Article 140 of the Basic Law had always meant, and which had even entailed a certain "reduction of the right to self-determination" (Muckel 1995: 314)?

A rights-focused interpretation of the public law clause is even inconsistent with some classic-institutional elements in the Constitutional Court's own *Zeugen Jehovahs* decision. Note that the court conceded that the corporate religion's "increased influence in state and society" made it "closer than other religious communities to the special duties of the Basic

Law to protect the rights of third parties."[40] In this sense, the corporate religion was more obliged by than entitled to fundamental rights. This hinted at the corporate status clause's (in fact, the entire Staatskirchen-recht's) "institutional bias, which defies its framing in terms of individual rights" (Korioth 2007: 66). Furthermore, the reinterpretation of the corporation clause in terms of a "means to unfold religious liberty"[41] rendered the constitutionally required "proof of durability"[42] test *ad absurdum*. "Proof of durability," after all, privileges "old and renowned," which is hard to reconcile with a rights-focused interpretation of the corporation clause. If the latter was carried to the end, the corporation clause should instead favor the young and fledgling religions, in a kind of "support-young-businesses" *(Existenzgründerhilfe)* attitude—which is clearly against both the letter and the spirit of the law (Hillgruber 2007: 210).

Islam's Long March through the Courts

To put in perspective the reluctance of the German state with regard to granting public law status to Islam, it is important to realize how much Islam's legal integration has proceeded apart from the organizational-level or corporatist track on the individual rights track. The legal literature even speaks, critically, of a "hypertrophying of the constitutional right of religious liberty" (Janz and Rademacher 1999: 708).

Legal Multiculturalism. A precedent-setting case for placing religious liberty above all other considerations, in effect institutionalizing a kind of legal multiculturalism in Germany, has been a 1993 decision of the Federal Administrative Court to exempt a twelve-year-old Turkish girl from coeducational sport lessons.[43] Germany's leading left-liberal newsmagazine, *Der Spiegel,* later dubbed this decision a "major transgression [*Sündenfall*] on the road to the legal protection of an Islamic parallel society."[44] The girl's parents had expressly stated in court that they "did not wish their daughter to be emancipated as Westerners understand that term" (Albers 1994: 987). The court assented to the parents' wishes, putting the girl's "fear of losing her headscarf," accommodated by Article 4 of the Basic Law, above the state's educational mandate, articulated in Article 7. Certainly, as always when two constitutional principles came to a head, a "practical concordance" between both had to be reached. But the public school administration's "obligation to exhaust all organizational possibilities to offer separate sports instruction for girls above the age of twelve"[45] had to be met. In times of chronic budget shortages and streamlined curricula, this was no easy thing to establish. The legal representative of the federal government in this case wisely foresaw that "a one-sided preference for the religious needs of pupils and their parents" would lead to a "total collapse" of the state mandate to "educate in common the children of many nationalities and religions."[46]

Reports from the front suggest that this fear was not without foundation. For instance, the principal of a primary school in Frankfurt am Main, in a part of this heavily immigrant city still not known to be "too difficult," calls it "business as usual" when "Muslim kids don't appear at swimming lessons; girls don't show up on the morning of a class excursion; pupils are picked up by their parents before sex education classes; classrooms are empty on Islamic holidays, before the beginning or after the end of vacation, and sometimes for weeks thereafter."[47] A sports teacher at the same Frankfurt school describes the local reality: "Practically no Muslim kid knows how to swim; physical activity is avoided. Girls don't have bicycles or inline skates."[48]

Crucially, the readiness of German courts to grant exemptions from the curriculum for the sake of religious liberty has become public knowledge at the Muslim grassroots. Interested parents can download from the popular Muslim-Markt.de Web site a standard letter with which to request their daughter's exemption from coeducational swimming lessons. The letter quotes the benchmark 1993 Federal Administrative Court decision but also a 1991 decision of the Upper Administrative Court of North-Rhine Westphalia that had even ordered a primary school girl's exemption from coeducational swimming lessons.[49] The 1991 court ruling explicitly condones the "Islamic fundamentalists'" extension of the sexual shame barrier far into the prepuberty phase of development, so that a girl of "ca. 8.5 sun years" was said to have reached "religious maturity" and was thus supposed to "hide her body (except face and hands) for non-related men and male youth."[50] For the court, this followed from the principle of state neutrality, which denies the state an evaluation of religious beliefs.[51] Certainly, a "careful balancing" of the state's education mandate against religious liberty rights had to be achieved in keeping with the "principle of concordance," but it is astonishing to see how little weight the state's education mandate seems to have had.[52] What today one would call a concern for "integration" was deliberately ignored: "It is irrelevant whether the Islamic dress code . . . is to the detriment of women by Western standards, relegating them to an outsider role in our society. This is because the societal effect of a belief is of no importance whatsoever in light of the need to protect a subjective religious belief." More than that, this way of protecting religious liberty explicitly discarded the interest of the child. If the

Muslim girl was forced to be an outsider, with "negative effect on the development of her personality," she had to "accept" it if "her parents insist on her behalf on the unhindered exercise of religion."[53] If some have argued that multiculturalism is "bad" for vulnerable members of minorities (Moller Okin 1999; Shachar 2001), here was a particularly pertinent and shockingly court-sanctioned example of the problem.

Since "integration" became a major public policy concern in the aftermath of the terrorist attacks of 2001, there has been a certain moderation of court-ordered multiculturalism under the cloak of religious liberty rights. When having to decide whether a nine-year-old Shiite Muslim girl should be exempted from the religious affront of coeducational swimming lessons, the Administrative Court of Hamburg reinstated the distinction between "children" and "youth" with respect to religious dress norms,[54] which had motivated the Federal Administrative Court in 1993 to establish the threshold of separate sports instruction for girls at twelve years. The 1993 court decision was incidentally "respected in Hamburg schools," yet legally savvy Muslim organizations sought in cases like this to push things further down the separatist road.[55] Not this time. In its rejection of the desired exemption, the Hamburg court gave an emphatically stronger rendition of the state's education mandate than in the past, where it might have been mentioned but then ignored. Now subjects as trivial as swimming and sports were deemed important for the "formation of responsible citizens, who are to participate equally and responsibly in the democratic processes of a pluralistic society."[56] To commit minority groups to this experience was a remedy to the threat of "parallel societies" and a tool of "integration," which was no longer discarded as a relevant concern.[57] And if back in 1991 Muslim females' "outsider role in society" was to be accepted for the sake of religious liberty, in 2005 an upgraded educational mandate included a concern for equality of the sexes, in accordance with Article 3(2) of the Basic Law.[58] Finally, children were no longer the pawns of their parents, so that children's religious rights in reality boiled down to their parents' religious rights; instead children were endowed with their "own dignity and the right of the free development of [their] personality," protected by the first two articles of the Basic Law.[59]

Although it reflected the new "integration" rhetoric of the post-2001 period, the 2005 Hamburg lower court ruling was no reversal of German courts' typically liberal line on religious exemptions from general laws—no high court has ever reversed the benchmark 1993 decision of the Federal Administrative Court. Instead, a limit was set to extreme demands emboldened by this decision. Consider the refusal of the Administrative Court of Düsseldorf, also in 2005, to exempt from coeducational swimming lessons a fifth-grade Muslim boy. This claim, novel in extending a Muslim dress code to male children, was advanced despite the availability of separate locker rooms for boys and girls and despite the fact that the school had allowed the boy to wear a special, navel-to-knee swim dress. As the court argued, giving in to such a demand would amount to obliging the school to insulate the Muslim child, who was "not yet a man," from an "everyday activity in this society," and the court insisted further that, if there was a problem, it could be resolved as in everyday life—by "looking away."[60] But even if there was an "objective conflict of conscience," which the court denied, its accommodation through the religious liberty and parental education clauses of the Basic Law still would have to "recede" behind the state's mandate to provide an equal education for all.[61] Referring, as the Hamburg court had done before, to a 2003 Federal Constitutional Court decision that had prohibited home schooling to adherents of fundamentalist Christian sects, the Düsseldorf court enlisted public schools in the "formation of responsible citizens,"[62] adding: "Schools are not insulated but part of German society. . . . In everyday life there are always situations in which Muslims are confronted with more liberal values, which they cannot avoid dealing with. The same holds true for public swimming lessons, which have the advantage of teachers around to reduce the tensions."[63]

Mosques and Ritual Slaughtering. Short of achieving public corporation status, Islam could profit from expansively construed religious liberty rights not just as individually but also as collectively practiced religion. A pertinent example is the construction and operation of mosques. Certainly, only corporations under public law get priority permits in residential areas, while all other religious organizations are forced into less restrictive industrial or "mixed" zones. However, a clause in the *Baugesetzbuch* (Building Code) requiring respect for the "social and cultural needs of the population" in the granting of construction permits approximates the status of mosques to that of churches (Oebbecke 2009: 237). Land use planning, argued the Upper Administrative Court of Rhineland-Palatinate against local opposition to a minaret in 2001, "can and shall not be milieu protection" (p. 239). Already in 1992, the Federal Administrative Court had decided that residents of a neighborhood near a mosque had to "accept in principle" that they might be awakened before dawn by religionists driving up to attend the early morning prayer (quoted in Lemmen 2002: 136), because the free exercise of religion ranked higher than the need for sleep. So much have mosques "in effect" been equated to churches and synagogues that "legislation would not help resolving or attenuating stillexisting conflicts in this area," according to a report by the Deutsche Islam

Konferenz (2008: 8). Even the muezzin's public call to prayer, which according to the Sunna is to occur five times per day, is protected by religious liberty rights. Its ritual text being considered part of the prayer itself, the call to prayer differs from the sound of church bells, with which it is legally equated, in that the latter is neutral in itself and may also serve some other function, say, to indicate the hour. By ritual prescription intoned in Arabic, and the first of its seven parts announcing that "Allah [God] is the Greatest" (to be repeated four times), the muezzin's call to prayer, especially if supported by loudspeakers, has repeatedly stirred conflict, the bone of contention being less the noise (the typical nuisance of church bells) than the verbal "attack on Christian culture."[64] Perhaps aware of the provocation, most mosques have "voluntarily abandoned their right" in this respect.[65] There is, in general, little case law on the construction and operation of mosques in Germany—instead, Muslim claimants here have mostly preferred informal "negotiations and discussions" to costly and contentious litigation (Oebbecke 2009: 240).

The same cannot be said about a second collective, organization-requiring aspect of practicing Islam, namely, ritual slaughter (for the production of halal meat). The right to kill animals without prior stunning, which would have to involve an exemption from the animal protection laws, has been fought all the way up to Germany's highest courts, ultimately with success. This issue also constituted a test case concerning how much (or rather how little) church-type organization on the part of Muslims was required to allow them to live in conformity with their perceived religious precepts. Article 4 of the 1986 Animal Protection Law grants an exemption from the general prescription of stunning, which is intended to minimize the animal's suffering, "if binding rules [*zwingende Vorschriften*] of a religious association forbid its members the consumption of flesh from non-ritually slaughtered animals." Jews had always been granted such an exemption but not Muslims.

In 1995, the Federal Administrative Court refused an Islamic exemption from the prohibition on ritual killing *(schächten)* for two reasons.[66] First, as there was no religious prescription to eat meat, the requirement of stunning could not be construed as a denial of religious liberty, according to Article 4 of the Basic Law. Muslims were not carnivores qua being Muslim. As the court advised them, not without sarcasm, they could eat "vegetables or fish" instead.[67] Brian Barry would have smiled, because this ruling confirmed his distinction between restricting "opportunities" (alone reprehensible from a liberal point of view) and reducing actual "choices" within a set of equal opportunities (which was the issue here): "Nobody is bound to eat meat" (Barry 2001: 45). But why were Jews allowed what

Muslims weren't? Back in 1983, before the 1986 Animal Protection Act would formalize the granting of exemptions, a local administrative court had held: "The permission for Jews to slaughter represents an act of . . . compensation to the Jews who are still alive. The Jewish religion has in Germany a greater historical tradition than the Muslims. . . . There exists no violation against the principle of equal treatment with respect to the Muslims" (quoted in Lavi 2009: 174). So blatant a violation of the equality principle in religious matters no German high court has ever dared to make.

Instead, the Federal Administrative Court resorted to a second, on its face more compelling reason to deny the Muslim plaintiffs their exemption: there simply was "no obligatory religious prescription" in Islam, said the court, that would prohibit the consumption of meat from animals that were stunned before killing.[68] This assertion pointed to Islam's weak spot in seeking entry into a Christian-dominated church-state regime, namely, its lack of a church-like, central, and hierarchical organization that sets binding rules for its members and which the state could consult in such matters. "The customers of the plaintiff [the cafeteria of a Hamburg mosque] are not members of a religious association that prohibits its members through binding rules the consumption of meat of non-ritually slaughtered animals," declared the court, reiterating that under Staatskirchenrecht a "religious community" (Religionsgemeinschaft) was one that "comprises the member of one and the same faith . . . for the comprehensive fulfillment of the tasks set by the shared faith" and which had to be "externally clearly delimited and internally capable of subjecting its members to binding rules."[69] A later decision by the same court on the protracted dispute over ritual slaughtering clarified that this could not mean that the religious association in question had to be formally a "corporation under public law,"[70] but the substantive requirement that it constitute a religious community came close to it.

It is true that there is no agreement among Muslim jurists about the strictness of the ritual slaughter requirement or whether one exists at all in non-Muslim lands. The influential minority *fiqh* of Yusuf al-Qaradawi, for instance, holds that Muslims are allowed the food of "People of the Book," that is, Jews and Christians, so that the entire issue disappears (see Bergeaud-Blackler 2007: 974–975). In 1982, the West German government obtained a fatwa from the religious Al-Azhar University in Cairo that electric stunning in itself was not illicit and that what mattered was that the animal's throat was cut while still alive—which is normally the case when the animal is stunned with an electric shock. Similarly, a fatwa by the Turkish religious state authority (Diyanet) held that slaughtering after electric stunning was not in violation of Islamic law. Whoever has watched the agony of throat-slashed sheep suffocating in their own blood would not find unreasonable the charge of animal rights activists that unnecessary suffering is inflicted on animals under the cloak of religious freedom.

The Federal Constitutional Court's eventual approval of ritual slaughter, in a landmark 2002 decision, is rather reserved about this aspect of the issue.[71] Its important innovation, a milestone in the accommodation of Islam in Germany, is to move from an objective to a subjective view of what religion prescribes, thus rendering irrelevant the question of its churchlike organization for achieving equality in this respect. Or, as one observer formulated the shift: "Religious freedom to slaughter no longer required public recognition of institutional affiliation and could be granted on the basis of individual belief" (Lavi 2009: 178). The difficulty with the 1995 Federal Administrative Court decision had been that the court had arrogated to itself a view of what Islam objectively prescribed (or rather did not prescribe): "The Koran . . . does not include a general prohibition of stunning."[72] In evaluating the content of a religious creed, this was a blatant violation of the requirement that the state maintain neutrality in these matters. By contrast, the Federal Constitutional Court in 2002 held that the "self-understanding" of a religious association, which could never comprise all members of the faith, had to be the benchmark of what religion prescribed and that the state had to "refrain from evaluating this faith": "The question of the existence of binding rules has to be answered by the concrete religious community within the larger interpretation of the faith [*Glaubensrichtung*]."[73] Unlike the Federal Administrative Court, the Constitutional Court did not further stipulate what constituted a "religious community," so that the question of what religion prescribed was effectively made a matter of subjective definition.

More in passing, the constitutional court also lifted the second pillar in the Federal Administrative Court's 1995 prohibition of ritual slaughtering, namely, that the consumption of meat was outside the scope of the right to religious freedom: "To ask of [Muslims] that they renounce the consumption of meat would be to take insufficiently into account the dietary habits of German society."[74] However, the court sidestepped the question of the scope of the religious liberty clause of the Basic Law (Article 4) by looking at the case primarily in terms of the denial of the "professional liberty" *(Berufsfreiheit)* of the plaintiff (a Turkish butcher who saw his business interests harmed by the prohibition of ritual slaughter). In an interesting twist, as Article 12 of the Basic Law, which guarantees Berufsfreiheit, is notionally a right reserved for Germans, the court resorted to Article 2, which protects individuals' "general freedom of action" *(allgemeine Hand-lungsfreiheit),* without any nationality constraints.

Alas, this was not the end of the matter. While the court-going Turkish butcher, Rüstem Altinküpe, from the idyllic town of Asslar in Hesse, became a household name for his eight-year-long legal struggle, his victory quickly turned sour. The animal rights lobby now had found an obvious target, and it quickly achieved, with the help of the then-governing Christian Democratic Party (CDU), constitutional status for the principle of animal protection, by way of a reformed Article 20a of the Basic Law. Now two equally valid constitutional principles clashed with one another. With the animal rights lobby breathing down their necks, local administrations now resorted to a strict practice of granting permits for ritual slaughtering (if a permit was granted at all). This meant requiring the presence of a public veterinarian; requiring written requests from each individual customer indicating that, for religious reasons, none but ritually prepared meat would do; and prohibiting the sale of halal meat to nonprivate customers, such as mosques or other butchers. "This is like under communism," the Muslim butcher from Asslar complained,[75] and again the courts were called to the rescue. In 2006, the Federal Administrative Court decreed that the recently granted constitutional status of animal rights, according to the amended Article 20 of the Basic Law, "did not preclude" the granting of exemptions from the animal protection law for ritual slaughtering, even though it allowed severe restrictions on granting these exemptions.[76] The hassles with pedantic local administrations were at least partially eased by another 2009 decision of the Federal Constitutional Court, which found that no public veterinarian had to be present during the ritual slaughtering.[77] This also ended Altinküpe's legal battle, which by now had dragged on for some fifteen years. An editorialist celebrated the media-shy but legally savvy Muslim butcher as "de facto German" and "constitutional patriot," while conceding that "his strict Sunni faith marks the limit of assimilation."[78] German courts have helped mightily to keep this limit in place, so that the sociological "limit of assimilation" also marks Islam's successful legal integration.

Limits of Inclusion (I): Public Corporation Status

Islam's impressive march through the German courts, helped by "extensively interpreted and practiced" religious liberty rights (Janz and Rademacher 1999: 708), must be kept in mind when considering the extant limits of inclusion, especially the denial of public corporation status. As we saw, an "extensive" religious liberty right, which relegates what religion is and what it prescribes to the subjective view of the believer, makes public corporation status less important—this has been the result of the protracted conflict over religious slaughtering. Moreover, the progression of the religious liberty right, in terms of contemporary Religionsverfassungsrecht, has affected the definition of the corporate status itself, as an "expression of constitutional liberty" (Korioth 1999: 231).[79]

So why has public corporation status still been denied to Islam? A concise and influential legal discussion of the mid-1990s concluded: "Muslim communities . . . don't yet have a 'constitution' that would enable them to develop a relationship to the state that is grounded in partnership and enduring cooperation" (Muckel 1995: 317). This formulation is less innocent than it may appear, because it combines the consensual and the controversial. Consensual, though as such no less astonishing, is the couching of the public status question as a "not yet," an interim that cannot last, to be decided more on the formal-organizational than on the creedal-substantive terrain. Controversial, however, and expressive of a nagging substantive concern, is the claim that "partnership" and "cooperation" are not merely a possible result but a hard legal prerequisite of corporation status. After the Constitutional Court's 2000 Jehovah's Witnesses decision, this part of the explanation appears outdated. In direct opposition to the Federal Administrative Court's 1997 view that corporate status was "an offer of the state to cooperate,"[80] the Constitutional Court argued there that it was unconstitutional for the state to "lure religious communities into cooperation through the offering of privileges"[81]; instead, these communities were free to "keep distant from the state" if that was their wish. To hand out privileges as reward for cooperation, in a kind of deal-making tit-for-tat, Stefan Magen (2004: 151) admonishes, is a "civilist scheme" that is "foreign to the Basic Law."

However, this legal evolution has been so radical, disempowering the state and empowering the religious individual, irrespective of her citizen status, that even its proponents often shrink back from the consequences. After arguing, cogently, that "loyalty" could be at most an "ethical expectation" but not a "legal-constitutional obligation," a partisan of liberal Religionsverfassungsrecht suddenly pushes back, opining that "the lack of will and capacity [of Jehovah's Witnesses] to cooperate with the state rendered perhaps in effect correct" the Federal Administrative Court's denial of public corporation status in 1997 (Korioth 1999: 245). This is plainly contradictory but also a recovery of common sense against a bizarrely self-referential legal evolution—why should the state bestow statelike privileges on organizations that reject the state?

It is helpful to rehash here some oddities of public corporation status, at least as applied to religious organizations. A corporation *(Körperschaft)* is usually defined as a "personal association with legal capacity which, by sovereign [*hoheitliche*] means and under state supervision, administers state tasks" (Magen 2004: 128). However, at the latest with the abolition of a state church *(Staatskirche)* in the Weimar Constitution, this definition does not even fit the historical churches, which are neither "under state supervision" nor "administering state tasks." If the concept was still applied to them, this was a distant echo of the churches' historical role in governing European societies. When the corporation clause was included in the Weimar Constitution, its purpose was deliberately left vague, and it came to be tellingly denounced by Carl Schmitt as "dilatory formulaic compromise." "Not to concretize the public function of the churches," as Stefan Magen finds (2004: 169), "was the basis of the Weimar Church Compromise."

As the public corporation status should be "no privilege of the Christian church" and be open for all "sects" and "new religions," and as it should not express "a special dignity"[82] of the institutions endowed with that status, the original understanding of the criteria for conferring this status was deliberately formalistic: the sole criterion was to be the anemic "durability test" *(Gewähr der Dauer)* that would exclude ephemeral "one-day foundations of the day before yesterday."[83] As if this were not thin enough, the durability test was at first defined only in terms of "the number of members," that is, in terms of size. The concept "constitution" was added at the eleventh hour, thus bringing in a modicum of substantive "dignity" considerations (Muckel 1999: 585). Note that Stefan Muckel's (1995: 317) concern about organized Islam's inability to provide "partnership and cooperation" with the state is expressed as a concern about its "constitution," which allows him to smuggle in substantive concerns within an otherwise formalistic status-granting procedure.

In fact, an initially "formal" procedure of conferring public corporation status became "materially" loaded only in the context of an increasingly "multi-religious and a-religious society" (Korioth 1999 235). Now the focus in the conferral practice and its legal commentary shifted from the very limited "written" criteria to the rather more amorphous "unwritten" ones, the only uncontroversial requirement among the latter being the religious community's "faithfulness to law" *(Rechtstreue)*. In addition to this *Rechtstreue,* and more controversially, a variety of "thicker" unwritten criteria were proposed, such as "'recognition-worthiness'" *(Anerkennungswürdigkeit),* to ensure the new religion's compatibility with the "constitutional cultural basis of the political community" (Albrecht 1995: 210);

Hoheitsfähigkeit, or the capacity to carry out statelike functions (Kirchhof 1994: 682–684); and, of course, the one criterion that for a brief moment was hard legal reality, namely, "loyalty." In Weimar, when the range of new religions did not go beyond candidates from within the Christian fold, it could be taken for granted that new claimants would meet these more substantive concerns, so there was no need to belabor the obvious. As one deputy during the constitutional deliberations nevertheless did, the grant of public corporation status was said to be the "valuation of the social forces of religion and of its meaning for public life."[84] Yet today, in the face of extensive doubt about the civic value of some of the new religions, there has been a scramble to explicate the previously taken for granted.[85]

However, the problem with most of the proposed unwritten criteria, for which the short career of "loyalty" stands as an example, is to "erase the necessary difference between law and the presuppositions of law" (Korioth 1999: 244). Or, as Stefan Huster (1998: 119) criticized the "loyalty" requirement imposed in 1997 by the Federal Administrative Court, it "transforms the precondition of the constitutional order into a constitutional obligation." Recall Böckenförde's (1991: 112) evocation of the "great gamble" *(Wagnis)* that is the liberal state's incapacity to reproduce the "culture of liberty" that it requires for its existence. Accordingly, it is futile, if not destructive of the liberties that are meant to be preserved, to move from risk to legal certainty in this respect.

Claims for corporation status have repeatedly been made by a variety of Islamic organizations since the mid-1970s. Most of them failed because of the formalistic component of the "durability" requirement, that is, an insufficient "size of membership," rather than because of its crypto-substantive component, the claimant's "constitution" (Walter 2006: 593)—not to mention that the expressly substantive "unwritten criteria" remained completely in the background (for an exception, see Albrecht 1995). Most Länder, which have authority over religious and church affairs under German federalism, require that a would-be corporation has been in existence for at least thirty years, to guarantee its intergenerational continuity; and they require a personal membership that is at least one-thousandth of the population of the respective Land, which again requires a degree of church-like centralization and hierarchical ordering that is foreign to Islam. However, to the degree that Germany's immigrant population reproduces itself over generations and that Muslim organizations have understood that federation is the sine qua non for corporate status, these formal-organizational obstacles are bound to wither away.

Because formal-organizational grounds for rejection were always at hand, there was perhaps no need to move to the much trickier substantive terrain flagged by the "constitution" requirement or even the "unwritten" requirements. However, if even the latter are as thin as the "faithfulness to the law" (Rechtstreue) formula decreed by the Federal Constitutional Court in its 2000 Jehovah's Witnesses decision, Islamic organizations cannot but succeed in the long run. As success on this front would shower considerable state privileges on rather dubious entities, it is bound to re-open the debate over the meaning and wisdom of public law status for organized religion at large. Consider only one of the most persistent and vocal claimants for corporate status, the so-called Islamrat (Islamic Council). Although it is nominally a federation of over thirty member organizations with some 140,000 individual members, and it controls about 700 of the estimated 2,500 to 2,800 mosques in Germany (International Crisis Group 2007: 10), it is in fact dominated by only one of its member organizations: the Islamische Gemeinschaft Milli Görüs. This is an offshoot of the Turkish Refah (Welfare) Party, which was founded by former prime minister Necmettin Erbakan and has been prohibited in Turkey since 1997 for its advocacy of an Islamic state. While fashioning itself as a religious community (Religionsgemeinschaft) for purposes of its corporation status request, it is "to a considerable degree economically active" (Lemmen 2002: 81), with the dominant Erbakan and El-Zayat families (tied by a marriage alliance) controlling a complex empire of real estate, supermarkets, trade, and travel agencies, all geared to the needs of Germany's Muslim population (the second largest in Europe, with an estimated three million).

For its political views, Milli Görüs has long been on the index of the Federal Office for the Protection of the Constitution (Bundesverfassungsschutz, the German equivalent of the FBI). It is not difficult to understand why. Literally meaning "national view," Milli Görüs advocates a "new greater Turkey," modeled on the Ottoman Empire, with its French-style laïcité abolished and an "Islamic social order" put in its place (Bundesministerium des Innern 2006: 240). The speeches and writings of Erbakan and other Milli Görüs leaders denounce "Western imperialism," "destructive Zionism," and "racist imperialism." If the West is out to "enslave and exploit" the world, Milli Görüs offers rescue, its message being not "reform" but "revolution": "*Milli Görüs* does not want to cooperate with the existing system . . . *Milli Görüs* believes it is not possible to reform the existing system. *Milli Görüs* says the system is rotten to the core and that nothing good can come from it. *Milli Görüs* wants to save and bring happiness to all humanity."[86] This diatribe was addressed to a Turkish audience. Toward German interlocutors, however, an integrationist rhetoric prevails, yielding frequent charges of doublespeak reminiscent of those often leveled at Tariq Ramadan (see Fourest 2004; Berman 2007). However, both stances converge on "entryism": "Our fundamental mission in this society is not to remain amongst ourselves but to find a place within the ruling elite" (quoted in Bundesministerium des Innern 2008a: 253). The "us" here is circumscribed by an "Islamic identity" that has to fend off the "rising danger of assimilation" (p. 252). Only an excessively formalistic understanding of corporate status would command granting state privileges to an entity such as Milli Görüs, whose open hostility to the liberal state is unmistakable.[87]

However, not all Islamic organizations intend to achieve corporate status, pointing to the significant opportunities that the private law of associations *(Vereinsrecht)* already offers to them. As a German Muslim jurist sees it, "With respect to some essential aspects of the lives of Muslims, the public-law quality of their community just is not important."[88] In addition, there is the risk of imposing a churchlike structure that is inimical to Islamic doctrines. The Zentralrat der Muslime (Central Council of Muslims), one of the leading national Muslim federations composed of eighteen organizations with an estimated 12,000 to 18,000 members spread over 400 mosques, much in contrast to the Islamrat, has always firmly rejected corporate status for precisely that reason. Its current leader, the German convert "Ayyub" Axel Köhler, criticizes the "official posture" *(amtliches Gebahren)* of some Muslim organizations and their attempts "to change Islam through a church structure that is alien to it." Instead, he deems the private law of associations better suited to the decentralized nature of Islam. All that "most Muslims" in Germany ask for is to "live and work freely according to their beliefs as part of a pluralistic society," which they could achieve simply by way of "more extensive use of their [private] association rights."[89]

Limits of Inclusion (II): Religious Instruction

If the quest for corporate status is dented by internal disagreement about its necessity, the second extant limit of accommodating Islam, the denial of religious instruction in public schools, knows no such disagreement within organized Islam; it is univocally perceived as a deficiency. Even the German state, from the Land to the federal level, has long been in favor of creedal Islam instruction in schools. However, some of the same formal-organizational obstacles that have stood in the way of achieving corporate status have also stood in the way of acquiring the right to teach Islam in public schools. Already in 1984, when the education ministers of the

Länder first agreed that Islam had to be taught as an ordinary part of the school curriculum, they pointed out that this required the existence of a "religious community" that met the "durability test"—which "at the moment cannot be observed among the Muslims in the Federal Republic of Germany" (quoted in Lemmen 2002: 162). This objection has constituted the main reason for rejecting this claim ever since, though—as we shall see—on ever-thinner grounds.

Accordingly, the reasons for rejecting both claims—for public law status and for Islam instruction in schools—are similar, reflecting the fact that the "material preconditions" for succeeding in either respect are the same.[90] However, there are two key differences that push in opposite directions. On the plus side, there is unanimous political support for Islam instruction in public schools, more than there has ever been for recognition of Islam's public law status. As one overview of the current situation in five Länder put it, "there is agreement across the political spectrum that Islam has become a part of German society and that this needs to be reflected in school curricula as well" (Hofhansel 2010: 205). This agreement is driven by a perceived need for integration, a particularly pressing issue after 2001, as well as for bringing the prickly business of Quran instruction under state control. In December 2001, the chiefs of federal and Land governments promptly expressed their "agreement" that Islam had to be taught as an ordinary subject in German language in public schools (de Wall 2008: 1).

Insofar as the issue is *Bekenntnisunterricht* (creedal instruction), in which religion is taught "in accordance with the tenets of the religious community concerned" (Article 7.3 of the Basic Law), this has created interesting schisms and alignments. The Turkish-Islamic Union of the Office for Religion (mainly known by its Turkish acronym, DITIB), the official representative of Turkish-state Islam in Germany, was the only Muslim organization ever to have favored noncreedal Islam instruction as it has been offered since the late 1980s in North-Rhine Westphalia (Stock 2004: 1402), while insisting that it had to be taught in Turkish. This position reflected DITIB's laicist-cum-nationalist agenda. By contrast, the other major Muslim organizations in Germany, especially the Islam Council and the Central Council of Muslims, had always supported the creedal variant but conceded it to be taught in German. The preference for German was not so much for the sake of promoting "integration," as especially Milli Görüs (dominant in the Islam Council) was fond of pretending,[91] but to weaken DITIB in the internal struggle for control over Germany's predominantly Turkish Muslims.

Interestingly, the organized Muslim majority's preference for the creedal variant is strongly supported by the Catholic and Protestant churches as well as by the center-right CDU. Again, this is not so much for the sake of "integration." Instead, it is because having Germany's second largest religion, after Christianity, partake on equal terms in religious instruction according to Article 7 of the Basic Law is the only way to save this increasingly anachronistic institution against the secular alternative of teaching ethics or cognitive *Religionskunde,* which has been gaining ground from unified Germany's more atheist and socialist-inclined East (the former German Democratic Republic). Even in the absence of a recognized Islamic "religious community," creedal Islam instruction has already been offered experimentally in Baden-Württemberg since the 2006–2007 school year and in Bavaria and Lower-Saxony since 2003–2004, intriguingly all under conservative governments (German Parliament 2006: 70–71).[92] In sum, religious instruction is the one aspect of the accommodation of Islam in Germany where the driving impulse has been more political than legal.

On the negative side, however, the bar for acquiring the right of religious instruction is also set higher than for acquiring public law status because it inevitably brings the involved religious community into close contact with the state. As Article 7.3 of the Basic Law stipulates, religious instruction has to occur "without prejudice to the state's right of supervision." While it remained subject to contestation whether corporation status implied cooperation and nearness to the state, there is no doubt that religious instruction constitutes a *res mixta,* geared toward "cooperation" between state and religious community (Langenfeld 2007). But from this it follows that mere "fidelity to the law," legally sufficient for corporation status after 2000, is not sufficient for the right of religious instruction. As the religious community moves from the private into the state sphere of education, which it is not forced to do, it must more actively "affirm" the liberal and secular principles on which this state is based—a "counter-instruction to the state's instruction" is "not acceptable" (Langenfeld 2007). Although homosexuality or nonmarital sex may still be "sin," as it is regarded also by the Catholic Church, the fundamental principles of the state's educational mandate cannot be put in question by any religion: toleration, equality between the sexes, and the separation of secular and religious spheres must be upheld without qualification. With respect to these principles, religious instruction "must be faithful to the constitution not just formally but materially" (Langenfeld 2007). One sees that Islam instruction as "part of the regular curriculum in state schools" (Article 7.3 of the Basic Law) opens up the Pandora's box of "unwritten," material requirements for achieving equality with the established religions, which Germany's highest courts had carefully sealed.

It is then no wonder that the key legal cases regarding the right of Islam instruction are largely mute on the substantive question, focusing instead on the formal-organization requirements. In 2005, the Federal Administrative Court ruled, for the first time, that a federation *(Dachverband),* whose "members" are not people but other organizations, could be a "religious community" entitled to teach Islam according to Article 7 of the Basic Law. Previously, all Muslim organizations' requests for Islam instruction had come to grief over their lack of credentials as "religious community." Now, their propensity to be organized as a "multilayered organization" *(mehrstufiger Verband)* no longer stood in the way of being a "religious community." Concretely, the case concerned the long-standing request by both the Islamic Council and the Central Council of Muslims to be granted the right of creedal Islam instruction in the Land of North-Rhine Westphalia, pioneer of the noncreedal Religionskunde that had been deemed insufficient by the claimants from the start. Both lower courts had declined this request in the traditional way, arguing either (like the Upper Administrative Court of the Land) that the claimants did not consist of "natural persons" and were not devoted to an "all-encompassing fulfillment of the tasks set by the shared faith"; or, even more beholden to the model of the Roman Catholic Church (like the Administrative Court of Düsseldorf), that there was no central interlocutor "empowered to articulate binding . . . basic principles [of the faith]" and connecting top and bottom of the hierarchy in an "interlocking chain of legitimacy" (quoted in Stock 2004: 1403). Taken together, the stipulated markers of a "religious community" were very much what a "church" is, which is difficult for Islam to meet because it is defined by (among other things) the very absence of a church.

The February 2005 Federal Administrative Court decision that umbrella organizations like the Islamic Council or the Central Council of Muslims "might" comprise a religious community "peculiarly mixes traditionalism and pro-religious reformism" (Stock 2005: 289).[93] Note that this was only virtual, not actual recognition of the claimants as a "religious community," referring the question back to the Upper Administrative Court to decide. Moreover, all classic elements of what constitutes a religious community are retained, the sole (if important) concessions being that a "division of labor" across the "various layers of the organization" was not prohibitive and that the Islam-specific "autonomy" of the local associations was no problem, given that "religious community life unfolds at the local level."[94] But traditionalism returned when the court required that "tasks essential" to the "identity" of a religious community had to be effected through the umbrella organization and that the majority of local membership organizations had to be not only "partially" but "comprehensively" religious. Reviewing a motley list of youth centers, unions, boy scouts, and student and cultural groups that were also represented by the claimants, the court at least flagged doubt in this respect.[95] However, when stipulating that in consideration of "planning and cost" the "material preconditions" of corporate status had to be fulfilled, the Muslim claimants could score a success—the "proof of durability" was considered "beyond doubt," which is no small matter if one considers that corporate status had previously been denied exactly on this ground.[96]

In loosening the organizational requirements for constituting a "religious community," the 2005 Federal Administrative Court decision is clearly a milestone for accommodating organized Islam in Germany. However, tacked onto the long and hair-splitting fine print concerning formal organization is a short and rather ambivalent statement about the additional, more substantive requirement of "faithfulness to the constitution." Considering that religious instruction in public schools goes along with "increased influence in state and society," organizations entrusted with this task were "especially obliged" to respect the rights of the Basic Law.[97] Although this passage was merely quoting the Constitutional Court's Jehovah's Witnesses decision, there is also stronger language that implicitly questions the "belief" versus "behavior" dichotomy outlined in the earlier decision: "The state cannot accept that a religious community which questions the elementary principles on which this state is based be allowed to shape the value-related part of the school curriculum," including the values of "human dignity," the "rule of law," and "democracy."[98] Pointing to the fact that Milli Görüs and organizations close to the Islamist Muslim Brotherhood were among the claimants, the court deemed their "fidelity to the constitution" an "open question."

"Fidelity to the constitution" moved from peripheral to key consideration in the Hesse Upper Administrative Court's September 2005 denial of the request by the Islamic Religious Community of Hesse (Islamische Religionsgemeinschaft Hessen, or IRH) to teach Islam in the Land's public schools.[99] Interestingly, the court pointed out that, compared with the granting of public law status, "a much closer cooperation between state and religious community" was required with respect to religious instruction. This in turn meant that mere "faithfulness to the law" was not sufficient; instead, "a special faithfulness to the law" was required, namely "faithfulness to the constitution."[100] And the IRH (which had been under surveillance by the Federal Office for the Protection of the Constitution since May 2001) did not meet this test, as it was dominated by Milli Görüs and by five members of the El-Zayat family, which in turn was suspected of being close to the Muslim Brotherhood. Moreover, the IRH subscribed to a "traditionalist," Salafi understanding of Islam,[101] with an exclusivist "claim to dominance" against other strands of Islam that "does not match the state's educational goal of a pluralist social order."[102] Furthermore, although the IRH might "affirm" the "secular state," it did so only tactically, in the Diaspora, and "not as a general principle."[103]

This is not to say that the usual formal-organizational concerns did not weigh heavily in the Hesse court's rejection of the Islamische Religionsgemeinschaft. On the contrary, this decision must be considered an astonishing setback after the Federal Administrative Court's loosening of the organizational screw only six months earlier. Characterizing the IRH as "merely an interest group for pursuing partisan religious and societal interests"[104] and as lacking a "spiritual leader"[105] capable of issuing binding rules on its followers, the court refused to see the IRH as a "religious community"; because the latter was less than ten years old, even the "proof of durability" was denied to it.[106]

While part of this reasoning may reflect the parochial Catholic Church model, calling the IRH a "religious community" may also be stretching the term under any circumstances. In its short life, the IRH, which was created for the sole purpose of acquiring the right to teach Islam in Hesse's public schools, went through frequent organizational changes, all opportunistically geared to fit the (evolving) requirements of German Staatskirchenrecht. Already the relabeling of its predecessor, the Islamische Arbeitskreis Hessen, an umbrella organization, into Islamische Religionsgemeinschaft Hessen, which since 2003 could include only natural persons, smacked of creating a Religionsgemeinschaft by the sheer act of so designating it and by manipulating the statute. After the Federal Administrative Court's 2005 recognition of *Dachverbände* as Religionsgemeinschaften, the statute was promptly changed to include, again, umbrella organizations, thus returning to the IRH's original profile. Now the IRH was made up of local groups like the Muslimischer Arbeitskreis Hanau (MAH)—"forum of a new generation of Muslims who understand themselves as an active part of society"[107] (a profile declared "representative" by the IRH)—which were evidently more politically or culturally than religiously oriented. Furthermore, however one may ridicule the much-deplored absence of a pope-like "spiritual leader," the fact that the IRH's chairman was a teacher in the Hesse

school system did not bode well for the "authoritative religious knowledge" that is required by law for shaping the religious curriculum.[108]
Finally, the IRH's barely ten years of existence, its frequent strategic organizational changes, and the refusal to present even a membership list
appropriately redacted for reasons of data protection raise doubt about
its "proof of durability."

The novelty in the Hesse court's rejection of the Islamische Religionsgemeinschaft nonetheless lay in moving the material, "unwritten" criteria to
the fore just when organized Islam sought influence on the public school
curriculum. This shift has not yet replaced the formal-organizational bias
in the recognition procedure, not to mention that no one has as yet addressed the problem that a "modern Islamic religious pedagogy, compatible with the protestant or catholic religious pedagogy, does not exist at
present" (Stock 2005: 287).

The Pandora's box of the compatibility of Islam with the state's educational mandate was first opened up in Berlin, where—due to a quirk of the
German Basic Law—religious instruction is not part of the regular school
curriculum but optional and provided under the complete autonomy of
the relevant religious community. In 1998, the Upper Administrative Court
of Berlin decreed that, against the stern opposition of the Berlin Senate, the
Islamische Föderation Berlin (IFB), yet another spin-off of Milli Görüs,
fulfilled "all requirements of a religious community" and thus was entitled
to teach Islam in Berlin's schools, and at the state's expense to boot. In a
decision as lax as can be imagined, a potential conflict with "fundamental
constitutional principles" and the state's educational mandate was categorically "excluded" in reference to the incontrovertible fact that an Islamic primary school, run by the IFB, had already been recognized (see
Lemmen 2002: 173).

After losing its appeal to the Federal Administrative Court in 2000, the
Senate (Berlin's City Council) tried to stop the IFB at the curricular level,
arguing that the "preliminary curriculum" presented by the IFB in 2001
clashed with two of the state's declared educational goals—namely, to allow schoolchildren to become "autonomous" and to learn to respect the
"equality between men and women." Alas, the Senate had to learn from
the Administrative Court of Berlin that, in Berlin at least, religious instruction was exclusively a "matter of the religious communities," which could
"not be influenced by the state in any way"; even under the stricter rules
of Article 7(2) of the Basic Law, in force elsewhere in Germany, the principle of religious liberty would "prohibit an ex ante control of instruction
by the state." The state may intervene only in the extreme case of

"counter-instruction" to the state's instruction, but this could be deter-
mined only after the fact, and considering that the IFB had "invited" the
Senate to attend its classes, there was no risk anyway.[109]

Imposing itself, with the help of local and national courts, on Berlin's
classrooms, the Berlin branch of Milli Görüs soon taught the Quran to
about 20 percent of Berlin's Muslim children, supported with significant
tax monies (1.4 million EUR in 2004) by a reluctant Senate. Apparently
the number of pupils taught, never high to begin with, has been shrinking
over time, which shows that the Islamic Federation is controversial among
Berlin's Muslims as well. Pointing to its more political than religious profile, a law professor defending the Senate in court likened the situation to
"the CDU entertaining the idea of teaching Christian religion."[110] Sealing
itself off from external scrutiny despite its self-proclaimed openness,[111] the
IFB's dubious school practices have repeatedly raised eyebrows. Parents
criticized the instruction as "missionary," while Berlin's head of schools
reported the circulation of "strange documents that fall behind the level
of tolerance that the [Christian] churches have imposed on themselves."[112] The IFB's initial report cards *(Zeugnisse)* carried the motto
that "there are two sorts of human beings: one, who are our brothers
and sisters in faith; and another, with whom we are connected through
being human." This was slyly formulated to fool the Federal Office for
the Protection of the Constitution (*Verfassungsschutz*), but placing the
"sorting" ahead of the "connecting" also undercut the liberal enlightenment standard of shared humanity.[113] And this was only the small part,
grudgingly corrected at the behest of a gutsy school director.[114] Observers found that, some three years into this court-ordered experiment, the
"climate" at the Berlin schools with an IFB presence had changed for
the worse: "Women are reduced in Islam instruction to the role of
housewives, and even very small children are obliged to fast during Ramadan. Suddenly there is anti-Semitism in the schoolyards, even young
girls wear headscarves, and the number of parents removing their
daughters from biology or sports instruction or from class retreats is
growing."[115]

Because outside Berlin (and Bremen) religious instruction is part of the
"regular curriculum" and thus subject to the state's "right of supervision"
according to Article 7 of the Basic Law, the Berlin experience cannot be
generalized to the rest of the country. But a clash between religious liberty
rights and the state's educational mandate is inevitable, should the formal-
organizational hurdles for being recognized as Religionsgemeinschaft be
cleared. The real conflict still lies ahead.

Toward a German Islam? The German Islam Conference

In September 2006, the federal minister of the interior, Wolfgang Schäuble, called into existence the Deutsche Islamkonferenz (German Islam Conference), which assembles fifteen representatives of the state and fifteen representatives of Germany's Muslims into a "dialogue" for "a better religious and societal integration of Muslims in Germany" (Bundesministerium des Innern 2008b: 1). This is part of the new European agenda of "institutionaliz[ing] a moderate, Euro-friendly Islam" (Yazbeck Haddad and Golson 2007).

As the accommodation of Islam thus moved from the legal into the political arena, the first thing to notice is that some of the same questions that had already been adjudicated by courts—more often than not in favor of Islam—now reappeared as essentially unsolved political questions: mosque construction, the headscarf, exemptions of Muslim pupils from the school curriculum, the role of girls and women, religious slaughtering, and—perhaps topping all other concerns—Islam instruction in public schools (see Amir-Moazami 2009). Indeed, the "strategy of long-term legal contestation" pursued by organized Islam in Germany may well have been "counter-productive," as it was "not accompanied by a broad societal dialogue about religious-cultural practices that are rejected by the majority society" (Kandel 2004: 9–10).

Accordingly, the federal interior minister's opening statement to the Islam Conference shows an ethical inflection that had been assiduously avoided, if not explicitly repudiated, in the legal system. The main purpose of the Islam Conference, argued the interior minister, is to transform "Muslims in Germany" into "German Muslims," "who feel at home in this country and who identify and engage with its societal concerns even more strongly."[116] Setting the parameters for the "dialogue" to come, he presents Germany as a country with "Christian roots and traditions," and claims that whoever wants to "call it home has to respect these roots." Predictably invoking the famous Böckenförde paradox, this self-consciously "Christian politician" hammered on the theme that a rational commitment to shared constitutional principles, which Muslims in Germany had learned to take advantage of only too well, and perhaps even identified with (Schiffauer 2010: 267–358), was not enough: "There has to be something to unite us at a deeper, human level: at exactly the level where religion and culture, values and identity are located."[117]

This was akin to asking for the "loyalty" requirement that German courts had thrown out earlier. No wonder the Muslim participants in the Islam Conference disagreed. In the first of four "working groups" that dealt with "German societal order and value consensus," no joint statement about a "German value order" could be reached. All that could be agreed on is that "integration" asks of the "Muslims living in Germany," next to learning the German language, the "thorough-going adherence to [*Beachtung*] the German legal order and to the value order of the Basic Law." As even one of the "secular" Muslims on the Islam Conference conceded, the "focus on the Basic Law is simply more precise."[118] But except for a compensatory zeal in the expected "completeness" of adhering to the law, this was a triviality that did not go beyond what had already been clarified in court. German Muslims, one might say, were "constitutional patriots" already, but they would not commit themselves to anything beyond it.

Here is a second statement about which no agreement could be reached: "Integration is a process that changes both parties involved, the majority society and the immigrants [*Zuwanderer*]. However, integration asks for a higher degree of adaptation on the part of the immigrants; it especially asks for their adaptation to the law, history, and culture of the receiving society" (Bundesministerium des Innern 2008b: 4). A minimalist version of the adage "when in Rome do as the Romans do," this is a sociological-cum-normative triviality, and it is astounding to see it refused. Such refusal seeks a perfect symmetry between the adaptive efforts of the vast majority and those of what is never more than a tiny minority, a stance that is as naive as it is self-aggrandizing. Were such symmetry stated as a "should" up front, no society, except one that hates itself, would ever take in a single immigrant.

Wrapping up what one interested observer described as a "horrendously vacuous talk" *(grauenhaftes Gequatsche),* "at best at the level of adult education,"[119] the first of five "theses" on which agreement could be reached opens up with something that was difficult to refute: "Germany understands itself as a European-rooted cultural nation and it is a liberal-democratic state of law [*Rechtsstaat*]" (Bundesministerium des Innern 2008b: 5). The only slight nontriviality was to point to certain "limits" of religious liberty, in the third of the five agreed-upon "theses": "The religious liberty of the individual finds its limits when it is opposed to the liberal-democratic order" (p. 6). This is a position that the German courts have not always upheld, in fact have sometimes blithely ignored, so that what was legally condoned now reappeared as an ethical-political "thou shalt not."

One of the declared goals of the Islam Conference has been the forging of Muslims into a "religious community" that is capable of "cooperating with the German state."[120] In this respect, it amounted to state help in overcoming the existing limits to the accommodation of Islam in Germany, which are all on the corporate, not individual side. However, in an ironic inversion with "laicist" France, which had actively sponsored the confederation of French Muslims in the CFCM, the otherwise less hands-offish German state prefers to hide behind its "neutrality" mandate, "welcoming" the making of a "central organization" among German Muslims, yes, but also pretending that the "right of religious self-determination" prevented it from being more active in this process.[121] When the four leading Muslim umbrella organizations with a seat in the Islam Conference (the DITIB, the Islamic Council, the Central Council of Muslims, and the ultraconservative, Ankara-steered Association of Islamic Cultural Centers [Verband Islamischer Kulturzentren]) overcame old animosities to found, in April 2007, the Muslim Coordinating Council (Koordinierungsrat der Muslime), they expected that the state would provide a "kind of roadmap toward the official recognition of Muslims in Germany." However, the federal minister of the interior coolly responded that "a *Verband* is not yet a *Religionsgemeinschaft*,"[122] and that "the broad majority of religious and nonreligious Muslims in Germany is not sufficiently represented" in the new federation.[123]

One wonders: how could "nonreligious" Muslims ever be represented in a would-be Religionsgemeinschaft, which the Coordinating Council aimed to be, with a particular eye on clearing the hurdle for Islam instruction in public schools? A fundamental ambiguity of the Islam Conference was its inclusion of "secular" Muslims—like all of its members handpicked by the Federal Interior Ministry—and this in a ratio of 2:1 over the "religious" Muslims, who were represented by the four large umbrella organizations and the Alevi Community. If the purpose was to mirror the "diversity" of Muslims in Germany, handing out five of fifteen Muslim seats on the Conference to "religious" Muslims was rather generous, considering that at most 20 percent of German Muslims are members of a religious organization.[124] However, it was also strange to include in an "Islam Conference" on the "Muslim" side a radical Islam critic like Necla Kelek, a kind of German Ayaan Hirsi Ali, who had become known for her view that the problem with Islam was, well, Islam (see her movingly authentic assault on arranged marriage: Kelek 2008). The government evidently mixed religious and ethnic Muslims in its composition of the Islam Conference, but then it should not be surprised to see both clashing severely. Moreover, it is unsurprising that the federating religious side would not include anyone who was not religious—as little, say, as the Catholic Church would want its legitimacy to hinge on having Madonna (the pop star, not the mother of Christ) in its ranks.[125]

When the Islamic umbrella organizations formed the Koordinierungsrat (Coordinating Council), the government suddenly realized that the "central organization" of Muslims favored by it played into the hands of those most adept at organizing, the religious organizations. The latter, like the conservative Central Council of Muslims, used the public attention generated by the Islam Conference to propagate the headscarf and religious exemptions from the school curriculum. In fact, when the religious groups refused to subscribe to the Islam Conference's statement, in its "Security and Islamism" section, that "Islamism" constitutes a "great danger," one might consider it logical (and revealing) that these very groups did not like to see themselves described as a threat. The arch-conservative profile of the Koordinierungsrat, denounced by Necla Kelek as a "congregation of Muslim tribal chiefs,"[126] proved that "Islamism is part of the mainstream"[127] in Germany (in contrast to France, whose mainstream is laicist).[128]

Note that, as the first Islam Conference went into its final round, the representative of the Islam Council, Milli Görüs chief Oguz Ücüncü, who had delicately participated in its section on "Security and Islamism," was forced to step down because of federal charges of "forming a criminal organization" engaged in tax evasion, document fraud, money laundering, and abuse of state funds to support the Palestinian terrorist Al-Aksa Brigade and Hamas. This charge was jointly raised against the notorious "financier of political extremism," Ibrahim El-Zayat, chief of the Muslim Brotherhood–oriented Islamic Community that dominates the Central Council of Muslims, and who was linked to the Milli Görüs boss through several real estate firms.[129]

It is little more than a footnote that the incriminated Islamic Council would not endorse the Islam Conference's "2nd Interim Resumé" statements on "German Societal Order and Value Consensus" and on "Security and Islamism," the former for its "problematizing of Muslim religiosity as a barrier to integration" and the latter for "categorizing Muslims as potentially dangerous without a concrete reason."[130] And none of the Islamic organizations in the Islam Conference, except the Alevi Community, would support a statement condemning Iran's "human rights violations" after its election fraud of June 2009. The leader of the Zentralrat für Muslime, "Ayyub" Axel Köhler, in the statesman's posture, declined to "interfere in the internal affairs" of another state.[131] The Second Islam Conference, called by Interior Minister Thomas de Maizière in March 2010, turned out a disappointment, with the Islamrat excluded for the pending criminal investigation against its leading functionaries and the other Islamic umbrellas closing ranks with the Islamic Council. In 2011, under a new interior minister, Hans-Peter Friedrich (Christlich Soziale Union) (CSU), the situation further deteriorated, as even the (usually moderate) nonorganized Muslim participants in the Islam Conference signed a protest note against the interior minister's call for a "security partnership" between Muslims and the state.

Judged by the sorry state of their religious (or, rather, political?) leadership, the transformation of Muslims in Germany into German Muslims remains unfinished business, as does the overcoming of the remaining hurdles for organized Islam to "cooperate" with the German state.

THIS CHAPTER delved deeper than the others into the intricacies of legal integration, thereby unavoidably deploying some of its technical language that may not be easy to follow for the nonjurist. We still feel that we scratched only the top of an iceberg that still awaits a more complete cartography. If anything, the chapter shows that the organizational-level or corporate integration of Islam is a slower and more arduous process than its individual-level integration, which works fast and symmetric for all religions. Perhaps corporate integration is forever incomplete,[132] because of the unavoidable asymmetries and compromises that mark historical state building. Organized Islam may be only an inch away from "cooperating" with the German state. But it also puts into question a church-state arrangement that dates from a time that is no longer ours. No wonder that the churches find it "not in [their] interest" if Muslims are denied public corporation status, because this denial puts into question their own privileges: "Alone the strict equal treatment of all organizations . . . protects the public reputation and continuation of this institution [public corporation status] into the future" (EKD 2006: 79 and 81).[133]

NORTH AMERICA

THE WESTERN EUROPEAN cases we have examined vary primarily in terms of the extent to which their church-state regimes may, when confronted with the problem of accommodating Islam, constrain religious liberty (France) or religious equality (Germany). In North America, the two cases we examine—Canada and the United States—differ in both parallel and divergent ways.

One parallel with Europe lies in the fact that, of the two countries, only in Canada has the state tended to follow the European pattern of seeking to substitute for the functions of a formerly established church. In this case, however, it has done so not only in terms of creating an extensive welfare state; it has also sought to manage ethnic and religious difference through a top-down policy of "multiculturalism" that seeks to accommodate cultural diversity by way of explicitly stated norms about how to handle such difference. The ethno-religious situation in Canada is not unlike that in Germany, where a nondenominational (but often Protestant) majority constitutes the federal government and most of the state governments while Catholics hold special sway in one province, Bavaria. In the German case, however, Bavaria has shown little inclination to want to leave the federation, in which it enjoys the symbolic status of *Freistaat* (Free State) and maintains a cultural distinctiveness that few begrudge it or want to deprive it of. In Canada, multiculturalism arose in the context of managing the anomaly of a French Catholic enclave with deep and persistent secessionist tendencies in the midst of a vast Anglo-Protestant sea. Even if multiculturalism nominally encompasses all of Canada's minority groups, it from the start centered on coping with cultural differences arising from immigration. The policy of multiculturalism offers special cultural rights to minority groups as a way of accommodating their differences from the mainstream population, while recognizing—in Will Kymlicka's (1995: 35–44) classic formulation—that there might well be tensions between "external protections" for group peculiarities and "internal restrictions" on individual group members.

The approach to accommodating Islam in Canada reflects this distinctive background. The advent of a quasi-constitution, the Charter of Rights and Freedoms, and the legal requirements of multiculturalism have watered down the earlier Protestant "shadow establishment"[1] in favor of greater religious equality. Yet the arrival of significant (though hardly large) numbers of Muslims has raised concerns about the degree to which internal restrictions may be emerging in a fashion that raises doubts about the policy as a whole. At the federal level, efforts to make "reasonable accommodation" of Islam have run into difficulties as more devout Muslims, taking advantage of Canadian laws affording a measure of legal pluralism, have proposed to institute "Shari'a tribunals" in personal law matters. In Quebec, following in certain respects its historical progenitor France, the controversy has centered around certain forms of clothing, especially the niqab and the charge that it removes the wearer from public interaction. While outside of Quebec the courts and legislatures have handled these issues at the federal and state levels, the Quebecois created their own commission to examine the meaning and implementation of "reasonable accommodation" against the background of their special circumstances. The commission has recommended dealing with religious difference by way of a nonlegalistic approach, but this is somewhat out of step with the preferences of the Quebecois public with regard to the matter of accommodating Islam. As we shall see, and in a pattern that can be found elsewhere in liberal democratic countries, the challenge of integrating Muslims and their Islam has generated serious misgivings about multiculturalism and the kinds of cultures these countries are actually prepared to countenance.

The other North American case, the United States, differs noticeably from its neighbor to the north but also from Europe on these matters, as there is nothing akin either to Canadian binationalism or to European church establishment or even quasi-establishment. Lacking any notion that there was more than one "founding nation," as long prevailed in Canada, the idea of an official policy of multiculturalism is practically inconceivable—even if the notion has met with considerable approbation "on the ground." And departing from the European experience of letting the state assume the functions previously carried out by the church, the United States prefers to let immigrants find their own way (for an analysis of the baneful consequences of this posture for naturalization rates, see Bloemraad 2006). Immigrants to the United States thus use preexisting social institutions as their route to inclusion; one of these, historically, has been religious affiliation. The constitutional guarantees of free exercise have thus been a crucial support to immigrant incorporation, and courts in the United States have generally sustained these commitments in regard to the immigration of Muslims in recent years.

The tricky difference in the United States is that Islam has also come in an anomalous indigenous version that was not always accepted as religion. The presence of a quasi-national variant of Islam, not necessarily regarded as the Muslim faith either by American courts or by other Muslims, has been the chief divergence from both the Canadian and the Western European encounters with Islam. Once the Nation of Islam's character as legitimate religion came to be established as a legal-constitutional matter, however, there has been little in the way of jurisprudential (as distinct from popular) discrimination against Islam. Indeed, as befits a country that regards itself as a bastion of religious liberty—to the point that this seems an embarrassment to the enlightened European—the legal accommodation of Islam in recent years has been relatively unproblematic, despite the existence of considerable anti-Muslim sentiment among the population at large.

In the United States, accordingly, we have a situation of relatively smooth legal incorporation of Islam against a background of significant public antipathy toward Muslims, especially since the attacks of September 11, 2001. With religion held distant from the state as a legal-constitutional matter, however, that popular antipathy has not been translated into law or policy. Tocqueville's oft-cited observation that, in the United States, every political matter is sooner or later translated into a legal matter thus redounds to the benefit of a religion that has faced real public opprobrium as a result of its association with heinous acts of violence within the United States itself. Meanwhile, to the north, insofar as the Canadian state has made minority integration into a matter of public policy and fundamental rights, the encounter with a potentially illiberal minority—a relatively small group that may not be interested in playing by the liberal rules of the game and may even want to get rid of them—has activated antipathy toward the multiculturalism policy as well as toward the minority in question.

The situation appears to vindicate the wisdom of the American founders in resisting the temptation to establish any particular religion as a constitutional matter. At the same time, it reminds us that the American constitutional distancing of the state from religion was intended in significant part to maintain the vibrancy of religion, whereas in France the aim was much more to maintain the secular purity of the state. In the American case, moreover, the "recognition" of religion as "public law corporation" à la Germany is not part of the picture at all; constitutional protection is afforded any religion that is recognized as such, however obscure and even doctrinally objectionable. And Islam now surely counts as religion, even if many people worry that it may be much more—or something other—than that as well. It is that fear, in North America as well as in Western Europe, that underlies the entire controversy about the faith of Muhammad. We turn first to the North American case that more closely resembles European circumstances, namely, Canada, and proceed to discuss the more "exceptional" American case in the following chapter.

CHAPTER FOUR

"Reasonable Accommodation" and the Limits of Multiculturalism in Canada

THE CANADIAN experience of Islam integration has overall been positive, in part because Muslims in Canada (much like their peers in the United States) tend to be better off economically and educationally than their counterparts in Western Europe. Moreover, the characteristically Canadian stress on multiculturalist policies has bolstered Muslim claims to acceptance of their different ways of life. These policies are more reminiscent of Europe than the United States, if only in the minimal sense that in the United States no immigrant integration policy of any kind exists at the federal level. In contrast to the United States, the legal guarantees of freedom of religion in Canada are as much a product of a policy commitment to multiculturalism as they are of any deeply ingrained tradition of religious freedom. Notwithstanding the relative advantages of Canadian policy stances and of Muslim socioeconomic well-being, however, the influx of Muslims—some of whom wish Canada to accommodate certain illiberal practices—has grown into a major challenge to the country's policy of multiculturalism.

In one important development that captured national attention, Canadian authorities in the summer of 2006 arrested eighteen men in the Greater Toronto area on suspicion of terrorist activity. Soon dubbed the "Toronto 18," members of the group were accused of plotting to storm the headquarters of the Canadian Broadcasting Commission (CBC, the Canadian equivalent of the BBC), the Canadian Parliament, and the offices of the

Canadian Security Intelligence Service (CSIS, the Canadian version of the CIA) and to kidnap and behead the prime minister. A number of the group pleaded guilty or were convicted in a jury trial that concluded in 2010.[1] The group was apparently inspired in part by videos showing the preaching of the Yemeni American cleric Anwar al-Awlaki, whose influence in American radical Islamist circles was substantial until his death at American hands.[2] Needless to say, Muslims and Islam have been subjected to heightened scrutiny by Canadians, both non-Muslim and Muslim, in the post-9/11 period as a result of high-profile events associated with Islamist radicalism.

Against this background, Canadians have sought to manage the tensions associated with cultural diversity through a variety of legal and policy measures, especially the originally Canadian but now widespread policy of "multiculturalism" and the more distinctively Canadian notion of "reasonable accommodation." Yet the demands of some Muslims, in particular, for accommodations widely regarded as unreasonable have challenged Canadian multiculturalism to clarify itself and what kinds of cultures it is actually prepared to countenance. In order to make sense of these developments, we begin with the adoption in the early 1980s of the Canadian Charter of Rights and Freedoms, which accorded to freedom of religion a constitutional status that it had not previously enjoyed and that brought demands for religious accommodation into the orbit of Canada's multicultural policy by underwriting claims for equal treatment and respect of religious difference. We will see in due course that the accommodation of religious freedom has collided head-on with the preferences of some Muslims in Canada for practices that undermine the liberty rights of others, resulting in a sharp questioning of the long-standing Canadian commitment to its much-vaunted multiculturalism.

The Charter of Rights and Freedoms

Although Canada has had extensive sovereignty since the British North America Act of 1867, the British monarch remained its head of state until long thereafter, and because Canada is still a member of the Commonwealth, she remains so to this day. Until the early 1980s, moreover, the country lacked a codified enumeration of constitutionally guaranteed rights of the sort that marked the revolutionary experiment to the south from its very inception. The early American devotion to rights-based liberalism, as compared with the Tory statism of Canadians, was one of the chief differences that underlay the "continental divide" between the two countries identified by Seymour Martin Lipset (1990). Yet in 1982, in a response not least to the spread of "rights consciousness" and especially of the idea of human rights in the aftermath of World War II, the British Parliament and the queen approved Canada's adoption of the Charter of Rights and Freedoms. The Charter mainly ensured the political rights and fundamental freedoms of Canadian citizens and the civil rights of all on Canadian soil. It did so by strengthening the judicial review that had been pioneered by those other former Britons south of the border. In keeping with Canada's "multinational" origins, however, the Charter also recognized group rights not sanctioned in American constitutional documents. In particular, Section 27 of the Charter enshrines the principle of multiculturalism in Canadian constitutional law, as follows: "This Charter shall be interpreted in a manner consistent with the preservation and enhancement of the multicultural heritage of Canadians." Together with the anti-discrimination injunctions in Section 15 of the Charter, this clause has been interpreted to entail the twin goals of "accommodation" of cultural differences, opening the door to an anti-racism interpretation that insists on the equality of all cultures, and the "autonomy" and survival of different cultures, opening the door to an illiberal one that legally guarantees "internal restrictions" on some members of the culture (Bhabha 2009: 49).

The Charter also upgraded the status of religion in Canadian constitutional doctrine. Religion was defined in the Charter as one of the "fundamental freedoms." It had not previously been viewed in this way. In 1963, the Canadian Supreme Court found in *Robertson and Rosetanni v. R.* that laws requiring businesses to close on Sundays were not inconsistent with religious freedom because they merely entailed a business inconvenience, not an impairment of the freedom of religion. The case involved the plaintiffs' opening of a bowling alley on a Sunday, in violation of the federal "Lord's Day Act," which mandated that businesses remain closed on Sundays in keeping with the country's Christian predilections. The plaintiffs brought their case on the basis of the older Canadian Bill of Rights, but the court held that the Bill had not been concerned with "human rights and fundamental freedoms" in a broad sense and found their claim wanting.[3] As a point of comparison, this decision came at almost exactly the same time that, in the United States, the Supreme Court found in *Sherbert v. Verner* that a Seventh-Day Adventist's refusal to work on Saturday, her faith's Sabbath, did not disqualify her from receiving unemployment benefits. The case established the rule that the government may not "substantially burden" religious exercise unless it has a "compelling interest" in doing so (Sullivan 2006: 26).

Following the 1982 adoption of the Charter of Rights and Freedoms, however, the constitutional priority of Canadian Christianity started to deteriorate. In the 1985 case of *R. v. Big M Drug Mart*, the Supreme Court struck down the Lord's Day Act and abolished federal Sunday closing laws on the ground that they violated Section 2 of the Charter, which guarantees a number of "fundamental freedoms," such as those of speech, belief, and religion.[4] The ruling was a significant step toward legal recognition of religious pluralism and away from the so-called shadow establishment of the Christian churches in Canada (see Martin 2005).

The 2004 case *Syndicat Northcrest v. Amselem* further diluted the legal hegemony of Christianity in Canada by recognizing an individual's right to religious practices that are based simply on that person's sincere conviction that the practice is related to a religious belief. In other words, the practice need not have been enjoined by religious authorities; the issue was only whether the individual felt compelled by his or her own religious beliefs to engage in the practice. The case had been brought by Jews who (like everyone else in the apartment complex in which they lived) had been proscribed from engaging in certain activities by the partial owner of their dwellings, Syndicat Northcrest. Relying in part on United States case law, the Canadian Supreme Court found that freedom of religion could not be constrained by a confining secular definition of religion and that examination of a person's religious beliefs must be only minimally intrusive. This consideration also entailed, according to the court, that an individual's previous beliefs should not necessarily be regarded as reflecting his or her current ones.[5] In short, the test of the sincerity of someone's religious convictions was to be rather relaxed, a shift toward making room for a more "postmodern" conception of religion in keeping with the existence in Western societies (and, some think, the spread) of "individual," DIY ("do-it-yourself") religiosity (see Torpey 2010).

Soon thereafter, the Canadian Supreme Court found in the landmark case of *Multani v. Commission scolaire Marguerite-Bourgeoys* (2006) that a Quebec school had violated the rights of a Sikh student by prohibiting him from wearing a *kirpan* (ceremonial dagger) that he believed he was required by his religion to carry. Contrary to claims that schoolchildren's safety was at issue, the majority found that there were many potential threats to students' safety and that one could expect only "reasonable" levels of safety without banning scissors and other objects commonly found in schools. The Supreme Court rejected the argument that the wearing of a kirpan could be said to violate the "reasonable limits" clause of Section 1 of the Charter, holding instead that the central matter at issue was religious freedom. Those who regarded the kirpan as nothing but a weapon were said by the court to be "disrespectful to believers in the Sikh religion" and neglecting to "take into account Canadian values based on multiculturalism." Those who felt that the decision meant that anyone should be free to carry knives of their choosing were rather sanctimoniously instructed that they should renew their study of the importance of religious freedom in a democratic society.[6]

In sum, religious pluralism has achieved considerably greater acceptance in Canadian constitutional law and jurisprudence at precisely the same time that the Canadian population has grown more diverse as a result of immigration—in particular, that of Muslims. The notion of "reasonable accommodation," which originated in labor law but gradually came to be associated with the practice of making limited exceptions to generally applicable laws in order to avoid infringing the equality rights of minorities, would soon come in for more intense scrutiny by legislatures and the Canadian population. Before exploring the legal and political responses to the heightened religious diversity that has come with the new immigration, let us first examine a number of measures of inclusion concerning the population that chiefly interests us—Muslims in contemporary Canada.

Muslim Attitudes toward Living in Canada

The purpose of any policy of immigrant integration is to make immigrants adherents of the society in which they have come to find themselves. With that fact in mind, a 2007 survey by the polling firm Environics queried Canadian Muslims concerning their views of life in Canada (Environics Research Group 2007). Their report found that Canadian Muslims were generally satisfied with the state of affairs in Canada—even more so than was the population at large. Four out of five Muslim respondents said they were satisfied with the country, as compared with only 61 percent of the population at large (p. 13).[7] Canadian Muslims also overwhelmingly indicated they are proud to be Canadian. For the country as a whole, a total of 94 percent of Muslim respondents said they were proud of being Canadian, with 21 percent stating they were "somewhat proud" and 73 percent pronouncing themselves "very proud." Muslims in the Canadian West (which includes the "prairie" provinces of Alberta and Manitoba, as well as British Columbia) suggested even greater levels of pride, while the proportion of those who were "very proud" was much lower in Quebec (47 percent). Unfortunately, the researchers do not share any results they may have had for the population at large, so it is unclear whether the Quebecois Muslims' response is atypical for Quebecois as a whole (p. 14). The series of efforts to make Quebec an autonomous entity suggest that Quebeckers, and especially the majority Francophones among them, are less likely to take pride in being Canadian than do Canadians in general.

The majority of Canadian Muslims perceived very little hostility toward Muslims in Canadian society. Three-quarters indicated that "just some" or "very few" Canadians are hostile to Muslims; only 17 percent said that "many" or "most" are. This number is much lower than that in the four European countries surveyed in a parallel study by Pew Associates, some results of which are indicated in the Environics report. The Pew researchers found that between 31 percent (Spain) and 51 percent (Germany) of Muslims said that many or most of their compatriots are hostile toward them, with France falling in the middle at 39 percent (p. 27). Other evidence suggests that Muslims have a very good sense of Canadians' views of them. Half the Muslim respondents said that Canadians' impression of Islam was positive, while 39 percent said it was negative; these numbers lined up almost exactly with the poll's findings concerning Canadians' actual views of Islam (p. 20). Although they highlight these upbeat findings, the pollsters also found that Canadian Muslims are more likely to report having experienced some form of discrimination than their coreligionists in Great Britain, Spain, and Germany (only in France were there more self-reported experiences of discrimination, at 37 percent) (p. 19). More than half of Canadian Muslim respondents (55 percent) said they believe that Muslims want to adopt "Canadian customs"; this figure was higher only in one of the other surveyed countries, namely, France (at a whopping 78 percent). Meanwhile, only 23 percent of Canadian Muslims said they thought Muslims wanted to remain distinct. In other words, Muslims think that Muslims want predominantly to assimilate culturally by a 2:1 ratio, but Canadians doubt this is the case in almost precisely the same percentages (p. 32). Muslims in Canada also tend to appreciate the opportunity they have to live in a free, democratic country that values multiculturalism (p. 15). As compared with Muslims in the other four countries surveyed, Canadian Muslims were most likely to believe that their country is "the place to be if you are a Muslim woman" (p. 25).

All of this appears very positive and suggests that Muslims are being accommodated successfully in Canada's ethno-religious "mosaic." Yet all is not necessarily well. More than half of the non-Muslim respondents to the Environics survey believed that Muslims want to remain distinct, and they would appear to have some warrant for that view. More than half of all Canadian Muslims surveyed—and more than three-quarters of those ages eighteen to twenty-nine—said that they regard themselves as Muslims first and Canadians second (p. 28). A plurality of Muslims—and just over half of Muslim women—wanted "traditional beliefs" about gender rights and roles accommodated (p. 34), whereas the vast majority of the overall Canadian population wants immigrants to adopt "mainstream" Canadian beliefs. Moreover, just over half of Muslims surveyed said that shari'a law should be used as the basis for resolving family disputes. These findings are particularly notable in that they decline only to 45 percent among Muslims who have been in Canada for more than fifteen years. In other words, attachment to relatively strict Islamic ways persists over time, despite longer residence as a minority in a Western society.[8] The overall population is strongly opposed to this sort of arrangement, with 79 percent against. We will see in due course that the envisaged application of shari'a law in family disputes in Ontario and elsewhere has polarized Canadians in the years since the terrorist attacks of September 11, 2001, and it is clear that that earlier Canadian controversy influenced these findings. Perhaps worrisomely, the numbers of those in the 18–29 age group who endorse the use of shari'a law were highest of all the groups broken out in the Environics poll at 59 percent. This result is mirrored in the finding that fully 77 percent of Muslims in this age group identify with Islam before Canada (p. 36).

Yet in a 2009 study of four different national-origin groups from "the Muslim world" in Canada (Iranians, Afghans, Pakistanis, and Palestinians), Moghissi, Rahnema, and Goodman (2009: 142) found that, despite being born outside the country, most Muslim youths regarded Canada as their "home" country. In general, they found that Canadian Muslim youths—and indeed Muslims in general—had assimilated well into the fabric of Canadian life. The fact that the CBC, the national television network, airs a sitcom entitled "Little Mosque on the Prairie" suggests a greater level of inclusion at the popular level than might otherwise be expected.[9]

Still, the persistent identification with Islam ahead of that with Canada that was found in the Environics poll and the enthusiasm for shari'a law even among those who have been in the country for some time suggest a persistent sense of differentness among Muslims. Whether this is a product of "positive" attachments to a religion qua "culture" or a product of a "negative" sense of exclusion in the post-9/11 context is difficult to say. Moghissi et al. argue that "when persons from ethnic or religious minorities feel they are not included in the social and cultural life of the receiving society, they may look back to their country of origin for inspiration, a sense of connection, and the social and political involvement they feel they have been denied" (2009: 168). Yet any sense of exclusion is more likely to result from these immigrants' "visible minority" status than from their religious affiliations (Reitz et al. 2009). In any case, it is not so much the old country to which people seem to be looking back as it is the old religion, although in its novel, "deterritorialized" form (Roy 2004, 2008). The suspicion that Muslims may remain more attached to other places and cultural commitments has sparked concern among Canadians that Muslims do not view multicultural integration as "a two-way street" (Adams 2007: 158).

Multiculturalism—surely Canada's most significant contribution to contemporary political theory and practice—has thus come under intensified scrutiny in the cradle of its birth, as indeed it has in other countries in which multiculturalism had once been regarded as a sort of gold standard for minority integration into the majority culture. In a recent contribution to the debate over Canadian multiculturalism, homegrown scholars Keith Banting and Will Kymlicka (2010)—the latter one of the chief progenitors of the political theory of multiculturalism *überhaupt*—insist that the model has come to be widely accepted as a basis of Canadian identity and continues to serve well the purpose of minority integration. Yet many Canadians—including, it should be noted, many Muslims—have worried that multiculturalism has entailed the reinforcement or even the creation of intergroup boundaries that are inimical to the promotion of common citizenship. By insisting on the preservation of putatively distinct "cultures," some have feared (see, for example, Resnick 2005), one may unwittingly be entrenching essentialist notions of belonging that lead unavoidably to ghettos inhabited by mutually unintelligible or even hostile groups. Discontent with the multicultural model has spread further in response to the greater pluralism of Canadian society that has developed on the basis of recent immigration. In particular, Muslim efforts to promote religious approaches to arbitration generated a controversy that heightened wariness among Canadians about the meaning and consequences of multiculturalism.

Shari'a Law in Ontario?

In the fall of 2003, Syed Mumtaz Ali, a Toronto lawyer and leader of an organization called the Islamic Institute of Civil Justice, announced with some fanfare that the Institute would shortly begin conducting arbitrations in accordance with Islamic personal law and that this endeavor was to constitute the nucleus of a shari'a court. The use of Islamic law for arbitration of personal matters had first been proposed in Quebec in 1994. Its proponents defended their plans by noting that they would operate along the lines of the rabbinical courts that already dealt with such matters among Jews, adding that they would likely produce the same results as Quebec's government courts and at a lesser cost. That earlier effort, which played out against the backdrop of a controversy over a Muslim school-girl's demand to wear a niqab (headscarf) to public school, was ultimately stillborn. The government said it would investigate, but no report was forthcoming and the would-be shari'a council dissolved itself soon thereafter. The issue lay dormant until the announcement by the Islamic Institute of Civil Justice almost a decade later (Khan 2007: 475–476).

Ali Mumtaz had a number of perfectly legitimate grounds for his proposal. He noted that he was proceeding on the basis of Ontario's Arbitration Act of 1991, which allows persons to choose among a wide variety of dispute resolution methods in their efforts to resolve quarrels. He also claimed that he was only insisting on the same right to develop an independent legal system that had already been accorded to Canada's First Nations groups (Boyd 2007: 466–467). But what made the proposal distinct from its predecessor was that its proponents suggested that, once the tribunals were in place, "good Muslims" would be bound to use them exclusively to resolve disputes, and their findings would be enforceable by Canadian courts. Still, the shari'a-based arbitration forums would be subject to provincial and federal law as well. In short, Ali was invoking the ideology and institutions of Canadian multiculturalism and legal pluralism in an effort to promote a greater role for his religion in certain judicial proceedings. But there was no massive departure from existing practice. Given that other religious groups were already doing what Ali had proposed, it was reasonable to conclude that "objection to Shari'a-based arbitration would amount to discrimination based on religion" (Weinrib 2008: 251).

No doubt in part due to the changed, post-9/11 context in which it emerged, the proposal caused an immediate uproar, provoking resistance from those who objected to what they saw as the nefarious designs of traditionalist Muslims. Opposition arose especially among Muslim groups, particularly the Canadian Council of Muslim Women and a newly formed International Campaign Against Shari'a Law in Canada. They objected that women and children would be particularly vulnerable if the arbitration panels came into existence. Further, refusal to use them might be regarded as a sign of disloyalty or even apostasy—with potentially severe consequences for the individual and his or (mainly) her family. Women and children suffer particular disabilities under Islamic personal law, these critics averred, and these could be made inescapable if the tribunals were the arbiters of family matters. Women would not be permitted to participate in the proceedings other than as subjects or objects of the law. Another disadvantage was that shari'a law is notoriously varied, depending for its interpretation on various schools of thought that have emerged in the course of Islamic history; such diversity would militate against consistency in outcomes. There was no provision in the proposal for training of the arbitrators under Canadian law, which was supposed ultimately to control the outcomes (Weinrib 2008: 251–254). In addition to these serious procedural concerns, a number of critics from within the Muslim community regarded the move to institute shari'a-based arbitration for family law matters as the "thin edge of the wedge," citing Ali's comment that he saw the creation of the courts as "the beginnings of a Muslim Civil Justice System in Canada" (Boyd 2004: 53–55).

The outcry about the proposal led the Ontario government to ask Marion Boyd, a former provincial attorney general and former minister responsible for women's issues, to conduct a review of the plan and of arbitration practices in the province generally. Boyd produced her report in December 2004, finding that there was no evidence of systematic discrimination against women in family law arbitration and recommending that alternative forums continue to be made available under the Arbitration Act. In an attempt to forestall such discrimination, the report made a number of recommendations intended to improve the procedural fairness of such forums (Boyd 2004: 133–135). The report asserted that "tolerance and accommodation must be balanced against a firm commitment to individual autonomy" (Boyd 2004: 92). Yet, as one analyst put it, the proposed procedural safeguards failed to override "the substantive concern that Shari'a-based arbitration would withhold hard-won entitlements under provincial and federal law that supported the liberty and equality of women" (Weinrib 2008: 255).

As a result, women's groups in particular were quite critical of the Boyd report. The Canadian Council of Muslim Women called Boyd's proposed changes to arbitration practice "well intentioned" but "naive." The group insisted that it would "continue to press for the removal of family matters from private arbitration . . . in order to protect women's and children's equality rights—as guaranteed under the *Canadian Charter of Rights and Freedoms* and other Canadian laws."[10] Meanwhile, the proponents of the shari'a-based tribunals dismissed their critics as biased or as unduly influenced by post-9/11 media influences. Confirming the fears of these critics, however, supporters of the Islamic courts often appeared imperious and quite comfortable with women's subordination. In response, a group of prominent Canadian feminists in 2005 thus fired off an open letter to the province's premier insisting on a single law for all Ontarians and worrying that acceptance of the shari'a panels would undermine Ontario's commitment to anti-racism and multiculturalism (Weinrib 2008: 256). Boyd's report seemed to make no one particularly happy, and the matter remained unresolved.

Eventually, however, Ontario premier Dalton McGuinty short-circuited the discussion of shari'a tribunals for family law matters when he announced in September 2005 that religious dispute resolution under the terms of the Arbitration Act would no longer be permissible for anyone: "There will be no Sharia law in Ontario. . . . There will be no religious arbitration in Ontario. . . . There will be one law for all Ontarians" (quoted in Fournier 2008: 156, n.13). Section 1(b) of the Family Statute Law Amendment Act of 2006, the relevant enabling legislation, required that any such arbitration be "conducted exclusively in accordance with the law of Ontario or of another Canadian jurisdiction."[11] McGuinty's decision sharply and unexpectedly reversed provisions for religiously based arbitration that had previously been regarded as unproblematic—when non-Muslims had been the ones availing themselves of the opportunities.

University of Toronto legal scholar Ayelet Shachar has argued that this case was an episode in a broader trend toward the "privatization of justice" and the larger "privatization of diversity." She notes that, in contrast to the general impulse of multiculturalism to include minorities in the mainstream by accommodating their practices in public, the creation of religiously based arbitration is an effort to secede ("contract out") from the laws governing everyone else, resulting in a situation in which legal systems may end up competing and militating against the common citizenship that multiculturalism was supposed to foster. The difficulty in such cases is that it may create a "split status"—for example, divorced in civil law but still married in religious law—that is likely to be most injurious to women. Shachar thus argues that, rather than an outright ban on religiously based arbitration that consigns such practices to the unregulated shadows, what is needed is a form of "transformative accommodation" that respects the reality that some persons may wish to avail themselves of an alternative, religiously based form of dispute resolution, knowing that that body is constrained by the secular laws of the state. "Against this background, permitting community members to turn to a faith-based tribunal may, perhaps paradoxically, provide the conditions for promoting a moderate interpretation of the tradition, as authorized by religious arbitrators themselves" (Shachar 2008: 602). Assuming such transformative accommodation actually came to pass, it would have the advantage of coming from "inside" the community rather than being imposed from outside. In view of their vigorous opposition to these bodies, however, many

Muslim women seem to have doubted that this sort of accommodation would be forthcoming from the tribunals.

In his response to the controversy, which surely trod on his dearest concerns, Will Kymlicka noted that the arrival of substantial numbers of adherents of Islam who are also "visible minorities" had led to a more severe testing of the Canadian commitment to multiculturalism. Initially a policy designed to integrate "white ethnics," he argued, Canada's multiculturalism policy had become transformed into a variant of anti-racism in response to immigration from non-European sources.[12] Kymlicka distinguished two forms of multiculturalism—the liberal version that defended both group rights and individual freedoms and a more "traditionalist," "communitarian" version that could lead to the oppression of members of cultural groups—and insisted that Canada's policy was a liberal one that had originally catered to groups not suspected of prior illiberal commitments. The attempt to create shari'a tribunals for family law matters raised hackles, Kymlicka suggested, because it appeared to many that Muslims were using the openness of the Canadian judicial system "as a first step towards securing broader exemptions from the normal constraints of liberal multiculturalism and pushing towards a more traditionalist conception" of the policy (Kymlicka 2005: 11–12). Kymlicka concluded that the move to create the shari'a tribunals under Ontario's Arbitration Act was thus more a case of "private arbitration run amok" than it was of "multiculturalism run amok," as Tarek Fatah of the Muslim Canadian Congress had charged (Kymlicka 2005: 13). But Kymlicka's view seems belied by Ali's justifications for the creation of shari'a tribunals in Canada. The available evidence indicates that Ali regarded what he was doing as a matter of multicultural recognition of his culture at least as much as one of expanding the available palette of opportunities for nonstate arbitration (Weinrib 2008: 255).

The Ontario shari'a debate began to canvass the limits of Canadian multiculturalism, a sense of where the accommodation of minority cultures may go too far for those concerned about the defense of individual rights in Canada today. Kymlicka is correct that the challenge to multiculturalism has arisen in response to the arrival in Canada of appreciable numbers of Muslims, some of whom bring with them illiberal practices regarded as unacceptable by the broader Canadian population—as well as by some Muslims themselves. The presence in Canada of Muslims making illiberal demands for accommodation has activated a concern that multiculturalism may be deployed as a way of justifying what Kymlicka (1995) earlier called "internal restrictions" on the members of a "culture" in a novel and disturbing way that had not arisen when multiculturalism was intended primarily for other groups not suspected of illiberal attachments. All multicultural cats, in other words, were no longer gray, and this shift has intensified doubts about how viable the policy really is.

As a result of the Ontario shari'a controversy, Canadian intellectuals, too, have increasingly begun to inquire into the limits of multiculturalism, either because it runs the risk of limiting individual equality rights or because it threatens social cohesion and (in the case of Quebec) regional identity. Surveying the political landscape in the aftermath of the shari'a controversy, leading political scientist Janice Gross Stein of the University of Toronto put the issues facing Canada succinctly as follows:

> Despite extraordinary successes, the Canadian commitment to multiculturalism is being tested in new ways. Recent immigrants to Canada are not doing as well as previous generations. Their incomes are significantly below those of Canadians with comparable skills. The commitment to multiculturalism is also being tested by worries about "homegrown" terrorism, the fear that acts of violence may be committed by Canadians against their own government. It is being tested by a resurgence of orthodoxy in Christianity, Islam and Judaism where lines of division between "them" and "us" are being drawn more sharply. And it is being tested because Canadians are uncertain about what limits, if any, there are to embedding diverse cultures and religious traditions in the Canadian context. (Stein 2006: 3)

Stein goes on to raise a number of questions, including, most significantly for our discussion, "How far can religious practice and celebration extend into public space? To what extent will the state, in the service of freedom of religion, continue to allow churches, synagogues and mosques the right to exclusive interpretation of religious law when they have impact on the fundamental rights of Canadians?" (Stein 2006: 4). Stein's concern is that the tension between individual rights to equality, on the one hand, and group-based rights, on the other, will lead to a curtailment of the former, and especially those of women, in favor of the latter. Although she framed the discussion in terms of her own struggles with a rabbi at her synagogue whom she regarded as sexist, the concerns Stein outlines have played a more prominent role in subsequent debates about the integration of Muslims into Canadian society.

The Bouchard-Taylor Commission in Quebec

After the contretemps over shari'a courts in Ontario, the Canadian spotlight on the accommodation of Muslims moved to Quebec. In early 2007, the small town of Hérouxville adopted a document outlining "Standards for Living" *(normes de vie)* for potential immigrants to the hamlet that provoked charges of insulting Muslims and others. The standards included an inevitably provocative insistence that it was inappropriate "to . . . kill women by stoning them in public, burning them alive, burning them with acid, circumcising them, etc." Having already antagonized the Muslim population, the standards went on to prohibit Sikh students from bringing their kirpans to school, despite the fact that such a stricture would violate the Supreme Court's decision in *Multani*.[13] The irony, of course, was that Hérouxville is a tiny crossroads of some 1,300 residents, situated a hundred miles north of Montreal, with exactly one family of immigrants at the time the standards were announced. The town council that promulgated the norms insisted that they were not "racists" but that they simply wanted to inform potential immigrants of "who we are" and what newcomers should expect if they were to move there.[14] Perhaps the town had simply taken a leaf from the Netherlands, who after the assassination of the provocative filmmaker Theo Van Gogh had begun showing videos of homosexual contact, nudity, and other features of contemporary Dutch life to potential immigrants, many of them Muslims, in order to forewarn them about what they were getting themselves into.[15] In any case, the dissemination of the Hérouxville standards provoked considerable public controversy. During the same period, the question of the "limits of reasonable accommodation" also arose in the context of a debate over whether women could wear the niqab or burqa to polling sites during the upcoming spring 2007 Quebec elections (Adams 2007: 158). Intentionally or not, Quebec had suddenly become "the crucible for a national debate over identity, values, and how far newcomers should have to go to integrate."[16]

The heightened awareness of the direction that greater religious diversity had taken the country was intensified in Quebec, which historically has been a bastion of ethnic separatism, linguistic conflict, and Catholic dominance. The overt influence of the Catholic Church in the province has declined markedly since the "Quiet Revolution" beginning in the 1960s, a process of secularization that was facilitated by the Second Vatican Council and the Roman church's acceptance of its status as a denomination among other denominations (see Casanova 1994: ch. 7). Whereas this watershed development strengthened the "Protestantization" of Catholicism in the United States, in Quebec—where it was the majority religion—secularization ensued instead, marked by a sharp, sudden desertion of the church. Until 2000, Quebec schools were confessional, run by Protestant and Catholic school boards in a replica of the "pillarized" system familiar from Dutch experience. After a long discussion beginning during the

1960s, however, in 2008 Quebec passed a constitutional amendment removing religious instruction from its schools and replacing it with a mandatory "Ethics and Religious Cultures" curriculum.[17] This shift is a further indication of the secularization of Quebec society since the Quiet Revolution. Yet the latently Catholic, French Canadian inflection of Quebecois society has remained, as have the strivings for political autonomy and linguistic primacy.

It was against this background that the government of Quebec in early 2007 created a commission under the leadership of Gérard Bouchard, a supporter of Quebec sovereignty, and the eminent "federalist" philosopher Charles Taylor to explore the meaning of "reasonable accommodation" of ethnic and religious minorities in the province of Quebec. After extensive hearings eliciting comments about the policy, the commission began its report by noting the universally recognized exceptionalism of Quebec in the larger Canadian picture: "the Canadian multiculturalism model does not appear to be well suited to conditions in Québec," it said, because in English Canada "there is less concern for the preservation of a founding cultural tradition than for national cohesion" (Bouchard and Taylor 2008: 39). Instead, it has been understood that the relevant framework in Quebec is that of "interculturalism," although this has never been officially adopted as a policy or its meaning clarified. The notion of interculturalism is understood to entail that the "nation" of Quebec, not all of Canada, is the relevant frame of reference for thinking about minority concerns and that the French language is expected to be predominant, even if multilingualism is encouraged.

The Bouchard-Taylor Commission's report thus outlined a peculiarly Quebecois model of minority accommodation. In particular, the commission sought to deemphasize the legal route to dealing with requests for appropriate arrangements for minority needs, which it explicitly equated with the term "reasonable accommodation." In contrast, its preferred approach of "concerted adjustment" would take the "citizen route" to accommodation. The basic idea is to avoid what the authors described as the "top-down" model of an antagonistic legal proceeding yielding winners and losers and to replace it with a "bottom-up" model based on negotiation and problem solving whose "objective is to find a solution that satisfies both parties." The report thus stresses a dialogical approach that is "contextual, deliberative and reflexive" and that seeks to promote "dejudicialization" (Bouchard and Taylor 2008: 52). The approach seems to be derived more or less directly from Jürgen Habermas's ideas about "communicative action" as a path to consensus and away from the "juridification of politics" (Habermas 1987: 357–366).

With regard to religion specifically, the Bouchard-Taylor Commission noted that during its public deliberations many Quebeckers insisted that "religion must remain in the private sphere." The authors argue, however, that this statement is less clear than it might seem at first glance; "private" may mean "not in the province of the state," or it may mean "not in public spaces." On the first interpretation, the notion of "private" religion may well correspond with a liberal understanding of the neutrality of the state, but this is not true in the second case: as a practical matter, it is simply not true that religions are denied permission to be present in Canadian public spaces. Moreover, the notion of state neutrality is ambiguous as well; the state must be even-handed with regard to different religions, but it must also be neutral with regard to religion and nonreligion. Indeed, "it must maintain its position of neutrality when faced with all deep-seated moral convictions, whether they are religious or secular." Ultimately, however, the secular, democratic state is based on a number of principles that are "not negotiable," whatever someone's "deep-seated convictions." These principles include political democracy, legal equality, and human rights (Bouchard and Taylor 2008: 44).

The commission thus recommended a model of "open secularism," a system of religious accommodation that accepts and does not seek to suppress religious identities, as preferred in some views associated with French republicanism (though not necessarily implemented there, despite a common perception that French secularism is a root and branch affair). In contrast to the stricter interpretations of French laïcité, some of which were echoed in the public contributions to the hearings the commission conducted across Quebec in preparing its findings, the report insists that there is no warrant for generally banning "religious signs" among public functionaries, except perhaps in the cases of higher officials who "by their very nature embody the State and its essential neutrality." In these very limited cases, there might only be said to be "a duty of self-restraint" (Bouchard and Taylor 2008: 48) but no across-the-board prohibition. The commission was clearly eager to defend the right to expression of religious belief in the context of a broader conception of state neutrality. In this regard, it appears to have been out of step with the preferences of many Quebecois, who incline toward a stricter secularism. In this regard, Quebecois also appear to diverge from the norms prevailing elsewhere in Canada.

The differences in outlook between the Canadian federation and the province of Quebec with regard to religious accommodation have led at least one legal scholar to argue that the two entities have fundamentally different conceptions of religion, which in turn has led to significantly dif-

ferent interpretations of the meaning of accommodation in the two jurisdictions. According to a study by Sébastien Grammond of four cases of
religious accommodation, the Quebec Court of Appeal has stressed the
private nature of religiosity and hence that "the State should not take religious factors into consideration when making decisions." In contrast, following the previously discussed decision in *Amselem*, the Supreme Court
of Canada regards religion as a matter of hard-won personal convictions,
not mere personal preferences, and hence must take more seriously the
individual's religious beliefs and practices. Grammond concludes that
"these diverging conceptions have a major impact on the degree of accommodation that judges are prepared to recognize" (Grammond 2009: 1).
Still, the predominance of federal law and the application of the "fundamental rights" clauses of both the federal and the Quebec charters to some
extent neutralize Quebecois idiosyncrasy (Grammond 2009: 1). The recommendations of the Bouchard-Taylor report are more in line with the
holdings of the Supreme Court than with those of the Quebec Court of
Appeal, but popular sentiment in Quebec is more secular in orientation.
We will see shortly that popular attitudes are less inclined even toward
Bouchard-Taylor's do-it-yourself vision of religious accommodation, despite the creation of a so-called 1-800-Accommodation hotline to field
queries seeking to achieve "concerted adjustment" and to defuse the "crisis" in Canadian multiculturalism.[18]

From a more theoretical perspective, the report is marked by a strange
conundrum. The commission begins by asserting that the supposed "crisis" of Quebecois identity is an overstatement but then bends over backward to accept the claims of the Quebecois that their stance toward minority integration should be that of "interculturalism" aiming at French
Canadian cultural survival rather than the less anxious stance of "multiculturalism." The commission thus accedes to an attitude toward integration—
namely, that it is something other than a two-way proposition—that it
would not find acceptable if it came from among immigrant minorities
themselves. More to the point for present purposes, the commission insists that the state must be neutral about "individual convictions" but cannot be neutral about certain "non-negotiable principles," such as democracy, human rights, and equality. "What happens," asks Ingrid Makus
(2010: 59–60), "when deep-seated convictions such as religious ideas on
the position of women in private and public spaces come into conflict with
liberal principles on gender equality?" We shall see in what follows that
such conflicts have dominated the recent politics of Muslim integration in
Quebec.

Veiling and the Limits of Multiculturalism
in Quebec

In view of Quebec's similarities with its distant progenitor, France, it is not entirely surprising to discover that a good deal of the debate about the accommodation of Islam in Quebec has revolved around the issue of headscarves or "veils." For example, at about the same time that the hamlet of Hérouxville promulgated its "Standards for Living," the Quebec Soccer Federation forbade a Muslim girl from wearing a headscarf while playing in a soccer game. The action, implemented in a nice irony by a Muslim referee, set off a controversy that drew even Quebec Prime Minister Charest onto the field of debate. Notwithstanding his empanelling of the Bouchard-Taylor Commission to explore the meaning of "reasonable accommodation," Charest announced his support for the referee's application of the rules on safety grounds. One commentator on the affair noted that an earlier consensus backing a wide ambit for religious accommodation was now "crumbling a bit[,] so every little incident is going to . . . spark questions."[19]

Indeed, the question of the veil—that is, the niqab, a head-to-neck covering that leaves only a slit for the eyes—has generated a striking effort to clarify and limit the range of religious accommodation in Quebec. In March 2010, the Quebec Commission on Human Rights ruled that women applying for a Medicare card would be required to remove any facial coverings for purposes of identification. Such a requirement, the commission said, does not infringe on the freedom of religion guaranteed by the province's Charter of Rights and Freedoms. This ruling, in turn, followed on the earlier expulsion of a niqab-wearing woman from not one but two different French language classes. First, the woman was ejected for declining to give a presentation to the class because there were men in the room; the second time, the teacher had asked her to remove her niqab for "pedagogical" reasons, which she refused to do on religious grounds. A representative of the conservative Muslim Council of Montreal saw the episode as unfortunate in that the woman was trying to acquire language skills that would better allow her to integrate into Quebec society. Raheel Raza of the Canadian Muslim Congress insisted, on the contrary, that wearing the niqab or burqa would itself make it difficult for Muslim women to integrate into Canadian society successfully, whatever their language skills.[20] Her comments echoed those of British Labour Party stalwart Jack Straw, who not long before had argued that the wearing of the face-covering veil would contribute to the creation of "parallel communities,"[21] as indeed it seems extensively to have done in the United Kingdom. In all events, the conflict between an individual's right to practice her religion as she sees fit and the public's interest in identification of individuals is manifest.

In response, in a move of unprecedented scope, the government of Quebec in late March 2010 proposed (the still-unrealized) Bill 94, which would require all recipients of public services to reveal their faces for purposes of "security, communication, and identification." Although no mention is made of Islam, as in the French law banning the veil from public spaces, the point of the law is not lost on anyone; it is intended to compel the handful of Muslim women in Quebec who wear the niqab to remove their facial coverings in any official public setting. The first legislation of its kind to have been proposed in North America, it has received a massive show of support both within and outside Quebec. According to a survey by the well-regarded Angus Reid polling firm, some 95 percent of Quebeckers and three-quarters of non-Quebecois Canadians supported the bill.[22] Endorsement has ranged across the political spectrum from conservative to liberal; even the well-known human rights defender-turned-Liberal politician Michael Ignatieff said he supports the idea as a "reasonable" effort to find the "balance" necessary for mutual accommodation of mainstream and minority cultures.[23] Quebec Justice Minister Kathleen Weil described the controversial legislation as the government's first attempt to codify "reasonable accommodation" in legal terms.

Not surprisingly, some segments of the Canadian Muslim population have endorsed such measures as consistent with the legal rights of women. The progressive Muslim Canadian Congress has pressed the Canadian government to outlaw the niqab and the burqa as "political symbols of . . . Islamic extremism" that are not required by Islam; the organization dismisses the burqa out of hand as "a medieval misogynistic practice."[24] That is not to say that the congress is opposed to head coverings across the board. But it must be understood, congress spokespersons Farzana Hassan and Tarek Fatah insist, that wearing the hijab is a purely optional matter and should not be understood as the definitive sign of a Muslim woman's piety.[25]

More broadly, however, the proposed law suggested to some observers that Canada had arrived at a turning point in its devotion to multiculturalism. Although substantial majorities have indicated continued support for the idea of multiculturalism, there is considerable uneasiness about what that term means in practice. The concern is exacerbated in a context in which immigration continues to transform the country's demography and against a background of intense international scrutiny of Islamist terrorism. Because the law is phrased in practical, security-minded terms, it cannot be known how much public support for Bill 94 may be an expression of anti-immigrant sentiment or of Islamophobia. But a set of polls conducted for the Association for Canadian Studies over the last several years has found that between 2007 and 2010, the percentage of those who believe that newcomers to Canada "should be urged to give up customs and traditions and become more like the rest of us" has grown from approximately one-third to approximately one-half. In addition, whereas 80 percent of Canadians told pollsters in 2001 that they thought multiculturalism enhanced Canadians' sense of identity and citizenship, by 2007 that number had declined to 69 percent. "If we still believe in multiculturalism," concluded the influential magazine *Macleans,* "we believe in a version with limits."[26]

One indication that something like Bill 94 may ultimately find legislative favor comes from a recent policy shift in regard to air travel in Canada, according to which all passengers are required to show their faces for purposes of security screening.[27] Notwithstanding the indications of public support for the bill and the disquiet concerning the realities of multiculturalism, however, commentators have suggested that, were it to pass, Bill 94 would be headed for a Supreme Court challenge because it would encroach on "fundamental freedoms" outlined in the federal Charter of Rights and Freedoms, as indeed it would. Even in Quebec, the legislation would likely face a challenge insofar as it goes beyond the recommendations outlined by the Bouchard-Taylor Commission with regard to educational settings. For example, the law would require both teachers and students to leave their niqabs and burqas outside the schoolhouse, whereas the commission recommended a considerably more open stance on this sort of question, as we have seen and as Canadian federal law would seem to require.

The problem with prohibiting the face-covering veil in certain settings revolves once again around the extent to which the state is unfairly depriving its citizens or residents of the freedom to express themselves in religious terms, assuming that that expression is freely chosen. Many, especially women, object to these forms of clothing as symbols of oppression imposed on them in some way, even if not by direct force. Louise Beaudoin of the Parti Quebecois, for example, said, "They say it's their choice, but I don't believe it. You know, at the time of slavery, there were slaves who didn't want to be freed, who praised their chains, but that's not a reason to not abolish slavery."[28] Leaving aside the veracity or otherwise of the claim about slaves applauding their shackles, Beaudoin and those who share her view adopt a Rousseauan understanding of freedom, as something that may have to be forced. Yet there is no easy way to demonstrate that the niqab wearer's choice of garb is involuntary. Beaudoin's stance is not easily squared with the Canadian Charter of Rights and Freedoms or indeed with any liberal constitution endorsing individual rights. For their own part, some opponents of the bill saw the niqab ban as creating "a climate of shame and fear" that would detract from Muslim women's "empowerment."[29] Both sides' perspectives make clear, however, that women's equality and women's rights are the central stakes in the controversy.

Notwithstanding the extensive public enthusiasm for Bill 94 when it was first floated, a recent ruling in Ontario suggests the difficulties such a bill would likely face in Canadian courts. The October 2010 decision of the Ontario Court of Appeal held that a witness must remove her niqab if failure to do so would jeopardize the possibility of a fair trial. But compelling a witness to remove a niqab can occur only on a case-by-case basis after the court probes whether that is really necessary under the circumstances. Courts must respect a person's sincerely held beliefs about his or her religious practices and, if necessary, accommodate those beliefs in some fashion if the situation warrants. This might include limiting the number of people in the courtroom or seeing to it that most or all of those persons are female. The court insisted that Charter rights are not "absolute" and must be interpreted in light of the "context" of their application.[30] Unsurprisingly, the conservative Muslim Council of Montreal greeted the decision warmly. Whether the broader "Muslim community" felt the same way, or whether the decision granted "the right to wear *niqab,*" as the headline of the group's press release put it, seems fancifully self-serving on the Council's part.[31] Still, the court's decision very much reflects the spirit of "concerted adjustment" as articulated in the Bouchard-Taylor report, and of previous liberal Canadian multiculturalism as well. It also seems to be more religion-friendly than the jurisprudence analyzed in Ran Hirschl's 2010 work on "constitutional theocracy"; the Court of Appeal ruling in this case is by no means as secularist in orientation as Dalton McGuinty's earlier decision, in the face of the attempt to create "shari'a tribunals" in Ontario, to insist that only Canadian law would reign in Ontario (see Hirschl 2010: 195–202).

No Consensus Within: The Varied Landscape of Canadian Islam

We have already examined some of the survey data concerning ordinary Muslims' views of their place in Canadian society. The aim here is to consider statements on this matter by at least some of the more authoritative spokespersons among Canadian Muslims. We should bear in mind that these views are not necessarily indicative of majority viewpoints; recall Goffman's dictum (1963: 27) that "representatives are not representative" because they are by definition more concerned with the issues under consideration than the ordinary member of the "community" in question. In any case, it is extremely important to note that there is considerable contention among Canadian Muslims themselves concerning the proper interpretation of Islamic tradition and its application to life in Canadian society. The different perspectives on the place of Muslims as a minority in Canadian society do not appear to have generated a "minority fiqh," as has occurred in the United States and elsewhere. That may simply be a result of the relative size of Canada and of the Canadian Muslim population and of the easy availability of relevant discussions of the United States and Europe online. In any case, let us briefly examine the published views of some of the principal Muslim groupings in order to get a sense of the range of perspectives that one encounters among Canadian Muslims. Irrespective of their views on the saliency of Islamic precepts in everyday life, they tend to be active in anti-discrimination work oriented to lessening Islamophobia in the post-9/11 period.

At one end of the spectrum, the Islamic Institute of Civil Justice (IICJ) and its head, Syed Mumtaz Ali, articulates a traditionalistic attitude toward the place of Muslims in Canada that emphasizes that these spaces are *dar al-harb* (usually translated "House of War" but referring to territories not controlled by Muslims). "Muslim minorities living in non-Muslim countries like Canada are like wandering Bedouins for whom the *Shariat* applies irregardless [*sic*] of where or when they live. Although they are free to live according to the Divine Law, to practice their faith unhindered in their homes and *masjids* [mosques], they have practically no say in the making of the laws of the land, and governmental institutions do not cater to their needs."[32] His remedy, as we have seen, was to propose the inauguration of Muslim courts of arbitration for family matters and thus to strengthen the reach of Islamic institutions in Canada. Alongside the IICJ, we should note that the Muslim Council of Montreal and its president, Salam Elmanyawi, similarly defend a more conservative version of Islam, in which the niqab is a sign of piety rather than of oppression.[33]

At the more liberal end of the continuum, we have a number of organizations especially concerned with the individual rights of Muslim women in Canada. We have already noted the opposition to shari'a tribunals and to the niqab of the Muslim Canadian Congress and two of its leading figures, Farzana Hassan and Tarek Fatah. Spokespersons for the congress have also insisted that Muslim extremism be taken seriously. They assert that "terrorism has too often been brushed aside as a conspiracy against Muslims" and that Muslim leaders must insist on the separation of church and state.[34] Likewise, as we have seen, the Canadian Council of Muslim Women was strenuously opposed to the IICJ's proposed family law arbitration panels and was sharply critical of Marion Boyd's report on the matter as being too soft on the request for special accommodation of Muslim demands. The Council's position is very much in line with the Ontario government's move to quash the use of any jurisprudence other than that of the Canadian federation or of the province in question.[35] If it were Jews who were under discussion, one would at this point expect the epithet "self-hating" to appear.

From a more abstract, philosophical perspective, we would be remiss to ignore the published views of Tariq Ramadan, because of his notable influence elsewhere and because he has written an article on the position of Muslims in non-Muslim societies in a volume directed specifically at those (interested) in Canada. Moreover, Sheema Khan, a Canadian Muslim liberal, favorably discussed Ramadan's views in her critical analysis of the IICJ's attempt to create a shari'a tribunal in Ontario. Khan (2007: 479) noted Ramadan's stress on three points:

1. that Muslims should recognize the constitution of the country in which they live (an accepted stricture upon Muslims);
2. that Muslims should undertake that loyalty "in conscience"—i.e., that one enters the agreement to support the constitution in full conscience; and
3. that one should participate in the society.

Ramadan makes these points again in his discussion of "Religious Allegiance and Shared Citizenship," a contribution to a 2007 volume on citizenship and multiculturalism in Canada today. But here he also stresses that the consensus among Islamic scholars that a Muslim should be loyal to the country in which he or she lives does not mean that that loyalty should be blind; rather, it should be a "critical loyalty" (Ramadan 2007: 456). This position seems perfectly consistent with liberal democratic understandings of citizenship; the notion of "my country, right or wrong" is hardly in good odor among democratic theorists.

What may be less consistent with democratic theory is Ramadan's insistence that as a matter of "philosophy of life," "I am a Muslim, and then I am a citizen—Canadian or French or British." It is of course true that many religious believers would put their religion ahead of their earthly attachments. Is that choice incompatible with life in a liberal society? Gérard Bouchard and Charles Taylor suggest that it might be, if it infringes on the bedrock Canadian values of democracy, legal equality, and human rights. Whether Ramadan advocates such infringement is often extremely difficult to pin down in his writings, which have a strangely elusive quality about them.[36] A liberal society must live with such views, however, at least up to the point where they can be shown to incite violence—even if that, too, is a difficult determination to make.

INASMUCH as Canada may be regarded as the original spawning ground of the very idea of multiculturalism, the Canadian experience is a bellwether for other countries pursuing minority integration policies understood in multicultural terms. This review of the vicissitudes of Muslim accommodation in recent Canadian experience highlights the challenges facing "multiculturalism" in contemporary liberal democracies. A traditionally construed Islam, whether involving the use of religiously based tribunals in family law or the wearing of certain kinds of clothing understood by some as incumbent on the pious, raises a number of red flags for defenders of individual rights. These challenges chiefly involve concerns about women's equality and women's subordination—concerns raised by Muslims as well as by non-Muslims.

But the desires by some Muslims to make use of shari'a courts or to wear a headscarf or facial covering also raise questions of individual freedom, for some might wish to do these things voluntarily—irrespective of whether others think them manifestations of these women's oppression or a display of their "false consciousness." These practices challenge skeptics of multiculturalism to accommodate unfamiliar differences more than they might otherwise be inclined to do, even if—indeed, precisely because— they find these practices abhorrent. As with the freedom of expression, freedom of religion can be realized only if it forces us to accept views we dislike and may dismiss as anti-egalitarian, authoritarian, retrograde, or otherwise undesirable. The problem is how to make those who prefer illiberal "inside" laws more inclined to accept liberal "outside" laws (see Esau 2008: 131–135).

At the same time, there seems little doubt that women who currently enjoy the individual equality rights enjoined by liberal constitutions have reason to be concerned about traditionalistically interpreted Islamic practices, insofar as these are not a matter of choice by the individuals themselves. And choice can be constrained not only by threats or actual violence but also by material circumstances of various kinds that might limit a person's options (see Fournier 2008). As a practical matter, however, in the absence of manifest physical violence, there are serious hurdles facing an outsider wishing to determine whether such practices are freely chosen.

Even if an outsider believes that these practices are intrinsically oppressive, as long as they are adopted without discernible external compulsion, a liberal society must accept them. Every effort should be made to undermine any such compulsion, of course, but short of the use or threat of physical violence, there is little basis for state intervention. The courts should intercede to ensure that individual rights are not being abrogated, while ensuring that religious freedom is being protected as well. Notwithstanding the requirement of accommodating even illiberal practices, a liberal society must defend the rights of individuals who seek to escape from such practices.

Finally, and perhaps most important, it must be emphasized that the debates in Western societies about the accommodation of Muslim beliefs and practices parallel a major dispute within the Canadian Muslim "community"—a term that inappropriately projects harmony where there is none—over how Islamic teachings should be interpreted and implemented. This is a struggle that must be nurtured and facilitated, as some interpretations of Islam (like those of other religions) are manifestly inimical to liberal democratic norms, especially with regard to women's equality. To borrow a line familiar from Islamic teaching, there can be "no compulsion in matters of religion."

In sum, a chastened Canadian multiculturalism is groping its way toward accommodation of a religion some of whose adherents are in fact not interested in making accommodation a two-way street, as many Canadians worry. So far, it appears to be succeeding reasonably well, but that is in part because Canada shares no borders with any sources of large-scale, "problematic" immigration—least of all of Muslims. Banting and Kymlicka (2010: 56) have noted that Canada has not faced Islamic radicalism to the extent that is feared in some European countries, and Kymlicka has elsewhere (2005: 8) averred that "the debate in Canada might have been very different if, as in Europe, ninety percent of our immigrants were Muslim." The fact is that the debate over multiculturalism in Canada needed only a small number of Muslims making demands for accommodation of illiberal practices to tip in a less enthusiastic direction. Size matters, and the relatively small size of the Canadian Muslim population means that the issue of accommodating Islam has so far been comparatively minor. Under other circumstances, it might become a major issue—and it has clearly also generated a certain degree of controversy in the heretofore happily multicultural Great White North.

CHAPTER FIVE

The Dog That Didn't Bark

Islam and Religious Pluralism
in the United States

IN 2010, the United States witnessed a remarkable spasm of concern about the place of Islam in American society. The event that precipitated it was the announcement of plans to build the so-called Ground Zero Mosque in lower Manhattan. Whether or not this is an apt name for a building to be constructed a couple of blocks from the site of the World Trade Center towers, destroyed by world-changing Islamic terrorism in 2001, this framing of the project concretized many people's objections to the endeavor. Many commentators found the project to erect a mosque so close to the location of the Islamist-inspired attack on American soil an affront to the memory of those who perished in that catastrophe. Others—ultimately including President Barack Obama—defended the rights of all law-abiding citizens to pray and worship in any way that was consistent with constitutional principles. A third, more moderate camp agreed that the backers of the project had the right, in principle, to build the mosque but saw the building's propinquity to the hallowed ground of what entered the lexicon as "9/11" as a needless provocation that prudence required them to renounce.

Although the episode generated much intense feeling, and even led a previously obscure Florida pastor to threaten to burn a Quran before the eyes of the world, the controversy was largely a product of electoral timing and manufactured for political consumption. The mosque project, otherwise known more innocuously as "Park51," had originally been proposed a year earlier, to little public notice or response. Imam Feisal Abdul Rauf, the cleric leading the project, told the *New York Times* that a Muslim presence so close to the World Trade Center site "sends the opposite statement to what happened on 9/11. We want to push back against the extremists." New York Mayor Bloomberg signaled his support, as did a number of religious figures in the city and in the neighborhood of the proposed mosque site. They were aware of the delicacy of the undertaking and even wondered whether it might not lead to backlash against Muslims, but they decided to move forward nonetheless.[1]

The 2010 midterm congressional elections supplied the context for just the backlash the project's endorsers had feared. A variety of politicians and activists, not least the ill-fated Republican gubernatorial candidates Rick Lazio and Carl Paladino, outdid each other in their denunciations of the mosque and the supposed "Islamist" impulses behind it. In the process, they conveniently ignored the fact that the FBI had attested that it had had positive, productive relations with Imam Rauf, who in any case is an (inward-looking) Sufi and hence not a likely enthusiast of Islamist plans to take over the world. It might be noted that, just as these developments were taking place, actual Islamists bombed an important Sufi shrine in Pakistan, killing several people and injuring dozens more in another display of the terrorists' lack of concern about "collateral damage" in pursuit of their aims.[2]

One of the outgrowths of the mood of anti-Muslim hysteria that attended the run-up to the 2010 midterm elections was a proposed amendment to the Oklahoma constitution that would ban courts from considering Islamic or international law in their decision-making processes—a slightly more serious (because legally consequential) version of the hilarious Hérouxville "standards" in Canada (see Chapter 4). As in that Canadian hamlet, the fact that consideration of shari'a law could not be shown ever to have occurred in the Oklahoma courts did not deter the proponents of the measure. In view of the proposition's stated intention to discriminate against one set of religious beliefs in particular, it offered an obvious target for a judicial challenge. The Oklahoma chapter of the Council on American-Islamic Relations (CAIR) promptly sued. Although the law was approved by more than 70 percent of the state's voters and took effect briefly, a federal judge stayed the certification of the election results until she could make a final ruling regarding its constitutionality. Contrary to its backers' protestations of even-handedness, Judge Vicki Miles-LaGrange of the Federal District Court in Oklahoma City found the amendment to be a transparent attack on shari'a law, which may be used in certain civil proceedings in the United States, and hence incompatible with the safeguards provided in the First Amendment. Many Muslims were concerned that, if the amendment had been adopted, their private law provisions—such as their wills—might be invalidated. In a telling vindication of American constitutional principles, the head of the Oklahoma branch of CAIR, Muneer Awad, noted with satisfaction that the judge's ruling meant that "the majority vote cannot take away my constitutional rights."[3] The lower court judge's decision was affirmed in a January 2012 ruling by the Tenth Circuit Court of Appeals. It is a signal confirmation of the American constitutional and legal endorsement of religious pluralism and hence of the accommodation of Islam. The Oklahoma bill had soon been followed by others in a number of states, including Arizona, Louisiana, and Tennessee, but these appear to have gone nowhere as well—perhaps as a result of the rough treatment the Oklahoma law received in the courts.[4]

In what follows, we explore the integration of Islam in the United States against the background of the country's fabled traditions of religious pluralism. We therefore not only examine the ways in which the American government and constitutional legal apparatus have responded to the presence of Muslims on American soil but also consider Muslim responses in the United States as members of a minority religion. The latter side of the coin is all the more important as, more than in any other case considered in this book, the "state" (always a bit suspect in the American context) stands aloof from civil society and, as Tocqueville knew, "where in France you would find the government . . . , in the United States you are sure to find an association" (Tocqueville 1969: 513).

Moreover, as Jocelyne Cesari astutely observed, in the context of America's foundational "religious pluralism," there is no point for Muslims to seek "establishment in official institutions"; instead, the attempt is to search for entry in "American civil religion" and to stretch the latter from "Judeo-Christian" to "Judeo-Christian-Islamic" (Cesari 2004: 84). To anticipate the conclusion, we find relatively little reason that Islam in the United States cannot find its place in the already existing chain "Protestant–Catholic–Jew," and we also find that authoritative Muslim commentators have been inclined to argue that Muslims can and should live successfully *as* Muslims in this setting. Despite the perception in far-flung parts of the world since the early Bush years that the United States is at war with all Muslims, Islam in America seems to have been the dog that didn't bark—a nonproblem, at least from a constitutional-legal perspective, if not necessarily from a popular one.

Religion: Defining What Must Be Protected

In both of the continental European cases, as we have seen, but also to a degree in Canada, accommodating Islam in legal terms revolves around the question of the relationship of religion to a putatively neutral state, whose neutrality is always a bit in question. In France, the point of policy efforts is to ensure that religion keeps its distance and avoids sullying the supposedly pristine areligiosity of the republican project. No tawdry superstition may besmirch the sacrally secular state, which, as we showed, may pose a risk to religious freedom. In Germany, by contrast, the problem of accommodating Islam arises from the fact that the state has historically reserved the right to recognize some religions but not others and has provided those so recognized with rights and privileges denied others. It must now decide whether it will officially recognize Islam as a "corporation under public law" and thereby place it on an equal footing with the other religions it has already recognized; this in turn requires Islam to assume a corporate form that is not native to it historically. In the German case, the critical issue is equal inclusion of organized Islam in public space by the state, whereas in France, where all things religious are equally excluded, the critical issue is the impairment of individual religious freedom that may be entailed by this exclusion. Canada resembled some European states to a degree, in that a "shadow establishment" and concomitant legal-constitutional privileging of the Christian faith had to be chased away and neutralized, as they eventually were.

In the United States, the religion-state constellation is different from all other cases, European and Canadian, considered in this book. The legal foundations of religious freedom lie in the "establishment" and "free exercise" clauses of the First Amendment. It is this strict and formal separation of church and state *ab ovo,* combined with the outspoken endorsement of any and all forms of religious belief, that characterizes an American context that appears schizophrenic (or perhaps "neither fish nor fowl") to European but also to Canadian eyes. The fundamental legal question concerning all religious activity in the United States is thus simply whether it really constitutes religion and not something else. If so, the Constitution requires that it be accorded the fullest possible legal protection. As a result, the U.S. government is always and unavoidably confronted in First Amendment religion cases with the problem of determining whether that on which it rules is, in fact, religion, because that is what the American Constitution must protect.

The problem of defining religion has emerged, among other instances, specifically in regard to Muslims in the United States, although presumably no one now doubts that Islam is a religion. The problem is that there has been a version of Islam in the United States that is not found elsewhere and that historically has had as much to do with cultural nationalism as with the universalistic faith centered on Mecca. In 1962, the question arose with regard to a number of black Muslims who claimed they were denied the right to exercise their religion as inmates in the Lorton Reformatory in Virginia. The director of the District of Columbia Department of Corrections, Donald Clemmer, denied said prisoners the right to practice their faith because of his view—"not without support in the record," as the court put it—that the black Muslims espoused "racial hatred." In response, the U.S. District Court for the District of Columbia applied the "theistic test," holding in *Fulwood v. Clemmer* that Muslims believed "in the existence of a supreme being controlling the destiny of man" and that, as a result, "the Muslim faith is a religion."[5] Still, the court was in some doubt about whether "the [black] Muslim faith is an authentic offshoot of the Islamic religion of the Moslems." Over time, as we shall see, the division in Islamic practices reflected in that perplexity would gradually be overcome, at least to some degree.

However, recent juridical practice has been less open-handed about accommodating religion than many religious activists and some scholarly critics would prefer (see, e.g., Nussbaum 2008 and Witte 2005). Questions concerning black Muslims have been an important part of this trend. As a result of the growth of a black Muslim population in prisons (where they have been successful at converting criminals, as most famously in the case of Malcolm X but also, more recently, boxing champion Mike Tyson), the matter of protecting the religious freedom of prison inmates, in particular, has received considerable attention from the courts. The Black Muslims were regarded with suspicion because of their sometime advocacy of violence against whites, and prison officials' concern for safety and security were given considerable latitude with regard to them.

In *O'Lone v. Estate of Shabazz* (1987), notably, the Supreme Court upheld a decision by a lower court denying Muslim prisoners' allegation that prison policies inhibited their freedom of worship and hence denied them their constitutional rights. Not so, said the court, which held that "the policies challenged here are reasonably related to legitimate penological interests, and therefore do not offend the Free Exercise Clause."[6] Prior to the decision in *O'Lone v. Shabazz*, however, courts had generally been inclined to accept claims that Muslims had been treated discriminatorily when their religious practices were denied by prison officials. "Most courts have ruled," wrote Kathleen Moore (1995: 86), "that suppression of religious liberty—for instance, the prohibition of prayer meetings and other forms of discriminatory treatment—if applied unequally at the expense of Muslim inmates" violated the First Amendment.

While *O'Lone* may chiefly have affected Muslim prisoners, the decision would soon emerge as part of a broader trend toward more restrictive judicial interpretations of constitutionally protected religious activity under Chief Justice William Rehnquist, who took office in 1986. In the preceding years under Chief Justices Warren and Burger, the court had gradually broadened the scope of what counted as "religion" for legal purposes. In particular, the 1965 decision in *United States v. Seeger*, a draft-exemption case, articulated the "ultimate concern" test, which focused less on the content of a person's belief and more on whether it is "a sincere and meaningful belief occupying in the life of its possessor a place parallel to that filled by the God" of other believers.[7] This holding opened the door wide to forms of "religion" that had little to do with the traditionally recognized faiths.

But the tide turned in 1990 with the famous Supreme Court ruling in *Employment Division v. Smith,* around which much of the recent legal debate on religious freedom in the United States has turned. In that case, two plaintiffs who were working as drug counselors had ingested the hallucinogenic cactus peyote as part, they claimed, of their religious observance as members of the Native American Church. The court was not amused, finding instead that "the right of free exercise [of religion] does not relieve an individual of the obligation to comply with a 'valid and neutral law of general applicability.' "[8] This determination constituted a notable departure from the previous, more capacious understanding of protected religious activity and provoked a storm of opposition among pro-religious activists.

Now a strange dynamic evolved that pitted a religion-friendly legislature against a religion-unfriendly high court, the exact opposite of the legal-political pattern otherwise observed in this book. Opponents of the ruling organized together in the Coalition for the Free Exercise of Religion, and they persuaded legislators in Congress to turn the tide in a more expansive direction. In 1993, Congress passed the Religious Freedom Restoration Act (RFRA), which sought to overturn the court's holding that religious actors could not seek an exemption from laws of "general applicability," as *Employment Division v. Smith* required. Yet by passing the RFRA, Congress had taken it upon itself to overrule the Supreme Court's interpretation of the Constitution, setting the stage for a major battle between the branches of the federal government. The Supreme Court fired back. In 1997, in the case of *Boerne v. Flores,* the court found the RFRA an unconstitutional usurpation of its authority to interpret the Constitution. Then, in 2000, Congress passed the Religious Land Use and Institutionalized Persons Act (RLUIPA), which prohibits restrictions on land use that would infringe on free exercise and limits the discretion of prison officials in imposing constraints on the religious exercise of prisoners; President George W. Bush signed the bill into law in 2004. Soon thereafter, the statute was thrown into doubt when a lower court held that the law violated the establishment clause. In *Cutter et al. v. Wilkinson* (2005), however, the Supreme Court surprisingly overturned the appeals court decision that found the RLUIPA a constitutionally impermissible promotion of religion. To the contrary, according to the court's majority, the government had sharply restricted the inmates' freedom of religion by incarcerating them, and the law was their only recourse to regain their rights to religious observance, and this was particularly so insofar as the petitioners were adherents of "nonmainstream" religions, such as Satanism and the white-supremacist Church of Jesus Christ–Christian.[9] The decision marked a shift back in the direction of the courts' more religion-friendly stance prior to *O'Lone.*

Meanwhile, religious activists also responded to *Boerne v. Flores* on the legislative front by exploiting the federal structure of the American state. Arguing that states were not bound by the Supreme Court's rejection of the application of RFRA at the federal level, they succeeded in encouraging more than a dozen states to adopt so-called mini-RFRAs, which seek to sustain a broader interpretation of the free exercise clause in these states (on these developments, see Sullivan 2006: 26–31). These laws typically require the government to demonstrate a "compelling interest" before placing any "burden" on religious beliefs or practices (a test arising from the famous 1963 case of *Sherbert v. Verner,* in which the Supreme Court held the government to this standard for denying unemployment benefits to a woman fired as a consequence of her religious convictions). Moreover, even under the more restrictive standard of free exercise set by *Smith,* any state or federal statute that may be regarded as an infringement on religious freedom is subject to "strict scrutiny" by the courts (Davis 2004: 227). Accordingly, although *Smith* has generated great hostility from among many pro-religion activists and their sympathizers, by no means everyone with an opinion on the matter regards the judgment in that case as the Waterloo of religious freedom, as we will see below in regard to at least one important case involving the legal integration of Muslims.

Public Hostility and State Repression after 9/11

Since the events of September 11, 2001, the presence of Muslims in the United States, which had previously been mainly associated with the indigenous Black Muslim population, has become much more strongly associated with immigrant populations and with questions of national security. In the wake of the attacks, there was an "overwhelming and relentless" (Bakalian and Bozorgmehr 2009: 1) backlash among the general populace directed particularly against Muslim and Middle Eastern Americans or individuals with Arabic- or Islamic-sounding names. Within days of the September 11 attacks, there were four confirmed cases of murder motivated by ethno-religious animosity. Seven further murder cases were also suspected to be hate crimes. Human Rights Watch found that there had been "a nationwide wave of hate crimes against persons and institutions perceived to be Arab or Muslim" that distinguished itself from previous hate crime waves "by its ferocity and extent." However, most of the incidents occurred soon after September 11, "with the violence tapering off by December" (Human Rights Watch 2002: 14–15).

Meanwhile, the list of repressive government initiatives against Middle Eastern and Muslim Americans at the time was extensive and worrisome. According to one authoritative account,

> the administration subjected 80,000 Arab and Muslim immigrants to fingerprinting and registration, sought out 8,000 Arab and Muslim men for FBI interviews, and imprisoned over 5,000 foreign nationals in antiterrorism preventive detention initiatives. As part of this program, the government adopted an aggressive strategy of arrest and prosecution, holding people on minor charges—in fact pretexts—such as immigration violations, credit card fraud, or false statements, or, when it had no charges at all, as "material witnesses." . . . Virtually all of the cases in which the government has actually charged individuals with a crime relating to terrorism allege not acts of terrorism per se, but only "material support" to a group the government has labeled terrorist, a term expansively defined to include financial assistance, training, services, and even expert advice. (Cole 2006: 39)

Then, in a 2006 decision in *Turkmen v. Ashcroft,* a district judge in Brooklyn granted the government wide discretion under immigration laws to detain noncitizens on the basis of race, religion, or national origin and to hold them indefinitely without explanation.[10] More recently, the extreme vagueness of the "material support" charge has not kept the Supreme Court from upholding the relevant law in 2010 when it was challenged by a human rights group seeking to advise the separatist Liberation Tigers of

Tamil Eelam of Sri Lanka and the Kurdistan Workers' Party, both designated as terrorist groups by the U.S. State Department, with regard to the peaceful resolution of the conflicts in which they have been engaged.[11] Although this case did not involve Muslims directly, it clearly bears on U.S. legal approaches to dealing with those the government seeks to prosecute as supporters of Islamic terrorism.

Bakalian and Bozorgmehr (2009) have found that the cumulative effect of the governmental and popular backlash against Arab Americans and Muslims has been widespread fear, emotional turmoil, and psychological distress. Chishti et al. (2003) argued that the government overemphasized immigration policy as an antiterrorism instrument, that immigration enforcement is of little effect in stemming terrorist attacks, that the arrest of noncitizens serves only to give a false sense of security, and that immigration actions have threatened fundamental civil liberties. He and his collaborators also argued that the targeting of Arab and Muslim Americans undermines national unity, which does not advance the cause envisioned by those lashing out at Arab Americans and Muslims. Indeed, the backlash has backfired: mistrust of the government in the affected communities, most of whom are unsympathetic to terrorism and could thus play an important role in helping to stymie it, rose in the wake of these measures (see Cole 2006). This approach thus seems misguided insofar as one of the main aims of counterterrorism policy is presumably to reduce the size of the population that may tacitly support Islamic terrorism, depriving extremists of the "moral oxygen" that sustains their activities (see Saggar 2010). The law enforcement focus on immigration policy also seems less and less appropriate as the United States has begun to generate its own "homegrown" Muslim terrorists, a notable shift from the foreign origins of the 9/11 terrorists.[12]

Despite the clear and extensive violations of civil liberties and the counterproductive backlash they have stimulated, a leading historian and sharp critic of the World War II internment of Japanese and Japanese Americans, Roger Daniels, warned that one should not exaggerate the similarities between Roosevelt's policies toward these groups after Pearl Harbor and the policies of the Bush administration toward Arab Americans and Muslims after September 11, 2001: "Many commentators have compared the two cases—some seeing a disturbingly similar pattern in reaction against a feared nonwhite population, others praising what they see as the relative moderation of today's government. . . . But compared with what was done to Japanese Americans during World War II, government actions before and after September 11 do not seem to amount to very much" (quoted in Bakalian and Bozorgmehr 2009: 60–61). Indeed, despite the strong domestic response to 9/11, which resulted in ubiquitous admonitions of heightened watchfulness ("if you see something, say something"), the federal government's actions can hardly be said to rival the precedent set by the World War II–era internment policy. Middle Eastern, Arab, and South Asian Americans met with increased hatred and discrimination in their everyday lives, and Muslims have been vilified in public, but Islam and the religious practices of Muslims were by no means subjected to systematic state repression on a scale comparable to the internment of 120,000 Japanese and Japanese Americans. Indeed, it has been widely noted that President George W. Bush repeatedly avowed his respect and appreciation for Islam, which he claimed to regard as a "peaceful religion."[13]

Notwithstanding these conclusions concerning the government's response, the perception among Americans that Muslims adhere to a bellicose religion and the popular desire for greater limitation on Muslims' freedom have remained high. For example, a 2004 Cornell University survey of Americans found that 44 percent of all respondents agree that "at least one form of restriction should be placed on Muslim American civil liberties." The researchers also found 47 percent of respondents agreeing that "the Islamic religion is more likely than others to encourage violence among its believers." Moreover, the survey found that these opinions were relatively stable over time, despite a sharp decrease in the perceived likelihood of another terrorist attack since September 2001 (Nisbet and Shanahan 2004). In 2006, a Gallup poll found that 39 percent of Americans believed Muslims were not loyal to the United States, and a full third said that Muslims living in the United States were sympathetic to al-Qaeda. Some 44 percent of all respondents believed that Muslims were "too extreme" in their beliefs.[14] The public also made a connection between security concerns and questions of immigration policy. In a 2007 *Newsweek* poll, 46 percent of respondents agreed that "this country allows too many immigrants to come here from Muslim countries."[15] A January 2010 Gallup poll found that half of Americans have an unfavorable view of Islam, with 31 percent indicating their opinion of Islam is "not favorable at all."[16] An August 2010 Pew Research Center poll found that only 30 percent of Americans hold a "favorable" view of Islam, down from 41 percent in July 2005 (the month of the 7/7 bombings in London); meanwhile, 35 percent of those polled believe Islam is more likely than other religions to encourage violence.[17] Given the "social-desirability effects" that frequently lead respondents to underreport sensitive responses such as prejudice toward certain groups, anti-Muslim sentiment may well be even more widespread in the general population than these figures indicate. In short, the perception remains widespread among Americans that

Muslims are uniquely or unusually predisposed toward violence, views that were much encouraged by certain politicians during the run-up to the 2010 elections.

Islam's Smooth Legal Sailing

In the post-9/11 climate, Muslims may have had greater difficulty defending their religious practices in the court of public opinion, but they have generally not had such difficulty in the courts of law or in public policy. The question of whether Islamic practices deserve constitutional protection pervades the American preoccupation with Islam since 9/11, in part because it is often disputed whether those attacks were motivated by religion as such or simply by extremists with grievances against American foreign policy who use religion as a cloak for their actions.

Testimony to Islam's smooth legal sailing in the United States is the non-issue of veiling. Surely, in recent years the wearing of Muslim religious garb in schools has emerged as a matter of contention in some instances. Although that issue has inflamed opinion and occasioned dramatic state action in France, Germany, and Canada, however, the consequences of such action have been rather limited in the United States. In 2003, for example, school officials in Muskogee, Oklahoma, suspended a Muslim girl who wore her headscarf to school. Press accounts noted that complaints about the student's headscarf first arose on September 11, 2003, the second anniversary of the terrorist attacks, despite the fact that she had been wearing the headscarf to school for a significant period beforehand. In response to the action of the school authorities, she and her family sued in federal court, claiming that their right to religious freedom had been violated. Notwithstanding the widespread international image of the Bush administration as having been at war with all Muslims, the U.S. Department of Justice joined the lawsuit on the plaintiff's side in March 2004. Soon thereafter, the school district settled with the family, agreeing that they should change their dress codes to allow exceptions on religious grounds.[18] The case vindicated the notion that people should be at liberty to exercise their religious freedom, even in a politically overheated environment deriving from unprecedented attacks on the country by persons acting under the putative color of Islamic religious motivations. More generally, a 1997 case arising in a Texas public school undergirds students' rights to wear the religious dress of their choice.[19] These cases of school dress code violations tend to be handled on a local, case-by-case basis, and the competing considerations—as in prisons—typically concern safety and order. The question of whether a particular practice constitutes religious expression is frequently at the heart of the matter; if it is so deemed, the practice will in all likelihood be protected.[20]

Muslims have also sought other types of accommodation in schools. Much of this activity has resulted from the efforts of the Muslim Students Association (MSA), along with the Islamic Society of North America, one of the oldest and most prominent organizations in the country promoting Muslim interests (see Smith 2009: 34). The MSA has successfully pushed for prayer baths at the University of Michigan, with many more such requests in the works. The group has also persuaded a number of universities to provide rooms "for Muslims only," complete with prayer rugs. These accommodations have caused controversy among those concerned about the separation of church (or mosque) and state. At least one Muslim, Zuhdi Jasser, chairman of a group called the American Islamic Forum for Democracy, objected that the accommodation of Muslims in these cases seemed to be one-sidedly providing Islam with privileges not accorded to adherents of other religions. Similarly, despite the American Civil Liberties Union's reputation for defending even some who would destroy the country's democratic foundations, Jeremy Gunn, director of the group's program on freedom of religion and belief in Washington, D.C., worried that the provision of Muslim foot baths and prayer rugs is "a difficult one, and it's right on the edge," legally speaking.[21]

With so much equivocation from likely sympathizers, it will not be surprising to learn that these accommodations have incited the ire of conservative gadfly Daniel Pipes, who has become well known for his opposition to anything that he believes smacks of official accommodation of radical Islam. Pipes and others objected to a proposed Brooklyn school that would teach Arabic language and culture and thus, according to Pipes, was effectively a "madrassa," which is simply the Arabic word for "school" but which has come to have associations with the Taliban and other extremist Islamist endeavors. Many of the parents involved objected not on any religious grounds but because they worried that the school would have taken away classroom space from the school building where the program was to have been housed. Despite the fact that the U.S. government has precious few speakers of Arabic through whom to communicate with the Arabic speakers of the Middle East, and despite the further fact that the designated principal—though a Muslim—was widely regarded as a religious moderate, the project was abandoned in 2007.[22]

In a case reminiscent of the Canadian *Multani* decision (involving, as we have seen, the constitutionality of the carrying of a ceremonial dagger by a Sikh schoolboy), Muslim men have also sought and received jurisprudential accommodation of what they believed is a religious requirement to wear beards. In the 1999 case of *Fraternal Order of Police v. City of Newark,* two Muslim police officers challenged a requirement that they be clean-shaven on the basis of the fact that the policy already made exceptions on other grounds, namely, medical ones. The plaintiffs won in district court, and the ruling was affirmed on appeal by the Third Circuit Court of Appeals, which found that the city had failed to make clear why it could not make an exception to its policy on religious grounds. In reaching its conclusion that the police department's policy was unconstitutional, the Circuit Court explicitly invoked the *Smith* requirement of "strict scrutiny" in cases in which the free exercise of religion is said to be curtailed. It may not be irrelevant for future legal developments that one of the judges on the Third Circuit panel that delivered that ruling was Samuel Alito Jr., now on the Supreme Court.[23]

Clearly, the presence of Muslims on American soil in the recent past has posed difficult challenges in an environment of much post-9/11 distrust and unfamiliarity with Islam. But the legal response has been overwhelmingly accommodating where laws and regulations have been shown to have a discriminatory impact on Muslims in violation of the First Amendment guarantee of the free exercise of religion.

A New American Minority

Having examined popular, government, and court responses to the presence of Muslims and Islam in America, let us now examine the matter from the reverse angle. How do authoritative Muslim commentators and ordinary Muslims themselves see the prospect of integrating into the American setting, in which they are not in the majority?

But first it is worth recalling that the Protestant hegemony in the United States during the nineteenth century, and the Catholic Church's unfamiliarity with a context in which it was not the established religion, led to a resolution that created a limited parallel society of religious schools, hospitals, and other institutions that were both refuge and ghetto for Catholics until well into the twentieth century. Only with the *aggiornamento* of Vatican II did the Catholic Church finally accept that it was only one denomination among others and thus make its peace with liberal democracy (see Casanova 1994: ch. 7). To what extent is the encounter between Islam and American liberal democracy comparable? However committed many of them surely were to illiberal forms of politics and practices, Catholics were not initially associated with terrorism when they arrived on American shores. The Irish were seen as incorrigible drunken brawlers, giving rise to the infamous "paddy wagon." Later, Italians were sometimes connected in the public mind with anarchist and other strains of radicalism, some of which had a violent streak—as in the case of Sacco and Vanzetti. But Catholics in general were not seen as progenitors of religiously motivated violence in the United States.

By contrast, the question of the integration of Muslims into Western societies has been vexed by a context in which some Muslims have conducted high-profile terrorist acts while proclaiming themselves defenders of the faith. Against this charged background, one might identify two basic scholarly perspectives concerning the place of Islam in nonmajority contexts. One, represented by such commentators as Bassam Tibi (2006, 2009a, 2009b) and typical of much secular opinion in parts of the Islamic world, is the view that Muslims cannot accept rule by non-Muslims and that Muslims will take every opportunity to seek political dominance in order to ensure that they are not so ruled. Similarly, Steve Bruce (2003) argues that wherever Muslims appear in substantial, concentrated numbers, they seek to assert the primacy of shari'a law and act illiberally toward other religions. Taken as a group, these Muslim proclivities are regarded as reflecting a refusal to separate church and state on the Western model or, worse, as evidence of an undemocratic, aggressive, and potentially violent quality within Islam that is an essential and intrinsic part of the religion's way of being in the world. Strikingly, Tibi (2006: 213) claims that even if one were to interview imams (prayer leaders in mosques) to learn about their views of Muslim relations with the non-Muslim world, they would not tell the truth because their aims are illiberal. If this guarded—not to say overwrought—perspective is correct, Mustafa Kemal (aka "Atatürk") was not the radical Orientalist one might be inclined to see him as but rather a clear-eyed analyst of his Muslim countrymen's religious and political culture with a sensible if draconian set of prescriptions for transforming them into modern Westerners.

The alternative view insists that Islam is, like all world religions, an extremely variegated phenomenon that has been compatible with a multiplicity of political forms and that is only marginally connected to the terrorists who act in its name. John Esposito (e.g., 2010) has been a leading exponent of this understanding. He and others sharing this perspective (perhaps most prominently Stepan 2000) note that Islam has come to dominate the religious landscape across an enormous swathe of the earth stretching from Morocco to Indonesia and from the Caucasus to Kenya; that it is divided into many forms (especially Sunni, Shi'a, and the generally more easygoing Sufi strands, not to mention the many schools of legal interpretation—Hanbali, Maliki, etc.); and that the tendency to associate Islam with the Arabic-speaking Middle East and its undemocratic political systems is profoundly misleading. Rather, such commentators insist, Islam is a religion enjoining peace, almsgiving, and the well-being of its adherents, and it has deep continuities and shared premises (not to mention holy figures) with its progenitors, Judaism and Christianity.

What is the situation of Muslims in the United States in this regard, and how do Muslims view that situation? For reasons we have already addressed, analysts of Islam in the United States routinely distinguish between "indigenous" and immigrant Islam. The indigenous braid of American Islam, in turn, actually has several strands. It includes those deriving from the earlier slave population, some of whom brought Islam with them across the Middle Passage. Then there were the relatively small numbers of Middle Eastern Muslims who began arriving in the United States a century and more ago from the declining Ottoman Empire, settling often in the Detroit area but remaining fairly inconspicuous—by adopting the widespread immigrant practice of changing their names to sound more American, for example.[24] Finally, and perhaps best known to most Americans, are the various black Muslim groups. Founded by Elijah Muhammad as the Nation of Islam, the Black Muslims made a reputation for themselves for being militantly anti-white but also for having turned around numerous wayward young men, most famously Malcolm Little (better known as Malcolm X). Under Elijah Muhammad's son, Warith Deen Muhammad, who assumed leadership of the movement upon his father's death in 1975, the Nation evolved very much toward a synthesis with the orthodox Sunni Islam practiced by many recent immigrants to the United States. It eventually dropped the Nation of Islam rubric, opting instead for the label American Society of Muslims. The more flamboyant and prominent Louis Farrakhan thus heads a declining remnant of black Muslims under the Nation of Islam moniker. The Nation's outspoken embrace of an identity understood as a reaction to the white, Christian domination of the country's slave populations has in the past raised questions about its religious status, as we have seen in the case of *Fulwood v. Clemmer*. Its star seems fated to fade as African immigrants—some of them Muslims—enter the American melting pot and as the American Society of Muslims links arms with Muslims whose roots lie elsewhere than in the United States.

In contrast to the indigenous strain of Islam, the immigrant variants have grown dramatically with a shift in the sources of migrants following immigration reform legislation in 1965. The principal streams of Muslims have come from South Asia, which contains one of the largest Muslim populations in the world, and from Iran. Whereas South Asian Muslims are generally Sunni, Iranian Muslims are overwhelmingly Shi'ite in orientation. In contrast to the Muslim populations in France and Germany, which tend to come from the Maghreb and from Turkey, respectively, American Muslims, much like Canadian Muslims, thus tend to come from a variety of different sending areas and thus to be more diverse in their religious and homeland orientations. Especially in the first (immigrant) generation, they may place a higher priority on politics in their regions of origin. Iranian and South Asian immigrants in general tend also to come from a higher segment of the class and occupational structure, a fact that distinguishes them noticeably from their African American coreligionists.

Also akin to their Canadian peers, Muslims in the United States generally fare much better economically than their European counterparts, and this is a crucial consideration when it comes to integrating persons from other cultural groups. A 2009 study found that 70 percent of Muslims in the United States were employed—a percentage higher than the American average of 64 percent—whereas that was true of only 53 percent in Germany, 45 percent in France, and a miserable 38 percent in the United Kingdom. Remarkably, though perhaps not surprisingly in view of its less generous welfare state, Muslims in the United States were actually more likely to be employed there than in any Muslim-majority country. Moreover, reflecting their higher class background, 31 percent of nonemployed Muslims in the United States are full-time students, as compared with only 10 percent of the overall population.[25] This enviable employment picture, combined with the disproportionate pursuit of advanced educational opportunities, apparently contributes to Muslims' positive assessment of their prospects in American society. Reflecting a stereotypically American outlook on life, more than 70 percent of American Muslims thus agree that "most people who want to get ahead in the United States can make it if they are willing to work hard." This view is not shared by African American Muslims, however, whose adherence to Islam is often precisely a product of the historical racial subordination of the black population and who correspondingly do not share other Muslims' optimism in this regard. Despite the division between indigenous and immigrant-origin Muslims regarding their chances in American society, a majority of Muslims said in 2007 that they find it more difficult to be a Muslim in America since September 11, 2001. Still, by a nearly two-to-one margin (63 to 32 percent), Muslim Americans questioned in the 2007 poll said they do not see a conflict between being a devout Muslim and living in a modern society.[26]

In a further reflection of Muslims' integration into American life, the number and size of mosques is growing apace. Contrary to images of the mosques as a breeding ground for jihadism, there is also little evidence that mosque-goers—more frequently of South Asian than of Arab origins—are hotbeds of religious and political extremism; instead, they are dominated by what Ihsan Bagby calls "contextualists" who hold that the Quran and Sunna (the sayings and way of living of the prophet Muhammed) must be closely followed in everyday life but in a flexible fashion consistent with contemporary circumstances. Conversely, though not surprisingly, Bagby's so-called secularists, who think the Quran and the Sunna must be accepted but not necessarily followed, are virtually absent from the mosque-going Muslim population. Consistent with the views of those who see Islam as asserting a claim to primacy among the various religions, 55 percent of mosque attendees disagree with the statement that "All the different religions are equally good ways of helping a person find ultimate truth"; in contrast, only 31 percent of churchgoers disagreed with that statement. Meanwhile, in a mirror image of these findings, only 30 percent of the Muslims surveyed agreed with it, whereas 52 percent of churchgoers did so. A majority of mosque-goers—presumably the more devout Muslims—thus "reject the liberal theological view" (Bagby 2010: 130). By a two-to-one margin, Muslims find the United States "immoral," but this position is disproportionately held by African American mosque attendees, whose religious convictions have historically been a form of anti-American nationalism rooted in their tragic saga in American history, while the immigrant second generation is more likely to hold this view than are their immigrant parents. Ultimately, however, 55 percent of mosque-goers regard the United States as "a better country than most other countries in the world" (Bagby 2010: 132–133). African American Muslims undoubtedly depress this figure; immigrant Muslims are more inclined to view the situation from the immigrant point of view, which tends to be a more positive one. But Muslim immigrants have particular reasons to be thankful: greater prospects of employment, often greater religious freedom than was available in their countries of origin, and greater freedom and access to meaningful political participation in general than is likely to be available in those countries as well.

Against this background, what do authoritative Muslim commentators say about living in minority contexts, especially that of the United States? It is important to recall here that Islam is a highly legalistic religion, in which jurisprudential interpretations resulting in fatwas (rulings) handed down by religious scholars (the ulema) constitute the crucial basis of right living. The ulema are more or less trained in Islamic law, perhaps at such leading institutions as Al-Azhar University in Cairo or, in the Shi'a world, at the seminaries in Qom, Iran, but by no means necessarily at such prestigious and authoritative schools. Moreover, there is no institutionalized structure of Islamic theological authority that can be likened to that of the Vatican and hence no absolutely authoritative source of doctrine in Sunni Islam. By contrast, Shi'ites have developed a more hierarchical form of organization in which the ayatollah has a status comparable to that of a bishop or cardinal in Roman Catholicism or to a chief rabbi in Judaism. As a result of the relatively decentralized character of Islam, Muslims can therefore pick and choose among any number of commentators and rulings as they search for answers to their questions about how to live their everyday lives. The easy accessibility of various perspectives via the Internet facilitates (or, depending on your point of view, exacerbates) this chaos of opinions.

According to Olivier Roy, a leading commentator on global Islam, this eclecticism is one of the most important sources of an increasingly detraditionalized, deterritorialized Islam that is more open to the eccentric interpretations of the doctrine that are associated with Islamic fundamentalism (see Roy 2004, 2008). Others, however, see the matter of divergent scholarly opinions more positively. In 2006, for example, Ben Biya, then vice president of the World Council of Muslim Scholars, argued that "the very divergence of fatwas is a blessing because it gives greater room for adapting *fiqh* to changing contexts" (quoted in Bowen 2010: 144). In contrast, Taha Jabir al-Alwani, a highly influential scholar-cleric and leader of "minority fiqh" in the United States, has bemoaned the fact that if "ordinary people can select the scholar whom they wish to follow" on any given matter, it is no wonder that Muslims find themselves in a "sea of confusion" as a result of the "differences of opinion among jurists" (al-Alwani 2003: xiv, 7).

Notwithstanding the varied sources of authoritative Muslim opinion, there are a few institutions and figures that appear to have emerged as more influential than others. Their geographical designations are somewhat misleading, as they interact with one another across national boundaries and oceans, and may in any case be turned to for guidance by anyone with access to the internet. In Europe, the European Council for Fatwa and Research (ECFR), led by the famous cleric Yusuf al-Qaradawi, has been an authoritative source of rulings on Muslim practice in that region. It is connected to the Islamic Society of North America, especially by way of the Fiqh Council of North America, in which Taha Jabir Al-Alwani has been a leading figure. Two of the leaders of American Islam, Salah Sultan and Jamal Badawi, have attended the meetings of the ECFR, but one of the most influential, the aforementioned al-Alwani, has not (Caeiro 2011: 16 n.51). In short, much like Judaism and very much in contrast to Roman Catholicism, Islam has no transnational structures of organization and authority whose dicta are universally recognized around the world.

In response to the emergence of substantial populations of Muslims outside the traditional Muslim-majority settings, some in the Islamic scholar-clerisy have been preoccupied in recent years with the problem of a "fiqh for minorities," including for those living in the United States. In one prominent contribution to this discussion in the United States, Khaled Abou El Fadl (2000), a law professor at UCLA, has argued that the primary question facing Muslims in the United States is whether they can live as Muslims in a non-Muslim territory or whether it is necessary to migrate to a Muslim-majority territory. Abou El Fadl insists that Muslims may live wherever they have the freedom to practice their religion. They must abide by the commercial and criminal laws of that country, while maintaining their religious observance. He summarizes the tension Muslim minorities experience as that between "the command to escape oppression, uphold Islamic law, [and] serve the public and individual interest of Muslims, and [the demand to] observe implicit and express promises made to a non-Muslim state" (Abou El Fadl 2000: 61). This is more or less the consensus view at present—Muslims make a pact with whatever state they live in and are bound to live according to its laws, while also doing their best to live as good Muslims in that context. Notwithstanding the seemingly "cosmopolitan" view of the place of Muslims in non-Muslim states, however, Abou El-Fadl seems to imply that Muslims are necessarily bystanders who can't really be part of the fabric of their country of residence; instead, they are contracting parties, standing apart from the entity with which they form a pact. One is also struck by the reference to the "command" to serve "the public and individual interest *of Muslims.*" Not unlike some other religions, perhaps especially orthodox Judaism, the universalism of the creed is often in fact limited to the universe of fellow believers. In addition, the wording of the passage makes it seem as though the bridge between "Muslims" and "a non-Muslim state" is impassable; according to Abou El-Fadl, either the state is Muslim or it is not, with seemingly little room for mutual accommodation.

Another influential statement of the Muslim position on the matter of Muslims' status in a non-Muslim state has been promulgated by Taha Jabir al-Alwani, previously chairman of the Fiqh Council of North America and more recently president of Cordoba University in Ashburn, Virginia, a Muslim institution. He is regarded as a cofounder, with Yusuf al-Qaradawi, of Muslim minority jurisprudence. In his pamphlet *Towards a Fiqh for Minorities,* al-Alwani dismisses the distinction between a "house of Islam" and a "house of war," frequently cited as an indication of Islam's bellicose inclinations, as a theological misunderstanding. Instead, he writes, "Islam knows no geographic boundaries; *dar al-Islam* [the House of Islam] is anywhere a Muslim can live in peace and security, even if he lives among a non-Muslim majority. Likewise, *dar al-kufr* [the House of Unbelief] is wherever Muslims live under threat, even if the majority there adheres to Islam and Islamic culture" (al-Alwani 2003: 28).[27] The issue in Muslim-majority lands, then, is not numbers but piety and the freedom to observe one's religious dictates; recall that until his death Osama bin Laden was at least as much at war with what he regards as an apostate Saudi regime as he was with the United States, although it was for allowing American troops into the Muslim holy lands that he was unhappy with the Saudis. Muslims can thus be in the "minority" even if they are sufficiently powerful to dictate the terms under which Muslims live (see Z. Badawi's introduction to al-Alwani 2003: viii).

Despite the upsurge of interest in working out the theological implications of Muslim well-being in what one would seem justified in calling "the Islamic diaspora," there has also been some disquiet among the Muslim ulema concerning the delineation of a "fiqh for minorities." The main reason has to do with the way in which this concern may undermine Islam's claim to universal validity (see Bowen 2010: 146–148). Al-Alwani (2003: 21) writes in such a manner as to transcend this concern, however. On the basis of the "Qur'anic concept of geography," he writes, "in reality, every country is either a "House of Islam" *(dar al-Islam)* as a matter of fact, or will be so in future. All humanity is the community of Islam *(ummat al-Islam)*, either by adopting the faith or as a prospective follower of it." Not unlike the United States itself, Islam is unabashedly universalistic, assuming that, sooner or later, the entire world will recognize and come to adopt "the way." It is this expectation that everyone else will sooner or later come to the (Islamic) truth that leads some commentators to suggest that Muslims will stop at nothing to make the world Islamic. But how will those current unbelievers come to see the truth? Salah Sultan (quoted in Caeiro 2011: 15) wonders, for example, "how many of them could become Muslims or think [well] of Islam and Muslims" if "the Muslims took upon themselves the mission of eradicating the illiteracy of 23 million Americans"?

Al-Alwani's statement about the prospect of a future world in which Islam holds universal sway certainly seems to reflect a boundless optimism about potential conversions to Islam, or a profound confidence in the Islamic message, or both. Others have read darker interpretations into words such as al-Alwani's, however, seeing in them a vision of long-term Islamic dominance. Similarly, the charge that he writes in "doublespeak" has persistently surrounded the Oxford University professor and advocate of a "European Islam," Tariq Ramadan, who is widely regarded as a

Muslim reformer. It was the murkiness of Ramadan's views on such practices as stoning adulterers as well as persistent charges of anti-Semitism that led the State Department in 2004 to refuse Ramadan entry in order to take up an academic position at the University of Notre Dame. Skepticism about Ramadan's positions has also arisen from his enthusiasm for the views of Yusuf al-Qaradawi, whose opinions also seem at times to be self-contradictory. Shortly after the attacks of September 11, 2001, Qaradawi and al-Alwani issued a joint fatwa condemning Osama bin Laden and approving Muslim participation in the U.S. military response in Afghanistan, even though it was clear that this would mean that innocent Muslims would likely die in the process (Esposito 2010: 32). Yet Qaradawi has also endorsed suicide bombing on the part of Palestinians and called for Palestinian Authority president Mahmoud Abbas to be stoned if he were found to have instigated the Israeli war in Gaza in 2007, as some have charged he did.[28] Nor is this mere idle speculation; an American diplomatic cable released by Wikileaks indicates that there is certainly collaboration between the Palestinian Authority and the Israeli intelligence services and it quotes the head of the Israeli intelligence service Shin Bet as saying in 2007 that "they [i.e., the Palestinian Authority] ask us to attack Hamas."[29]

It is contradictory views such as those of Qaradawi that have led some to wonder what to make of Islamic teachings and what it means to be a Muslim "moderate" in this context. Of course, this is not to say that Qaradawi's more extreme views are necessarily widely held among ordinary Muslims. But it is not ordinary Muslims who become suicide bombers; such persons are always and inevitably a tiny minority. Beyond questions about the accommodation of specific religious practices, the challenge of integrating Muslims in liberal democratic societies at present revolves to a considerable degree around ensuring that "fence-sitters" (Saggar 2010) do not drift into the extremist camp. Otherwise, Muslims are just another ethno-religious minority that is likely to go through the usual difficulties of finding their way in a new setting, which frequently involves a degree of skepticism—if not outright hostility—on the part of the receiving society, especially when the new arrivals look "different," have "strange" beliefs, and are associated, however unjustly, with terrorist activity.

The United States is no exception in this regard. The association in the public mind of Muslims with spectacular acts of terrorism on American soil does not simplify the challenge. The problem created when authoritative Muslim figures advocate violence grows more significant as some of those carrying out the violence are themselves American and perpetrating violence in the United States. The Fort Hood shooter Nidal Malik Hassan, the "Christmas Day Bomber" Umar Farouk Abdulmutallab, and the would-be Times Square car bomber Faisal Shahzad have all been said to have been influenced by the dual Yemeni American citizen and Muslim cleric Anwar al-Awlaki. In response to al-Awlaki's open and repeated threats against the United States, President Obama approved his assassination as a matter of national security, making al-Awlaki the first American citizen ever to be placed on a list of those whom the CIA was allowed to kill if and when the opportunity presented itself.[30] This directive in turn raised serious questions about the president's right to target American citizens for assassination without proper legal authority. One might even ask whether this decision does not call into question President Obama's claim that he "reject[s] as false the choice between our safety and our ideals."[31] In all events, al-Awlaki was, in fact, killed by a drone in September 2011. His persistent appearance in reporting about terrorist threats to the United States suggests that there was a legitimate concern here; the question is how to deal with such complicated cases within the confines of constitutional scruple.

But these sensational issues of violence clearly concern an infinitesimally small minority of Muslims. With regard to the Muslim mainstream, some Muslims ask: should Muslims engage in politics in the United States? Bagby (2010: 128) has found that mosque-goers and mosque leaders are "virtually unanimous" in their support for community involvement on the part of Muslims; more than seven in ten endorsed participation in "community service projects that benefit non-Muslims." As usual, it is the African American Muslims who are more skeptical about such participation. Bagby (2006: 31–32) had previously found that 72 percent of mosque representatives agreed with the statement that "Muslims should participate in the political process," arguing that they should do so to protect Muslim rights and interests and to strive for positive change. Again, however, this perspective is not homogeneously reflected among the different strands of American Muslims. Although all immigrant leaders interviewed in Bagby's study agreed that Muslims should participate in American politics, a significant minority of African American leaders (13 percent), almost half of whom were affiliated with the Black Power–influenced, historically Sunni African American mosques, objected to political involvement because they believed that it was corrupting (Bagby 2006: 33).

In sum, Muslim Americans are substantially integrated into the American economic and political order. Yet that picture must be qualified by the extent to which African American Muslims feel as though they are irremediably outsiders. But this is really a matter of race, not religion; sadly and remarkably, native blacks in American life continue to look more like immigrants in European societies with respect to the degree of their incorporation into the society and their view of their own situation. It may well be that the kind of Islam that most needs integrating into American life is that associated with its "indigenous" adherents, but that will require attention to the disabilities suffered by black Americans rather than those faced by Muslims per se.

At the same time, there are certain aspects of so-called minority fiqh that seem, despite an apparent openness to life in non-Muslim contexts, also to suggest that there are limits to participation in non-Muslim life beyond which Muslims cannot go and still remain truly Muslim. But this kind of stance is mostly a matter for religious virtuosos and probably has only a limited influence on ordinary believers—notwithstanding the fact that Islam seems to level the distinction between ordinary believer and virtuoso in favor of an (in its own way) egalitarian expectation that all will be equally devout. Insofar as the latter are from non-African American groups, they show every indication of wishing to be part of the American mainstream and in some ways are even more integrated economically than the average person in the non-Muslim majority.

GIVEN THE EVIDENCE that has been assembled in the foregoing pages, there is every reason to expect that the sort of Islam that is on everyone's mind at present—namely, the imported version—will be assimilated into the American fabric over time and that Muslims will in due course contribute their share to "remaking the American mainstream" (see Alba and Nee 2003). The arrival in recent years of significant numbers of Muslims, now increasingly identified as such rather than, as formerly, in ethno-national terms (e.g., as Arabs), seemed a genuine novelty in the United States. In part because the arriving Muslim populations do not raise as prominently the class issues associated with Mexican immigration, however, they are just another religious minority that promises to be assimilated in due course; moreover, because their numbers remain relatively small, Muslims are not generally viewed as a source of labor market competition by the existing population. One might even argue that Muslims are better off being defined in religious rather than in ethnic terms in the U.S. context, because much of the population of the United States has a historical self-understanding of the country as a refuge specifically for religious minorities.[32] And, as we have seen, even where the populace may have singled out Muslims for opprobrium, the courts have been vigilant in protecting Muslims from discrimination on account of their religious faith.

For some time to come, the question of Muslim integration in the United States will revolve less around legal niceties than around the causes of Islamic-inspired violence. The concern among Americans and others about Islam is part moral panic, generated by a media-induced fear of an unfamiliar "other," and part legitimate concern about acts of terrorism, although victimization by these is statistically rather improbable and, like the violence in American ghettos, in fact mostly afflicts fellow residents who populate those parts of the globe in which Muslims are much more numerous (e.g., Pakistan, Afghanistan, Iraq, etc.). In policy terms, perhaps the most important thing the United States government can do is to be sure not to stigmatize the Muslim population and thus to encourage a sense of apartness or special saliency. By and large, Muslims simply want to integrate and be Americans, extending the string "Protestant-Catholic-Jew" to include them in the American religious panoply—although the evidence suggests that this is less true of African American Muslims than of their immigrant coreligionists.

In addition, although it would surely not put an end to all Muslim grievances against the West, much could be achieved if the United States could help broker a peace settlement in the Middle East. Muslim extremists get enormous unearned mileage out of the misery and mistreatment of Palestinians in the occupied territories, even if the treatment of Palestinians in many of the Gulf Arab states is not much better and is often much worse. What the world sees and hears is that Israel, which seems to enjoy nearly unquestioning American support, allows Jewish settlers to displace Palestinians in the West Bank or massively restricts the normal operations of a society and an economy in Gaza. The United States could help integrate its small but growing Muslim populations—and those of other liberal democratic countries as well—by pressuring Israel to work out a lasting deal with the Palestinians, thus reducing one of the principal causes of Muslim disenchantment with the West. More generally, a more rational energy policy that reduces American dependence on the undemocratic oil states of the world—many of them in the Muslim Middle East—would also help reduce the perceived need to engage militarily in parts of the world where Muslims are predominant. The kinds of warfare in which the United States and its allies have been engaging in the Middle East and Asia are not likely to be "winnable" in any robust sense and are in the meanwhile likely to antagonize the populations in question, undermining the likelihood that they will assist us in stopping terrorist violence.

Ultimately, integration of Muslims in the United States thus depends on the successful management of foreign policies in which Muslims are the predominant populations as well as on the continued successful defense of constitutional rights to religious freedom. Here is an intriguing difference from the situation in Western Europe, where the problem has much more to do with integrating Muslims into the often difficult-to-enter labor markets of the countries involved and less to do with foreign affairs (even if these are hardly irrelevant). Unlike Europe, the United States, like all new settler states, did not originally gain its own self-definition out of a direct challenge from Islamic antagonists, so the contemporary encounter of the United States with its Islamic inhabitants lacks the historical resonance of that between a Europe widely understood as "Christian" and its recently arrived Muslim inhabitants.

In sum, although there are a number of contentious areas in which discrimination occurs or the question of accommodation arises, there do not appear to be any major obstacles to integrating Muslims as such into American society. Insofar as claims of discrimination are deemed to have a religious basis, they are generally resolved in favor of the complainant. Many conflicts about accommodation of Muslims in educational institutions and public services have remained localized and have not triggered divisive legal or policy outcomes. In short, nothing about the legal-political framework suggests that the accommodation of Islam as a minority religion should prove extraordinarily difficult as long as American foreign policy does not continue to be seen as unjustifiably targeted against Muslims elsewhere in the world.

CHAPTER SIX

Conclusion

Islam and Identity
in the Liberal State

THIS STUDY was not immune from an ambivalence that marks the abundant and fast-growing literature on Muslims and Islam in the West: not always to distinguish clearly between the integration of "Muslims" as social category and of "Islam" as religion. Of course, our interest was in the combination of both, as the nonreligious aspects of integrating yet another immigrant group was not our topic; instead, our subject was the lesser or higher hurdles met by individually practiced and organized Islam across Western host societies. Perhaps it is time to finish the obsession with religion as central to the integration of Muslim immigrants and to point to other, more mundane dimensions that matter more—jobs, education, residential mixing, etc. Alas, this will have to wait for another book, and other authors are better qualified to speak to this than we. But our focus on the religious dimension, however overextended, still yields an important message: liberal institutions have proved remarkably elastic in accommodating a religion that, judged by its worldwide politicization, may pose more of a challenge to liberal societies than others. Even though Islam and Muslim immigrants are a less hotly contested issue in North America than in Western Europe, there is no essential difference in the accommodating powers of liberal institutions on either side of the Atlantic.

Having said that, the reader will have noted a difference in tone and accent in the North American and European chapters: gloomier on the European side, more optimistic on the North American side, along with a propensity to talk about "Islam," an abstraction, in the European chapters, and about "Muslims," flesh-and-blood people, immigrants at that, who do not all think and act alike, in the North American chapters. Sociologists, like all people, are creatures of their societies, and it is not difficult to discern the different temperaments and proclivities of a European and an American author that mirror the comparatively relaxed and empiricist attitude toward Islam in North America and the more skeptical and principled stance in Europe. This is no excuse for lack of coherence. But two authors will never be one, and it is better to state the fact openly than hide or ignore it.

Immigrant Islam in Europe and North America: "Barrier" versus "Bridge"?

When comparing the processing of immigrant Islam in Europe and North America, a good way to start is to call immigrant religion a "bridge" to inclusion in the United States and "barrier" to inclusion in Western Europe (following Foner and Alba 2008). Indeed, it has been a classic motif in the American literature on immigrant assimilation that "in and through . . . religion . . . [the immigrant] . . . found an identifiable place in American life," to quote the most famous work in this genre, Will Herberg's 1955 classic *Protestant, Catholic, Jew* (quoted in Foner and Alba 2008: 365). This process seems to work just as well for the new religions entering the American scene after 1965, so that one now is "Becoming American by Becoming Hindu" (P. Kurien, quoted in Foner and Alba 2008: 366). The reason for this has remained the same over the intervening half-century: religion offers the three R's—"refuge," "respectability," and "resources"— that help newcomers find their way in the new land (C. Hirschman, quoted in Foner and Alba 2008: 362).

Upbeat though Foner and Alba (2008) are about the positive role of religion, old and new, in the American immigrant experience, they notably do not extend that enthusiasm directly to Islam: they make no claim, as it were, that one can "become American" by "becoming Muslim." Instead, they quote President Bill Clinton's pronouncement, already in the mid-1990s and later repeated in so many words by war-faring President George W. Bush, that "Islam is an American religion" (p. 380). Except for stating as an "is" what in Europe still appears more as a wishful "ought," this is not fundamentally different from European state leaders' calls for moving from an Islam that is "in" to one that is "of" their respective society. Whether stated as fact or as norm, the very stating that Islam is national or to be rendered thus betrays a certain uneasiness, even on the American side, and it concedes that Islam's integration into the national fabric is not the default position.

Particularly in the post-2001 period, Islam in America is probably not the "bridge" to inclusion that other religions may well be. Conversely, Foner and Alba (2008) provide sensible arguments as to why in Europe Islam is even more "a barrier or a challenge to integration and a source of conflict with mainstream institutions and practices" (p. 368). They offer three arguments for this. First, three-quarters (75 percent) of contemporary immigrants to the United States are adherents of Christianity, a religion that is not likely to be a source of friction, whereas the majority of immigrants to Europe are Muslim, where no such optimism is warranted (p. 374). Second, comparing the churchgoing inclinations and religious beliefs of Americans and Europeans, America is the most religious society in the Western world, with the exception of (a rapidly unchurching) Ireland (see also Norris and Inglehart 2004: 60, table 3.2). By contrast, Western Europe is arguably the most secularized region on earth (outside midtown Manhattan, of course), and a religiously mute majority is ill prepared to face a religion that makes expansive claims to public acknowledgment and asks a good deal in the way of others' adjustment to its norms and strictures. But third, and most decisively, Foner and Alba (2008) argue that European "societal institutions and national identities . . . remain anchored to an important extent in Christianity and do not make equal room for Islam" (p. 374).

The argument that European societies have somehow not managed to clearly and cleanly separate religion and state, and that they continue to espouse Christian identities with vitiating consequences for Muslim integration, can often be found in the American literature. For instance, Zolberg and Litt Woon (1999), in their insightful inquiry concerning why Americans are preoccupied with (Spanish) language in their integration debate while Europeans worry more about (Islamic) religion, attribute the latter to the fact that "European identity . . . remains deeply embedded in Christian tradition" (p. 7). Similarly, Martha Nussbaum (2008: 83), in her defense of "America's tradition of religious liberty," paints a grim picture of Europeans as "still inclined to think of nationhood as a matter of blood, soil, and religious heritage" and thus as incapable of offering equal space and liberties for new religions. If our previous analysis is correct, such statements confound public sentiment, which may well be as the authors describe, with public institutions, which due to the prevalence of liberal norms cannot operate unchallenged on an ethnocentric basis.

With respect to public institutions, Chapters 2 and 3, on France and Germany, cast doubt on the claim of a generic, incurable propensity of European states to favor Christianity and discriminate against Islam. One has to be aware, of course, that European states have been competitors with the Catholic Church for exercising public powers since their inception in the late medieval period and that the historical compromises struck in the process are by nature asymmetric, not open to everyone, and sticky (see Whitman 2008). But it is an exaggeration to call the few and shrinking institutional inequities, which are the inevitable byproduct of European state building, a major "barrier to inclusion." For France, to begin with, it is erroneous to speak of "deeply institutionalized religious identities" (Foner and Alba 2008: 381). The constraints on liberty associated with the *foulard* and burqa laws arise from France's secular, perhaps secularist, but not (or at least only indirectly) from its Christian identity. In Germany, as we saw, the one institutional privilege afforded the established religions, now including the Jewish religion, is to enjoy the status of a "corporation under public law," a privilege still denied to Islam—though the resistance to such recognition is on ever-thinner judicial ice. Moreover, this violation of equality on paper amounts to rather little in reality, because the main demand of organized Islam in Germany—namely, to provide religious instruction in Islamic doctrine at state expense in public schools—can be met short of granting Islam public law status, and political consensus in Germany suggests that it will, indeed, have to be met before long. In sum, religion, particularly Islam, may still be more "barrier" than "bridge" to including immigrants in Europe but only as a matter of mentalities, not of institutions.

In fact, as if to concede a flaw in their analysis, Foner and Alba (2008) conclude their instructive comparison by heralding "major changes" underway in European religion-state relations (p. 386). Britain, they correctly say, is becoming more "liberal" than ever (despite clinging to an increasingly moribund Anglican establishment, a quaint relic of its statebuilding process that does not seem to diminish its friendliness to new religions one bit) (p. 385); the Netherlands is "accommodat[ing] many Muslim religious demands" better than most other European states do, even in an extended moment of virulent populism (p. 385); and for France, they refer to the 2003 creation of the French Council on the Muslim Religion (Conseil Français du Culte Musulman), which has formally put Islam on a par with the established religions.

The picture is somewhat different when viewed not from the perspective of accommodating a new religion but of integrating immigrants—that is, of social as against institutional integration. Here informal host society perceptions and attitudes toward newcomers figure prominently. From this more sociological angle, our comparative study reveals patterns of convergence and difference that resonate with past sociological research. The prospects of integration of Muslims in North America are, on the whole, brighter than those of Muslims in Europe, and this is in considerable part a product of the historical trajectory of the two continents as comparatively friendly or uncongenial toward immigration in general and particularly toward groups defined chiefly in religious terms. We should not forget that, throughout much of its history, Western Europe has been torn apart by religious conflict in a fashion that simply has no parallel in North America. Moreover, the integration of unfamiliar populations in Western European societies has generally been perceived as more difficult than their integration in the United States and Canada, which are often described as "traditional countries of immigration." In contrast, in Germany the decades-long official refrain that "Germany is not a country of immigration" seemed absurd insofar as it manifestly was a major destination for immigrants (even post-1973, when most immigrants came as unsolicited asylum seekers or family unifiers, technically speaking). Nor does official French republicanism countenance anything that would undermine the supposed ethno-cultural unity of the French people, notwithstanding the actual story of the "French melting pot" (Noiriel 1996). It is for this reason that foreigners are counted as "persons of foreign birth" rather than according to ethnic criteria, as in North America. The absorption of a population of non-Christians in contemporary Western Europe presents particular obstacles, especially when those groups adhere to a religion—Islam—with which "Europe" was at odds for hundreds of years during the middle stages of Islam's history and in the formative years of Europe's own history as a distinctive entity (Pirenne 1970; Wheatcroft 2003; Pagden 2008).

It is worth noting, however, that it is only in recent years that immigrants in Europe and North America have been viewed chiefly in terms of their religion, as opposed to other characteristics of the relevant populations, especially their national origins. Algerian and Moroccan immigrants to France were for a long time "Harkis," "post-colonial migrants," "foreign workers," or just that—"Algerians" or "Moroccans." In Germany, they were Turkish "guest-workers" or simply "Turks" (see Bleich 2006). Until very recently, Muslims in the United States were virtually all African Americans and perceived in these racial terms. To this must be added that the Arabs in Detroit and Los Angeles were frequently Christians, so that even the equation of "Arab" with "Muslim" is not automatic here. In

Canada, due not least to distance from the source populations, Muslims were very thin on the (frozen) ground.

Since September 11, 2001, however, in all these cases these persons have become "Muslims"—a group identified by a religious label and often regarded as subversive, threatening, alien. Fear of Muslims has intensified with the string of attacks by Islamic terrorists and the discovery that some of the most dangerous of such people are actually home-grown—in the United States, Canada, Germany, and the United Kingdom, though much less so in France (see Leiken 2011). We need to bear in mind, however, that many terrorists in the United States are, of course, not Muslims at all—think of Timothy McVeigh of the Oklahoma City bombing, the Columbine and Virginia Tech attackers, and Arizona shooter Jared Lee Loughner. None of this kept a Long Island congressman who once enthusiastically supported the (terrorist) Irish Republican Army, Representative Peter King, from calling hearings to explore the alleged radicalization of (only) the Muslim population in the United States.

The fear of the religious "other," in North America and Europe alike, has grown exactly in the moment that the "golden age" of multicultural ideas and policies was dimming, and as we shall further argue, both developments are connected. In the United States, official multiculturalism policies are largely unimaginable, but the country has long been seen as a patchwork of ethnicities that are integrated by the society and the labor market rather than by anything the state might do (Bloemraad 2006). Muslims of immigrant background have been relatively well integrated into the country, but that probably has as much to do with their comparatively high economic and educational status as with other factors. And, of course, the very existence of an African American Muslim population was historically a product precisely of the sense of disenfranchisement harbored by many of the country's blacks, whose Muslim members on average are distinctly less well off than their coreligionists hailing from elsewhere. Canada, the headquarters of multicultural ideas and ideals, has undergone a swelling controversy about the presence and practices of Muslims, leading to a rethinking of multicultural objectives, despite the fact that it, too, has an unusually well-educated and well-heeled Muslim population.

The socioeconomic profile of the immigrant Muslim populations in each of the North American cases contrasts sharply with that of the Muslim populations in France and Germany. Drawn from around the Mediterranean basin or from Europe's Anatolian periphery, these groups can arrive easily by land, sea, and air and were long seen simply as reserve armies of labor power compensating for the postwar shortages of native European male populations. The comparable population for Americans is Mexicans; Canada has no border with massive numbers of comparatively poor potential immigrants. Europeans, however, are confronted with large numbers of prospective postcolonial or peripheral immigrants associated with a religion that at present is held in questionable esteem. The adherents of this religion may be different from the indigenous populations on any imaginable ground: ethnic, racial, religious, educational, cultural, and so on. Seeing a man of, say, Turkish origins walking down a Berlin street several paces ahead of his headscarved presumable spouse may be an object of perplexity for a number of reasons, only some of which are, strictly speaking, religious in nature. Yet this picture is nonetheless likely to be attributed by the ordinary observer to "Islam" rather than to the man's rural, ill-educated, peasant background. No doubt there is something to the religious interpretation of the tableau, but it is hardly the entire story. Yet particularly in unchurched, post-9/11, post-7/7 Western Europe, it is overwhelmingly the main story at present. It remains to be seen whether the chain of uprisings across North Africa and the Arabian Peninsula (the "Arab spring") will result in Muslims being regarded as more "like us" than has been the case in the period since September 11, 2001. Much will depend on the kinds of regimes that replace the despised secular dictatorships that came to be challenged by the Arab (and notably nonreligious) masses after a Tunisian fruit vendor set himself alight in protest, on December 17, 2010, against the heavy hand of the state. Judged by the recent electoral successes of Islamists in Egypt, Tunisia, and elsewhere, however, the prospects are not bright.

Islam in the Retreat from Multiculturalism

The difficulties associated with the integration of Muslims in Western societies have sharply undermined the legitimacy of multicultural doctrines and policies. There has been a retreat from multiculturalism wherever Muslims and Islam have come to dominate a country's integration debate, including even in Canada. As Will Kymlicka (2005, 2007, 2010) pointed out, multiculturalism requires a sense of security and shared liberal values. This premise no longer holds for Muslims, who are widely suspected of being "disloyal and illiberal" (Kymlicka 2010: 108). The general public fatefully confounds ordinary Muslims, who "prove every day that they can live as a minority in religiously neutral and laicist states" (Matyssek 2010: 228), and the Islam of the activists and doctrinaires, which often suggests otherwise. A Croat intellectual once described herself as "pinned to the wall of nationhood" (Drakulic 1993: 51): "That is what the war [between Serbia and Croatia] is doing to us, reducing us to one dimension: the Nation." Something quite similar occurs to "Muslims," who are pinned to the wall of religion, even though many of them may not feel the slightest religious inclination.[1]

But what exactly is the "multiculturalism" that is put to the test, if not rendered obsolete, by the perceived failures of Muslim integration? Not necessarily the official multiculturalism that only a few countries, like Canada, have ever practiced. Rather, "multiculturalism" at minimum is the quintessentially liberal approach to minority integration, an approach that refrains from intervening in a process that is best left to individuals themselves. Chandran Kukathas (2004: 13) usefully suggests that there is continuity between classical liberalism and multiculturalism, as the former "proclaims the importance of individual freedom to live a life of one's own." Under conditions of heightened pluralism (which are, of course, not so different from the conditions in which liberalism has historically emerged), classical liberalism must engender multiculturalism. Therefore one observes a declared retreat from multiculturalism even in societies, such as Germany or France, which had never had an official multiculturalism policy (see Joppke 2013b). Instead of an explicitly multicultural regime, most countries had a laissez-faire regime, perhaps even a "maximally tolerant regime" that "even accept[ed] within its midst those who are opposed to it" (Kukathas 2004: 14).

Of course, "complete tolerance," as Kukathas points out, is always a fiction in the world of politics, as "there cannot be such a thing as a political regime that is morally or culturally neutral" (2004: 20). We have also seen that liberal states cannot escape the requirement that they define religion in some way, if only in order to know what sort of activity demands constitutional protection. Under the reign of multiculturalism, however, there was little enforcement of nonneutrality, with the result that putatively cultural differences were treated with a degree of indifference that has now come to be regarded with alarm. The encounter with Islam brings to the surface the main problem of Kukathian "anarcho-multiculturalism," namely, that it is destructive of the liberalism that enables it. This is because multiculturalism requires liberalism but does nothing to regenerate it. Modern liberals like Brian Barry (2001) therefore have argued that the liberal state must not tolerate illiberal practices but should engage in an ethical project of forming liberal citizens. In the world of politics, this is what contemporary states' retreat from multiculturalism in favor of civic integration is all about.

Kymlicka (2010: 108) diplomatically reduces Muslims' presumed lack of liberal credentials and loyalty deficit to a perception problem and leaves it at that. However, it is implausible to completely exculpate Islam, at least not its politically visible and articulated versions, from the malaise. H. A. R. Gibb, in a classic work (1949), called Islam "not simply a body of private religious beliefs" but a creed that "involved the setting-up of an own independent community, with its own system of government, laws, and institutions" (p. 3). Such reasoning is today rejected as "Orientalist" or "essentializing" Islam, and it has become de rigueur to stress the "multivocality" of Islam, like that of all world religions (Stepan 2000). But one can carry this otherwise commendable stance too far and turn it into a taboo on anything that names and categorizes and thus by nature must simplify. Without falling into the untenable stereotype that Islam cannot distinguish between religion and politics—in its own ways, it can and this from early on (see Lapidus 1975)—one could more cautiously argue that Islam, like Orthodox Judaism, stresses orthopraxy over privatized beliefs, stipulating that ritual and belief are "inseparable" (Mahmood 2012: xv; see also Mahmood 2006). As the distinguished religious scholar Samuel Heilman noted in explicating "some parallels between Islam and Judaism," "fundamentalist-like Jews and Muslims refuse to be 'divided' between their social and religious selves" (Heilman 1995: 86).

In fact, the very notion of fundamentalism may be misguided for religions that reject "secular religiosity" (Mahmood 2012: xv) as we have come to know it in Christian lands. The liberal Muslim scholar Abdullahi Ahmed An-Na'im thus rejects the notion of "fundamentalism" in reference to Islam because it "would apply to such a broad spectrum of Muslims that it would cease to be useful as a tool for identifying a specific group" (An-Naim 1990: 3). More than any "Orientalist" would ever dare to say, An-Naim even holds that Muslims find it "difficult" to accept the secular concept of the nation-state because "the identity of religion and government is indelibly stamped on the memories and awareness of the faithful" (p. 3). But then we are back to Gibb's classic analysis that "Islam, as a way of life, stands or falls with the supremacy of the Sacred Law" and that one could never "reduce Islam to a body of private beliefs without practical issue in social relations" (Gibb 1949: 191).

No wonder that even the more flexible, reform-oriented versions of Islam, including the minority fiqh of Yusuf al-Qaradawi (1960, 1987, 1998) and the citizenship approach favored by Tariq Ramadan (2001, 2002b, 2004, 2007, 2009), both of which seek to accommodate Muslims' permanent existence in non-Muslim societies, depict Muslims as a people apart, a nation within the nation, and invest more effort in ensuring their separate groupness than on cultivating ties with the larger society. Various orthodox religious sects may do the same,[2] but there are not some twenty million of these others, as there are immigrant Muslims in European lands. Despite his citizenship rhetoric, according to which Western Muslims are not a minority but fully "at home" in the West, Ramadan envisions a "dialogue from equal to equal without inferiority complex" (2002b: 28). The units of this cannot be citizens but must be groups, which are separated by no less than a chasm of "civilizations" (2001: 219). To depict Muslims and Islam as part of a different "civilization," in fact, is not the invention of Samuel Huntington (1998) but runs as a red thread through many of Ramadan's writings (see also Allawi 2009). Not satisfied with mere "toleration," Ramadan resorts to the quintessentially multicultural rhetoric of asking for "respect" (2004: 110). However, "respect" is notably not to be reciprocated by Muslims themselves—at least one looks in vain for any passage in his works or sermons that would suggest otherwise. On the contrary, Muslims are called on to "resist" the West in terms of its spiritual impoverishment, material temptations, and its globalizing reach (Ramadan 2002a). Apart from this inconsistency, "respect" is an incoherent stance for a state to take in principle (as trenchantly argued by Peter Jones 2009).

The even less integrationist minority fiqh of the European Council for Fatwa and Research (ECFR), in which Yusuf al-Qaradawi is a leading figure, goes under the rubric of "integration without assimilation" (see Caeiro 2010: 444), with the emphasis being less on "integration" than on "without assimilation." The "integration" pursued by the ECFR is highly legalistic in character, using the ample legal repertoire of the liberal-constitutional state to protect religious belief and practice while rejecting any loyalty commitment that would go beyond the legally required minimum. In this legalistic spirit, German Muslims refused a commitment to the "German value community" *(deutsche Wertegemeinschaft)* that the interior minister had asked of them, during the Islam Conference of 2008 (Amir-Moazami 2009: 202). They could justify this refusal with the jurisprudence of Germany's highest court, which expects conformity with the law but not the right "disposition" *(Gesinnung)* toward the state (see Chapter 3).

But the crux of the matter is Islam's penchant for demanding that its adherents remain entirely and always within its religious framework and to accept secular law only if this is first commanded by religious law itself. This is, of course, no peculiarity of Islam but a feature of all monotheisms, where a transcendental God's command trumps the laws of society, if there is conflict. The complication is the immigrant situation, where ethnic difference is added to religious difference, thus doubling "difference." "Political liberalism" (Rawls 1993), which argues that an "overlapping consensus" in liberal institutions can be reached by always staying within one's "comprehensive doctrine" (as long as the latter and the people who adhere to it are "reasonable"[3]), has worked in favor of such position, and it has naturally been embraced by many Islamic reformists (e.g., Abou el Fadl 1996; Fadel 2008; An-Naim 2008). The problem is that it insufficiently considers the immigrant context, which pitches citizens (the default actor of "political liberalism") against strangers. In an immigrant situation, where religious difference is doubled by ethnic difference, the license to always stay within one's "comprehensive doctrine" feeds the main objection against multiculturalism, which is that it encourages group-insulating "segregation" instead of "pluralism" with crosscutting cleavages (see Sartori 2000). Concretely, Islam tends to make peace with non-Islamic settings by reinterpreting them in religious terms, so that "to act according to the law is in itself a way of worshipping" (Ramadan 2004: 95–96).

In light of the political history of Islam, with its prophet at the same time spiritual and political leader, such posture may be more than the monotheist stock-in-trade, certainly its Christian variant. It points to a particular uneasiness with differentiation, between religious and political, sacred and secular, individual and group. By way of contrast, the French philosopher of religion Marcel Gauchet (1985) found in Christianity a propensity for "dualism," which has allowed it to become the "religion to exit from all religions" (p. 11) and to easily blend with (if not to lay the historical roots for) liberalism, which has been precisely described as the "art of separations" (Walzer 1984).

In his insightful ethnography of French Islam, John Bowen (2010) calls "social pragmatism" Muslims' prioritizing of religious over secular law, while being extremely flexible in stretching the "religious" to bring under it the "secular." It works like this: as long as a nonreligious rule, like civil marriage (to which there is no religious alternative in laicist France), bears "positive social consequences" for Muslims, these positive consequences figure as the civic rule or institution's "Islamic justification" (Bowen 2010: 168). This functionalism in effect turns the entire world Islamic. As Tariq Ramadan illustrates its workings, "A civil marriage already is a Muslim marriage, I think, because it is a contract, and that is what a Muslim marriage is" (quoted in ibid.).

Bowen thinks that "social pragmatism" of this sort, which is akin to "political liberalism's" claim that one can find intrinsic agreement on common rules by always staying within one's "comprehensive doctrine," might lead "toward an ideal of shared respect for a common legal and political framework" (2010: 198), and he holds this sharply against the "ideal of value-monism" that the French state is said to impose on its recalcitrant Muslims. He reads an illuminating if arcane exchange between a secular Muslim intellectual, a professor at a Parisian banlieue university, and a well-known religious traditionalist, who is imam of a mosque in Bordeaux, as the secular protagonist aggressively imposing the "primacy of secularism" on the religionist, marginalizing the latter already in form, by always wanting to have the first word to which the latter is then forced to respond (Babès and Oubrou 2002, discussed in Bowen 2010: 189–190). But one may read the same exchange as the secular professor simply wishing to establish a distinction between "law" and "ethics," limiting Quranic prescriptions to the inner realm of the ethical (Babès and Oubrou 2002: 18), which the Bordeaux imam is apparently reluctant to make. Babès probes Oubrou about questionable aspects of Islamic law, such as corporal punishment (and worse) that is prescribed by the Quran for certain transgressions of the faith and which even an ultraliberal reformer like An-Naim (1990: 107) finds a hard nut to crack because there is "no Islamic authority for abolishing [it]." But rather than wishing to erase these antiquated elements of shari'a (as apparently advocated by An-Naim 1990: ch. 5) or at least creatively outinterpreting them (as more cautiously suggested by Abou El Fadl 2003: 17), Tareq Oubrou finds, in all seriousness, that "the pain inflicted by the punishment—physical or moral—serves only one objective: to improve the moral condition of the Muslim" (Babès and Oubrou 2002: 76).

The "value monism" that Bowen (2010: 198) attributes to Babès (and to French secularists at large), who in fact seems to espouse the exact opposite, that is, dualism and role switching, is more characteristic of the rector of the Bordeaux mosque. Oubrou may indeed be the self-described "easygoing and permissive imam" (Babès and Oubrou 2002: 176)—in fact, in other places he has taken progressive stances, defending homosexuals and refusing the claptrap of "Islamophobia," and his advice to young French Muslim women to "take off your veil" *(mets ton foulard dans ta poche)* because it is "not a cultic object"[4] has earned him the epithet "Republican imam,"[5] which was not meant to be a compliment. Only, in his exchange with Leila Babès he does not come across as a progressive, defending instead the unequal treatment of men and women in Islamic law as grounded in "their different natures" (Babès and Oubrou 2002: 110), attacking the mixing of the sexes in school and other public places as "banal" and "aggressive" (p. 161), and justifying polygamy on the grounds that the male of the species is the "producer of an infinity of spermatozoa" (p. 102).

The least to say is that the refusal to ever leave one's religious frame-work may be no less an instance of "value monism" than insisting on the primacy of secular law, which by nature is a law that does not suppress domain-specific logics, including in the religious sphere. It is not clear how one can arrive at a "shared respect for a common legal and political framework" (Bowen 2010: 198) from this starting point. Note that Tariq Ramadan, who became a celebrity for the liberal-sounding (because dualism-suggesting) claim that Muslims could be "European," quickly retreats from his apparent commitment to pluralism: "If for being a good Frenchman you have to be a bad Muslim, then I say no" (quoted in Four-est 2004: 224). The astonishing thing, to repeat, is not so much to put religion above worldly attachments—every serious religionist would do this. Instead, what raises eyebrows is the quasi-nationalistic language of peoplehood that juxtaposes "Frenchman" and "Muslim." Certainly, this juxtaposition is "at least as much *about* Muslims as it is *by* Muslims,"[6] so that it is difficult to say whether it is endemic to the creed or only reactive. However, a similar alternative between "Christian" and "French" (or be-tween Christian and any non-religion-forcing nationality you pick) would be equally difficult to imagine, because both affiliations simply do not compete on the same level.

Note that there is nothing akin in the Christian religion to Islamic ju-rists' extended discourse, ongoing since the eighth century, on "the status of Muslim minorities residing in non-Muslim territory," which throughout the ages has been considered "problematic" (Abou El Fadl 2006: 2). Note, moreover, Islam's peculiar dichotomizing of the political world into a "house of Islam" and a "house of war." However much it has been relativ-ized in recent reform efforts, the very existence of this dichotomy points to a political-territorial claim of the Islamic faith that makes its retreat into a spiritual or private realm not impossible but also not the obvious direction.

If "political liberalism" is the natural meeting point between Islam and Western host societies, its problem is to invite an only pragmatic or instru-mental attitude to host society rules and institutions.[7] In turn, these rules and institutions are likely to be skirted whenever they conflict with one's religious precepts—or this is the generic suspicion fed in such an environ-ment. Political liberalism, as one of the most impressive academic match-makers between Islam and liberalism concedes (March 2007: 249), "can-not require as part of a minimal doctrine of citizenship any robust or emotional attachment to one's community of citizenship." This is also the usual riposte against multiculturalism, and both—multiculturalism and political liberalism—live and die together.

Much as one might find fault with "social pragmatism" (Bowen 2010), to throw principles at Islam may not be the cleverest way to bind it into liberal societies. One may even ask: is there any alternative to social pragmatism? Of course, one wants Muslims to embrace secular law and principles for intrinsic and not just instrumental reasons. But this desired end point of integration cannot be forced by legislation, simply because "identity" cannot be legislated, least in a liberal state. An intriguing historical study of the making of "French" and "Spaniards" in the Pyrenees (Sahlins 1989) found that, initially, these new national identities were adopted by local people (dubbed "political amphibians") at first for purely instrumental reasons, as they furthered their local interests, and only later and imperceptibly did these "national disguises" wound up "sticking to their skin" (p. 269). This was a process that required generations, even centuries, and it isn't complete today, as vital Basque separatism in the region confirms. One should take this as a template for contemporary Muslim integration, which has barely exceeded one generation, and relax.[8]

Moreover, to repeat an important truth, Islam is not alone in prioritizing religious over secular law—latently all monotheisms do this, because otherwise God's powers are compromised, and all fundamentalisms do it as an unabashed matter of course. The U.S. Supreme Court dealt with the Christian variant in its famous *Mozert v. Hawkins County Public Schools* decision in 1987. The case concerned Christian fundamentalists who claimed that the exposure of their children to secular ideas in public school, especially Darwinian evolutionary biology, violated their First Amendment right to free exercise of religion. The plaintiffs claimed that it was their duty as parents, mandated by the Bible, to safeguard their children from the "eternal damnation" that awaited them for reading school books espousing such un-Christian doctrines. Religion appeared here not as subjective belief, as which the liberal state has to process it (thus requiring a reflexive, distance-taking attitude),[9] but as objective truth toward which there can be no choice. As a legal observer notes (Stolzenberg 1993: 612), the *Mozert* case thus dealt with the "truly radical assertion that . . . neutrality may itself constitute an assault on the plaintiffs' beliefs." The radical claim, which was rejected by the court, was that "mere exposure" to something, like the quiet reading of a biology book, constituted "indoctrination" and thus an "act" that violated a religious precept (p. 591).

The Christian fundamentalists' denunciation of the state's "neutrality" as de facto exercise of power is strangely reminiscent of radical multiculturalism (e.g., Young 1990). Giving in to it would be giving up on the idea that the function of public education is to prepare young people for citizenship, which is an idea cherished from America to France. Much like similar exemption claims raised by Islam, *Mozert* shows the archaic power of religion untainted by liberal precepts. Insofar as the idea of multiculturalism is thought to enshrine official acceptance of this insistent prioritization of "primordial" values, it has fallen into disrepute.

After Multiculturalism: Liberal or Christian Identity?

If multiculturalism is in retreat, what is stepping into its place? Representative of a general trend across Western states, British prime minister David Cameron recently suggested the alternative of "muscular liberalism" (see Joppke 2013b). The adjective "muscular" suggests that "liberalism" without such a modifier, which Cameron denounced as leading to a "passively tolerant society," is itself inevitably involved in the production of multiculturalism.[10] But what is liberalism's muscular variant? Continuing a central theme in British politics at least since the days of Labour prime ministers Tony Blair and Gordon Brown, the Tory Cameron calls for "stronger citizenship" to keep a centrifugal immigrant society together—and, of course, it is part of the project of sharply reducing the size of government in favor of a putatively self-activating "Big Society." It is not enough for a liberal society to "stand neutral between different values," according to Cameron; instead, one has to be "unambiguous and hardnosed about the "defence of our liberty." In the "civic integration" idiom that is now the standard rhetoric on immigrant incorporation across Europe, Cameron insists that "immigrants speak the language of their new home" and that "people are educated in elements of a common culture and curriculum."

Muscular liberalism is liberalism thickened into an identity (Joppke 2009; 2010: ch. 4; see also Tebble 2006). This is paradoxical because liberalism is normally understood as a recipe for reconciling and providing a common ground for many diverse identities, especially religious ones, without thus wanting to replace them with one of its own. Such liberalism, which undercuts the Kantian distinction between law and morality, is ultimately self-destructive, as it casts people into a standard mold and thus robs them of the freedom to decide who they want to be. As Jeff Spinner-Halev (2008) has convincingly argued, one cannot, from a liberal position, want to make liberalism and religion "congruent": "If liberalism is going to take the ideas of liberty and toleration seriously, it must be prepared to tolerate non-liberal religions. To happily announce that liberals will tolerate liberals is to hollow out the meaning of toleration" (p. 564).

But muscular liberalism, which is precisely the program to make religion "congruent" with liberalism, is still an understandable response to the challenge of Islam, because the latter requires liberalism in order to exist in the West but hollows out its principles from the outside. Make no mistake: Orthodox Jews, say, equally "hollow out" liberalism; only, apart from Israel, they do not happen to move in larger numbers into Western lands.[11] Unfortunately, no such qualification applies to Christian evangelists in the United States, who hollow out liberalism and mobilize in massive numbers and thus are much more threatening to liberal democracy than any Muslim minority ever could be (Goldberg 2006); but they are indigenous to the American society project and thus require a different and more sustained analysis than we can provide here.

As "muscular liberalism" is a contradiction in terms, doubts about its "muscles" are apposite, and despite exceptions here or there it mostly boils down to political rhetoric (see Joppke 2013b). By contrast, a second alternative to multiculturalism recently making headway in Europe, which is national particularism, seems to raise no such doubts. Therefore there is no need in it for rabid language. On the contrary, wherever this alternative appears, it immediately tends to deny itself and wants to appear in a mellower, more universalistic light. The difference between a liberal identity and one under the sign of national particularism thus may be more nuance than a difference of principle.

A fascinating example of national particularism that immediately denies itself is the defense by some European governments of Christian crucifixes in public schools, which has recently preoccupied the European Court of Human Rights (ECtHR) in the *Lautsi v. Italy* case.[12] Interestingly, after first finding that crucifixes in Italian schools violated the principle of separation of church and state, the ECtHR eventually allowed the cross with an argument that parallels the U.S. Supreme Court's argument for forcing the children of fundamentalist parents to learn about evolutionary biology: that mere exposure to a "passive symbol," as which the crucifix is taken by the ECtHR, does not amount to an act of indoctrination, in this case a forced "participation in religious activities."[13]

But there is more to the *Lautsi* case than this. It raises the fundamental question of whether the neutrality of the liberal state, its canonic stance on religious matters since the religious wars of the seventeenth century, is compatible with partiality toward the symbols of the majority religion, as the Italian state claimed it is. By contrast, the plaintiff, Soile Lautsi, an atheist naturalized Italian of Finnish origins, argued that "the concept of secularism required the State to be neutral and keep an equal distance from all religions."[14] Accordingly, the exposure of her children to the

Christian cross violated her right to educate her children in "conformity with [her] own religious and philosophical convictions" as well as her children's negative religious freedom, which are protected by Articles 2 and 9, respectively, of the European Convention on Human Rights (ECHR). The initial decision by the lower chamber of the ECtHR, in November 2009, affirmed Mrs. Lautsi's view, which is also the only view that takes the Christian cross seriously as a "predominantly" religious symbol[15]: "The Court considers that the compulsory display of a symbol of a particular faith in the exercise of public authority in relation to specific situations subject to governmental supervision, particularly in classrooms, restricts the right of parents to educate their children in conformity with their convictions and the right of schoolchildren to believe or not believe. . . . [T]he restrictions are incompatible with the State's duty to respect neutrality in the exercise of public authority, particularly in the field of education."[16] Echoing the German Federal Constitutional Court's very similar rejection of having to learn "under the Cross" in its famous *Kruzifix* decision of 1995, the European court argued in 2009 that the (negative) right of a minority not to be bothered by the cross deserved "special protection" because they "are placed in a situation from which they cannot extract themselves if not by making disproportionate efforts and acts of sacrifice."[17]

In their defense of the crucifix in public schools, the Italian government and Italian administrative courts took the cross as first and foremost a cultural symbol and one that represented an "identity-linked value" of the Italian people.[18] To transform, or rather reduce, an originally religious symbol into a cultural one has been a long-standing strategy of some European governments, notably of a number of German Länder, to defend the selective inclusion of Christian and exclusion of Islamic religious symbols from public space, especially schools (see Joppke 2009: ch. 3). This defense insists on a difference in kind between separating state and religion, which is the touchstone of liberalism, and separating state and culture, where "benign neglect" not only is not possible (as argued by Kymlicka 1995) but, as the very encounter with Islam brings to the light, also is not desired.

However, the Italian state's defense of national culture was also draped in strangely universalistic hues, which turned out viciously exclusive of other religions (read: Islam). Crisply, if without a sense of paradox, the Italian administrative court had argued in its first-instance decision that the Christianity incarnated in the cross stood for universal values such as "tolerance, equality and liberty, which form the basis of the modern secular State." Accordingly, "it would . . . be something of a paradox to exclude a Christian sign from a public institution in the name of secularism, one of whose distant sources is precisely the Christian religion."[19] But the real paradox here, undetected by the court, was to justify the cross in reference to secularism. This "confessional" or "post-secular" reading of the principle of secularism is a reductio ad absurdum of secularism itself, and it "occasioned considerable amusement among constitutional law scholars" (Mancini 2010: 10). Trumpeting Christianity as "uniquely" standing for values that "exclud[e] no one,"[20] this argument also advanced a none-too-subtle denigration of "other religions" that would not go that far toward inclusion—most notably, of course, Islam (p. 18).

Although one may ridicule the Italian state's defense of the Christian cross for the sake of secularism, the *Lautsi* case, much like the earlier German crucifix case, raises important questions about the meaning of secularism and state neutrality in a multireligious and multicultural but still irremediably national society where "the stench of history" is inescapable.[21] In the words of the Maltese judge on the ECtHR, concurring with the Grand Chamber's final approval of the cross in 2011, removing the crucifix "from where it has quietly and passively been for centuries would hardly have been a manifestation of neutrality by the State. Its removal would have been a positive and aggressive espousal of agnosticism or of secularism."[22] "Secularism" now figured more appropriately as an argument against the display of the Christian cross in public schools, and it was now also rightly dissociated from "neutrality."

What is striking is that all parties in the Italian crucifix controversy (apart from the plaintiff) favored "neutrality" but most emphatically not "secularism." As another ECtHR judge concurring with the court's 2011 decision put it, "Neutrality requires a pluralist approach on the part of the State, not a secularist one."[23] "Secularism" was attacked as an unhistorical intrusion on most European states. Various non-Western European governments—advised, ironically, by the iconic American Eurojurist Joseph Weiler[24]—warned of an "Americanization" of a Europe tilting toward a "rigid separation of Church and State," which was foreign to its traditions.[25] In the same vein, the Maltese ECtHR judge Bonello argued that "in Europe, secularism is optional, [but] freedom of religion is not."[26] And the plaintiff's "freedom of religion" was not affected in this case, Bonello opined, because the "silent and passive presence of a symbol in the classroom" did not constitute the sort of proactive indoctrination (or "teaching") that is prohibited under Article 2 of the ECHR.

The ECtHR's eventual acceptance of the Christian cross in Italian schools implicitly sided with the fierce condemnation of the lower chamber's prohibition of the cross, namely, that "a European court should not be called upon to bankrupt centuries of European tradition" and to "rob the Italians of part of their cultural personality."[27] Of course, this particularism still stood to be defended. But the European court did it in terms of a gentler pluralism (notably a key liberal value), not in terms of universalism, that is, the aggressive (though factually accurate)[28] claim that only Christianity had produced secular values and a culture of liberty, as the Italian government and Italian administrative courts had triumphantly argued. The only communality in both justifications of the Christian cross was to take the religion out of it, to reduce it to mere "tradition." In line with its previous jurisdiction, the ECtHR could then argue that the Christian cross's "perpetuat[ion]" by the state fell "within the margin of appreciation of the respondent State," which is the court's old formula for reserving for national governments the right to decide such culturally sensitive matters.[29]

However, more important than this legal continuity is the discontinuity established by this rule, as one now can no longer say that constitutional courts have "an inclination toward secularism and modernism" (Hirschl 2010: 162). As noted, the justification for being partisan in the 2011 *Lautsi* decision of the ECtHR consisted not in defending the alleged universalism of Christianity but rather in insisting that "Italy opens up the school environment in parallel to other religions," especially Islam:

> It [is] not forbidden for schoolchildren to wear Islamic headscarves or other symbols or apparel having a religious connotation; alternative arrangements [are] possible to help schooling fit in with non-majority religious practices; the beginning and end of Ramadan [are] "often celebrated" in schools; and optional religious education [can] be organized in schools for "all recognized religious creeds." ... Moreover, there [is] nothing to suggest that the authorities [are] intolerant of schoolchildren who believ[e] in other religions, [are] non-believers, or [hold] non-religious philosophical convictions.[30]

Assuming that these Italian government statements are indeed true, this conclusion offers a perfectly sensible way of reconciling the principle of state neutrality with a rejection of "cultural vandalism" or "historical Alzheimer's,"[31] and one that is inclusive of Islam and Muslims to boot.[32]

Lautsi stands for a trend across Western states to reassert national identities and particularisms, which may include Christian symbols. However, this has ironic, even uncomfortable implications for these states' stance on multiculturalism, which would need to be reconsidered. Remember that dissatisfaction with multiculturalism had pushed these states toward reasserting national identities in the first. However, as the ECtHR underlined in its 2011 *Lautsi* decision, the legitimacy of embracing the "identity-linked value"[33] of the Christian cross hinged on the reality of pluralism in Italian schools, that is, that minority religions are not suppressed in them. This is exactly the constellation addressed by "liberal multiculturalism" (Kymlicka 1995). It argues that the liberal nation-state cannot but privilege the culture of the dominant group; that this privileging puts minorities at a disadvantage; that this disadvantage creates a liberal justice claim on their part for multiculturalism policies; and that such policies can be adopted "without undermining more general principles of democracy and human rights."[34]

Do we then need to reconsider our analysis of multiculturalism in "retreat"? First, we only observed policy trends, or what some have argued is merely a change of political rhetoric (Vertovec and Wessendorf 2009); we did not take a normative stance "for" or "against" multiculturalism. Second, even in a book as short as this one, "multiculturalism" appeared in many different guises: "radical," "liberal," "communitarian," "legal," "official," and perhaps more. This may be our shortcoming, but it also reflects the many meanings of "multiculturalism" out there. In fact, "multiculturalism" is an almost meaningless category because it can mean too many different, even opposite things, depending on context. In everyday language and much of public discourse, "multiculturalism" still uniformly signals an approach that posits the "group" above the "individual" and thus as something that conflicts with liberalism. We stick to the position that this multiculturalism will remain controversial and under attack, particularly as an approach to deal with immigrant minorities (see Joppke 2004). By contrast, the "liberal multiculturalism" (Kymlicka 1995) that is required as antidote to nation-state particularism is an incontrovertible extension of liberalism, and it largely describes and justifies existing policy and legal reality in the liberal state—most often it exists not even qua "policy" but as "law" that constitutionally prescribes extensive individual liberty protections. However, and this is the point we wished to establish with the help of the *Lautsi* decision of the ECtHR, the multiculturalism that is required by liberalism may more easily coexist with a nation-state that is at ease with its particularism than with one that denies it under the cloak of militant secularism or "muscular liberalism."[35]

No Best Practice

In the end, one wants to know: who does it best? In our view, there is no "best practice" in accommodating Islam and Muslim immigrants. There is wisdom in each of the historical ways of linking (or rather separating) religion and state in a secular age, and all have made equally impressive strides in binding into them religions that were not originally an influential part of the formation of these states, most notably Islam. What raises eyebrows is not that Islam has not yet achieved the equal status that Muslims and their secular advocates want it to have. How could one realistically expect almost 400 years of post-Westphalian religion-state relations, be they under the opposite signs of separatism or cooperation (or even establishment), but always inevitably skewed toward the Christian religion, to be opened up to a significant but still decidedly minoritarian Muslim presence in little more than two decades (because the Islam debate has not been going on much longer)? The truly momentous historical novelty is that nothing less than full equality is the guiding principle of the inclusion of Muslims in liberal societies. It cannot be emphasized too strongly that a reciprocal equal treatment of the Christian religion in Muslim-majority societies is unthinkable. The *dhimmi* status allotted to other "People of the Book" (Jews and Christians) by all Islamic legal traditions, while still privileged if compared with dehumanized unbelievers or "polytheists" who are simply beyond the pale of law and morality, is inherently and unalterably inferior. Among many of the impairments that go with dhimmi status, there is a "categorical prohibition" on building new places of worship (Matyssek 2010: 187) and the famous poll tax *(jizya)* that is "intended . . . to signify . . . submission and humiliation" (An-Naim 1990: 89).[36]

An interesting new literature on "religious governance" has explored whether there is convergence or persistent divergence across Western states with regard to the management of religious difference (Bader 2007; Koenig 2007). The answer turns out to be "both," and our study confirms this finding. A legal scholar (Ferrari 2002) has observed the rise of a "Western European model of church and state relations" that converges on religious liberty rights, state neutrality, and "selective co-operation" between state and religious groups. However, this model is not provincially European but may equally be extended to the United States and Canada, so that it is in reality the liberal state model to which there is no alternative if the varieties of religious practice are to be equally respected and protected. At the same time, Veit Bader (2007: 881) has pointed to the persistence of "institutional diversity [that] does not seem to converge into one optimal or even predominant regime of religious governance." As demonstrated by the crucifix debates in Europe, there has even been a "reinterpretation of Church-State relations as symbols of national identity" (Koenig 2007: 928). This is not necessarily detrimental to Muslims, whose demands for "symbolic incorporation" can only gain weight in the process, as we suggested above.

In particular, one should be wary of lionizing the relatively relaxed North American attitude toward Islam and insisting that the Europeans follow it. As we demonstrated, the North American posture is strongly facilitated by a more fortunate profile of Muslim immigrants in the United States and Canada, resulting from a selective immigration policy that prizes skills and wealth over other criteria. If the United States were faced with a sizeable Muslim underclass leaning toward a strict practice of their religion, we suspect that the easygoing stance would quickly yield to more serious self-examination—of the sort that followed the publicization of the plans to build a mosque near Ground Zero. And Canada's fabled multiculturalism is cracking now that the quest is not for sari and samosa but for things that clash with its liberal underpinnings, including the primacy of secular law and equality of the sexes.

Finally, even if there is no answer to "who" does it best, is there perhaps one to the question of "how" one does it best, in the functional sense? If there is any commonality in the handling of Islam and of Muslims in Europe and North America, it is the pivotal importance of courts and the legal system. This confirms John Hart Ely's famous notion that "courts should protect those who can't protect themselves politically" (1980: 152), that is, minorities in majoritarian democracies. Most major advances that Muslims have made in regard to their religious needs have been achieved through the legal system, especially on the grounds of constitutional law that protects religious beliefs and practices. Although constitutional law has functioned as it was designed to function, to "represent the unrepresented" (p. 152), using the legal arena rather than the political one has its costs. On the part of court-going Muslims, it has fostered a legalistic-cum-instrumentalist attitude, exploiting the many conceptual and legal resources of the constitutional state only to better seal themselves off as a group and shying away from the court of public opinion. If one reviews German Muslims' stunning march through the German court system, which is perhaps the most protective of the legal systems considered in this study, this is the unavoidable conclusion to draw. With an eye on the European scene, Saba Mahmood (2009: 860) thus sensibly argues that "the future of the Muslim minority . . . depends not so much on how the law might be expanded to accommodate its concerns but on a larger transformation of the cultural and ethical sensibilities of the majority Judeo-Christian population that undergird the law." Only, this is a tall order that may well hit the limits of what the state can do by way of public policy, which cannot but proceed in the medium of law.

To "dejudicialize" minority accommodation had been the one good impulse of Quebec's Bouchard-Taylor Commission to find ways out of the Canadian province's deadlocked "reasonable accommodation," which is thus of interest beyond the narrowly Canadian context. The Quebecois experience shows that overdrawn legal protectiveness invites political backlash. So one might also read the making of the French burqa law of 2010; nay, the entire politicization of Islam in Europe in the past few years bears tell-tale signs of a political backlash against the quiet inclusiveness of the legal system. The backlash, in turn, has not left the courts unaffected. As we saw, the French Conseil Constitionnel has not dared to interdict the 2010 burqa law, and the ECtHR, in its *Lautsi* decision of 2011, seems to have heeded the Italian prime minister's rejection of the court's earlier prohibition of the crucifix as "not acceptable for us Italians" (Mancini 2010: 6). This is not to condone populism but simply to remind us that legal integration alone is not sufficient to grant Islam and Muslims the equal place in liberal societies that is unquestionably theirs.

Notes

1. Introduction

1. Here and in the following, we use the notion of "accommodation" interchangeably with "integration" or "incorporation," that is, with no connotation of a specifically difference-recognizing, multicultural way of responding to Islam. For a specifically difference-recognizing usage of the term, see Ford (2011); MacGarry, O'Leary, and Simeon (2008); or Nussbaum (2008).

2. See important recent works on "religious governance" by Bader (2007) and Koenig (2007); or, most recently, Laurence (2012) on the "neo-corporatist" institutionalization of Islam in Europe.

3. A notion invented by Karl Jaspers and later adopted and further developed by Shmuel N. Eisenstadt, "axial age" culture emerged in the first millennium B.C. in several civilizations simultaneously, in the form of philosophy (Greece) and religion (Israel, India, China). Bellah (2005: 88) defines it through the invention of "second-order thinking," which is "the capacity to examine critically the very foundations of cosmological, ethical and political order." In other words, the possibility of critique, of taking distance, of "choice," defines axial age religion.

4. See Parekh (2000: 161–162), who establishes the religion-culture distinction along this line indirectly, by arguing that "cultural communities are not voluntary associations. . . . We do not join but are born into them"; or Benhabib (2002: 94–100), who depicts the Islamic veil as "choice"; also Gutmann (2003: 24), who finds that "most religious groups . . . are voluntary." As Bedi (2007: 235) summarizes, "contemporary theory has come to see religious affiliations and practices as contingent, open-ended and freely constructed," in

short, as choice based. But see against this view Mahmood (2009), who criticizes as parochially Western the view of religion as "primarily about belief in a set of propositions to which one lends one's assent" and thus as "fundamentally a matter of choice" (p. 844). Instead, she proposes to view Islam, in particular, in terms of "affective and embodied . . . attachment and cohabitation" (p. 842). Her critique mixes the reasonable (that Islam, more than Christianity, may require a unity of belief and ritual) with the arcane (e.g., what is "cohabitation [with the Prophet]"?). Moreover, it is not clear why both stances (one cognitive, the other emotional) should be alternatives rather than equally possible and coexisting for every committed believer, the Christian included. A compelling metacritique is March (2012).

5. This qualification is important, as, of course, we do not endorse a reified view of culture as never subject to choice and evaluation. So one may, for instance, reject "European imperialism" but embrace the European "human rights tradition." As one anonymous reviewer of a draft of this book commented, "rejecting culture is not obnoxious in itself, particularly if one differentiates cultural attributes."

6. The locus classicus of this view is John Locke's (of course, very Protestant) *Letter on Toleration.*

7. Even though this banning of the Christian cross rested on a narrowly religious, noncultural reading of this symbol, which brought to bear the full weight of the state's neutrality obligation.

8. We refer to the famous U.S. Supreme Court decision *Employment Division v. Smith* (494 U.S. 872 [1990]) and Congress's retaliatory Religious Freedom Restoration Act, both briefly discussed in Chapter 5.

9. See Neil MacFarquhar, "Pakistanis Find U.S. an Easier Fit Than Britain," *New York Times,* 21 August 2006, pp. A1, A15.

10. There are, however, more of these "voices" in the North American than in the European chapters, also because about Europe there is simply more to tell from a legal-institutional point of view.

11. Already Cesari had claimed to "examine the instances and places of *reciprocal influence* between the cultural constructs of the European and Muslim worlds" (2004: 5). But when announcing to show how "rationalism and secularism . . . [were] transformed by Muslims," she mostly reports about Europeans' "essentializing discourse on Islam" and their denigration of Islam "as stigma" (ibid., p. 22). A more successful demonstration of "reciprocal influence," in our view, is Bowen (2010: ch. 8).

Western Europe

1. Laurence (2012: ch. 1) draws a similar distinction between integrating Muslims as "equal citizens" and their "corporate integration" (and then concentrates on the latter).

2. See the critical discussions of the new "politics of religion" by Liedhegener (2008) and Willems (2008).

2. Limits of Excluding

The first draft of this chapter was written in early March 2010, when Christian Joppke was visiting professor in the Nationalism Program at the Central European University in Budapest. He wishes to thank his hosts for their exceptional welcome and excellent working conditions.

1. Mostly worn in Afghanistan, and extremely rare to see in France, the *burqa* covers the entire body and face, with a finely woven mesh before the eyes. The *niqab* is common in Arabic countries and the one extreme veiling that one occasionally finds in France (when the word "burqa" is used here, it usually refers to the niqab); it covers only the head, with a slit for the eyes. The niqab is often worn in combination with a *jilbab,* a loose-fit outer garment covering neck to feet.
2. *Libération,* 22 June 2009, www.liberation.fr/.
3. Assemblée nationale, "Proposition de résolution," no. 1725, 19 June 2009.
4. Having been informed by a knowledgeable anthropologist that the burqa was practically nonexistent in France, Commission president Gerin ordered the relabeling of his enterprise as one intended to examine the "integral veil" *(voile intégral).* This neologism has since become the umbrella term for niqab and burqa in French political language. In the following, however, we use the terms "integral veil" and "burqa" interchangeably, following French everyday language.
5. "The Taliban Would Applaud," *New York Times,* 26 January 2010.
6. "Les dégâts collatéraux du débat sur le port du voile intégral," *Le Monde,* 5 February 2010.
7. Laurence (2012: 6) extends this argument to Europe at large, where post-2001 repressive measures "belie a broader trend toward greater religious freedom and institutional representation and toleration over the last 20 years."
8. Tariq Ramadan at the sixth meeting of the Burqa Commission (Mission d'information sur la pratique du port du voile intégral sur le territoire national), Paris (29 September 2009). The transcripts of all eighteen meetings are available at www.assemblee-nationale.fr/13/cr-miburqa/09-10/index.asp. I refer to them in the following as Mission, followed by the meeting number (1–18) and date. All meetings took place in Paris.
9. Mission, meeting no. 8 (14 October 2009), p. 19.
10. Mission, meeting no. 10 (28 October 2009), p. 4.
11. A French public survey done on the heels of the Swiss vote found 46 percent of respondents in favor of prohibiting minaret constructions in France ("Les Français de plus en plus hostiles à la construction de mosquées," *Le Figaro,* 3 December 2009, p. 11). If one considers that no poll had predicted the Swiss referendum outcome (presumably for respondents' reluctance to express hostility to Islam and Muslims), this figure is likely to be an undercount of minaret opponents.
12. Nicolas Sarkozy, "Respecter ceux qui arrivent, respecter ceux qui accueillent," *Le Monde,* 9 December 2009, pp. 1, 20.
13. Ibid., p. 20.

14. "La création de mosquées se banalise en France," *Le Monde,* 4 December 2008, pp. 1, 9.
15. Sarkozy, "Respecter ceux qui arrivent, respecter ceux qui accueillent," p. 20.
16. Ibid.
17. See, for instance, the Council of the European Union's (2004) "common basic principles" of immigrant integration policy.
18. Mission, meeting no. 18 (16 December 2009), p. 12.
19. *Libération,* 22 June 2009, www.liberation.fr/.
20. Mission, meeting no. 15 (2 December 2009), p. 2.
21. Mission, meeting no. 4 (9 September 2009), p. 9.
22. Mission, meeting no. 2 (8 July 2009).
23. Ibid., p. 5.
24. Ibid., p. 12.
25. UMP commission member Jaques Myard commenting on the Bouzar testimony, in ibid., p. 10. The "War of Gods," of course, is inevitable to a degree, because the protection of religious liberties requires that the state first defines what "religion" is (see Reuter 2007: 181).
26. Mission, meeting no. 8, p. 3.
27. CFCM president Mohammed Moussaoui, in ibid., p. 4.
28. Mission, meeting no. 18, pp. 3–4.
29. Samir Amghar of the Ecole des Hautes Etudes en Sciences Sociales, in Mission, meeting no. 11 (4 November 2009), p. 3.
30. Ibid. For the "hyper-individualism" of contemporary global, deethnicized Islam, see above all Roy (2004). Also Abdennour Bidar, "La burqa, symtôme d'un malaise," *Le Monde,* 24/25 January 2010, p. 14.
31. Quoted in "Vivre en France avec le niqab," *Le Monde,* 24 June 2009, p. 3.
32. Conseil d'Etat, 27 June 2008, *Mme Faiza M.,* req. no. 286798.
33. French Salafi expert Samir Amghar testifying before the Burqa Commission, in Mission, meeting no. 11, p. 6.
34. *Le Monde,* 24 June 2009, p. 3.
35. Michel Champredon, mayor of Evreux, in Mission, meeting no. 3 (15 July 2009), p. 21.
36. Ibid.
37. Ibid., p. 24.
38. Philippe Esnol, mayor of Conflans-Sainte-Honorine, in ibid., p. 22.
39. Xavier Lemoine, mayor of Montfermeil, in Mission, meeting no. 6, p. 8.
40. Sihem Habchi (Ni putes ni soumises), in Mission, meeting no. 4, p. 9.
41. The Burqa Commission report follows here the statement by law professor Anne Levade, in Mission, meeting no. 13 (18 November 2009), p. 10.
42. Rémy Schwartz *(conseiller d'Etat)* (state councilor) in Mission, meeting no. 7 (7 October 2009), p. 13.
43. In doing so we need only to follow the Burqa Commission report (Assemblée Nationale 2010: 87–122).
44. Rémy Schwartz, in Mission, meeting no. 7, p. 16.
45. Philosopher Abdennour Bidar, in Mission, meeting no. 2, p. 17.

46. UMP delegate Jacques Myard, in Mission, meeting no. 14 (25 November 2009), p. 6.

47. Mission, meeting no. 8, p. 25.

48. We follow here the succinct discussion of the "multiple and uncertain" contents of the concept of dignity in the Veil Commission report (Veil Committee 2008: 92–95), which—despite conceding the ambiguity of "dignity"—recommended inserting a dignity clause into Article 1 of the French Constitution.

49. Minister of Work, Xavier Darcos, at Mission, meeting no. 18, p. 8.

50. Ibid., p. 9.

51. Mission, meeting no. 18, p. 13.

52. Mission, meeting no. 14, p. 6.

53. Ibid., p. 6.

54. Ibid., p. 12.

55. Mission, meeting no. 13, p. 6.

56. C.E., Ass., 27 Octobre 1995, *Commune de Morsang-sur-Orge.*

57. European Court of Human Rights (ECtHR), *Laskey, Jaggard and Brown v. The United Kingdom,* 19 February 1997, at par. 50 and 45, respectively.

58. Ibid., at par. 20.

59. ECtHR, *K.A. and A.D. v. Belgium,* 17 February 2005.

60. Mission, meeting no. 14, p. 3.

61. Ibid., p. 12.

62. Denys de Béchillon, in Mission, meeting no. 8, p. 28.

63. Mission, meeting no. 14, p. 7.

64. Mission, meeting no. 7, pp. 15–16.

65. Rémy Schwartz, in ibid., p. 15.

66. Anne Levade, in Mission, meeting no. 13, p. 5.

67. Rémy Schwartz, in Mission, meeting no. 7, p. 13.

68. Anne Levade, in Mission, meeting no. 13, p. 7.

69. Denys de Béchillon, in Mission, meeting no. 8, p. 25.

70. Ibid., p. 25.

71. Guy Carcassonne, in Mission, meeting no. 14, p. 16.

72. Ibid., p. 13.

73. Ibid.

74. Copé's *proposition de loi* is reprinted in Assemblée Nationale (2010: 268–270).

75. Law professor Danièle Lochak, quoted in *Le Monde,* 13 November 2009, p. 13.

76. Denys de Béchillon, in Mission, meeting no. 8, p. 26.

77. Rémy Schwartz, in Mission, meeting no. 7, p. 15.

78. Ibid., p. 29.

79. The Socialist members of the commission even refused to vote on the final version of the commission report, in protest against the UMP law proposal launched separately by Jean-François Copé and to express their disagreement with the parallel "national identity" campaign conducted by the Gaullist government.

80. In an annex to Conseil d'Etat (2010), entitled "Fiche questions-reponses."

81. President Nicolas Sarkozy, quoted in "Burqa: Le chef de l'Etat reparle d'une loi," *Le Monde,* 26 March 2010, p. 9.

82. "De la difficulté de lutter contre le communautarisme par la loi," *Le Monde,* 31 March 2010, p. 12.

83. President Sarkozy, quoted in *Le Monde,* 26 March 2010, p. 9.

84. *Le Monde,* 2 April 2010, p. 9.

85. A Belgian parliamentarian, quoted in *Le Figaro,* 30 April 2010, p. 11.

86. "Voile intégral: Une loi votée avant l'été," France2.fr, 23 April 2010, www .france2.fr/.

87. *Le Monde,* 9 April 2010, p. 18.

88. Ibid.

89. Copé, quoted in Le Figaro.fr, 14 May 2010, www.lefigaro.fr/.

90. Ibid.

91. Ibid.

92. Ibid.

93. Ibid.

94. *L'Express,* 14 May 2010, www.lexpress.fr/.

95. Assemblée Nationale, *Projet de loi interdisant la dissimulation du visage dans l'espace public,* no. 2520, 19 May 2010, pp. 3–4.

96. Assemblée Nationale, *Compte rendu no. 75, Commission des lois constitutionnelles, de la legislation et de l'administration générale de la République,* 6 July 2010, p. 2.

97. Ibid.

98. Ibid., p. 8.

99. Mission, meeting no. 13, p. 7.

100. Assemblée Nationale, *Rapport fait au nom de la commission des lois constitutionnelles, de la legislation et de l'administration générale de la République sur le projet de loi (no. 2520), interdisant la dissimulation du visage dans l'espace public, par M. Jean-Paul Garraud,* no. 2648, 23 June 2010 (hereafter cited as Garraud Rapport 2010), p. 31.

101. Assemblée Nationale, *Compte rendu no. 75,* p. 4.

102. Glavany, quoted in ibid., p. 14.

103. Ibid., p. 15.

104. Ibid.

105. Manuel Valls, Parti socialiste (PS), in *Le Monde,* 1 October 2010, p. 20.

106. Conseil Constitutionnel, *Décision no. 2010–613 DC,* 7 October 2010 *(Loi interdisant la dissimulation du visage dans l'espace public).*

107. Patrick Weil, "La loi sur la burqa risque l'invalidation par l'Europe," *Le Monde,* 24 November 2010, p. 23.

108. Justice Minister Alliot-Marie, when audited by the National Assembly in June 2010 (Garraud Rapport 2010, p. 27).

109. Weil, "La loi sur la burqa risque l'invalidation par l'Europe."

110. ECtHR, *Affaire Ahmet Arslan et autres c. Turquie* no. 41135/98, 23 February 2010.

111. Garraud Rapport 2010, p. 21.

112. Ibid.

113. Weil, "La loi sur la burqa risque l'invalidation par l'Europe."
114. This has been Rogers Brubaker's reading of this chapter.

3. Limits of Including

1. France's *étatist* separation regime, which protects the state, is to be distinguished from the American "liberal" separation regime, which protects the individual and her religious freedoms. For the best available comparison between Germany, France, and the United States, see Walter (2006).
2. See Heinig (1999, 2008) and Heinig and Walter (2007).
3. Here and in the following, we will use the terms "public corporation status," "public law status," and "corporate" or "corporation status" as interchangeable shorthand for "status of corporation under public law."
4. "The right of religious communities (to teach religion in public schools) is conditional on the material preconditions according to Article 137.5.2 of the Weimar Constitution" (Decision of the Federal Administrative Court of 23 February 2005, Bundesverwaltungsgericht [hereafter BVerwG] 6 C 2.04 [*Dachverbandsorganisation als Religionsgemeinschaft*], p. 27). Article 137.5.2 lays out the conditions for being recognized as a corporation under public law.
5. Paul Mikat, quoted in Walter (2006: 551).
6. Joachim Wieland, quoted in Walter (2006: 539).
7. The Weimar Constitution speaks of *Religionsgesellschaften* (religious associations); the more recently used word for "religious associations" is "religious communities" (*Religionsgemeinschaften*). The meaning of both is identical.
8. Article 137(5) of the Weimar Constitution, incorporated in Article 140 of the Basic Law. For explications of the "durability test," see Weber (1989) and Tillmans (1999).
9. Social Democratic Party (SPD) deputy Quarck, quoted in Walter (2006: 122).
10. Liberal Party (Deutsche Demokratische Partei, DDP) member Friedrich Naumann, quoted in Korioth (2007: 56).
11. See also Hillgruber (1999: 547), who finds that it is "for the sake of self-preservation of this state to further the Christian heritage as a necessary spiritual possession." The tool for this is the public corporation clause of the Basic Law (Article 140).
12. Lepsius (2006: 348) argues that in Germany the religious liberty right from the start contains "features of a collective right to state-free self-determination," which he dates back to the corporate emancipation of *"bürgerliche Gesellschaft"* (bourgeois society) from a monarchical or princely state.
13. Bundesverfassungsgericht (hereafter BVerfGE) 24, 236 (*Aktion Rumpelkammer,* Decision of 16 October 1968).
14. Ibid., 242.
15. Ibid., 245.
16. Ibid.
17. Ibid., 246.
18. Ibid., 247.

19. BVerfGE, 1BvR 618/93 (decision on refusal of blood transfusion by Jehovah's Witnesses, 2 August 2001).
20. BVerfGE, 2 BvR 1436/02 (*Ludin* decision of 24 September 2003).
21. BVerfGE 93, 1 (*Kruzifix* decision of 16 May 1995), 16.
22. Ibid., 17.
23. Article 4(1) of the Basic Law protects not only positive but also negative religious liberty, as in the *Kruzifix* case, the right of a child of atheistic parents not "to be forced to learn 'under the Cross' " (BVerfGE 93, 1), 18.
24. "The following basic rights are binding the law maker, executive power, and the courts as directly valid law" (Article 1.3 of the German Basic Law).
25. BVerfGE 102, 370 (*Körperschaftsstatus der Zeugen Jehovas*), 20 September 2000, p. 7. Stefan Magen (2001: 888) approvingly characterized the constitutional court's stance in Jehovah's Witnesses as "basic rights realization through organization."
26. BVerfGE 102, 370 (*Körperschaftsstatus der Zeugen Jehovas*), p. 6.
27. On the question of "loyalty" in the granting of public corporation status, see Huster (1998), Thüsing (1998), Korioth (1999), and Morlok and Heinig (1999).
28. BVerfGE 102, 370 (*Körperschaftsstatus der Zeugen Jehovas*), p. 16.
29. Ibid., p. 13.
30. BVerwG 7 C 11.96 (*Zeugen Jehovas*), decision of 26 June 1997.
31. Ibid., p. 17.
32. Ibid., p. 10.
33. Ibid., p. 14.
34. Ibid.
35. Ibid.
36. Ibid., p. 15.
37. Ibid., p. 16.
38. For a critique, see Muckel (2001).
39. BVerfGE 102, 370 (*Körperschaftsstatus der Zeugen Jehovas*), 20 September 2000, p. 9.
40. Ibid., p. 15.
41. Ibid., p. 7.
42. This is according to Article 137.5.2 of the Weimar Constitution (incorporated as Article 140 of the Basic Law).
43. BVerwG 6 C 8/91 (*Befreiung einer Schülerin islamischen Glaubens vom koedukativen Sportunterricht*).
44. "Haben wir schon die Scharia?," *Der Spiegel* no. 13 (16 March 2007), pp. 22ff.
45. BVerwG 6 C 8/91, pp. 4–5.
46. Ibid., p. 4.
47. Susanne Kusicke, "Das Übliche," *Frankfurter Allgemeine Zeitung*, 22 December 2004.
48. Ibid.
49. Upper Administrative Court of North-Rhine Westphalia, 19 A 1706/90 (*Befreiung von Schwimmunterricht aus religiösen Gründen*), 12 July 1991.
50. "Befreiung vom Schwimmunterricht," Muslim-Markt, www.muslim-markt.de/.

51. Upper Administrative Court of North-Rhine Westphalia, decision of 12 July 1991 (unpaginated).

52. Ibid.

53. Ibid.

54. Administrative Court of Hamburg, 11 E 1044/05 *(Ein 9jähriges Mädchen aus der islamischen Glaubensrichtung der Ahmadiyya muss am Schwimmunterricht der Schule teilnehmen)*, 14 April 2005, p. 8. Parental authority in the education of their children is enshrined in Article 6 of the Basic Law.

55. As, in this case, the Shiite Ahmadiyya sect.

56. Ibid., p. 11. This passage is taken from a 2003 decision of the Federal Constitutional Court (FCC), which rejected home schooling in lieu of public or private schooling for the children of Christian fundamentalist parents (1 BvR 436/03, par. 7). The FCC decision was the first in which the state's education mandate, according to Basic Law Article 7, trumped the religious liberty and parental authority protections of the Basic Law (in Articles 4 and 6, respectively).

57. Ibid. The Hamburg court again quoted the FCC, 1 BvR 436/03, par. 8.

58. Ibid., pp. 12–13. Article 3(2) of the Basic Law stipulates: "Men and women have equal rights."

59. Ibid., p. 13.

60. Administrative Court of Düsseldorf, 18 K 74/05, 30 May 2005, par. 6, 32, 33.

61. Ibid., par. 38 and 39.

62. Ibid., par. 43.

63. Ibid., par. 45.

64. Stefan Muckel, quoted in Lemmen (2002: 140, fn.46).

65. "Haben wir schon die Scharia?," *Der Spiegel* no. 13 (26 March 2007), pp. 22ff.

66. BVerwG 99, 1 *(Schächten)*, 15 June 1995.

67. Ibid., p. 5.

68. Ibid., p. 6.

69. Ibid., pp. 2–3.

70. BVerwG 3 C 40.99 *(Ausnahmegenehmigung für betäubungsloses Schlachten)*, 23 November 2000, par. 32.

71. BVerfGE, 1 BvR 1783/99, decision of 15 January 2002. All it says in this respect is that the claim that stunning minimizes the animal's suffering can "at least be made" *(zumindest vertretbar)* (par. 39).

72. BVerwG 99, 1 *(Schächten)*, p. 6.

73. BVerfGE, 1 BvR 1783/99, par. 56.

74. Ibid., par. 44.

75. Jutta Rippegather, "Schächten unter Auflagen," *Frankfurter Rundschau*, 6 October 2009.

76. BVerwG 3 C 30.05, decision of 23 November 2006.

77. BVerfGE, 1 BvR 1702/09, decision of 28 September 2009.

78. Alan Posener, "Muslime vor Gericht: Stand der Dinge im Einwandererland Deutschland," *Die Welt* (online), 4 October 2009, www.welt.de/.

79. Korioth (1997: 231) thus anticipated the famous diction of the Constitutional Court in *Jehovah's Witnesses*, that public corporation status is a "means for the unfolding of religious liberty."

80. BVerwG 7 C 11.96 *(Zeugen Jehovas)*, decision of 26 June 1997, p. 9.

81. BVerfGE 102, 370 *(Körperschaftsstatus der Zeugen Jehovas)*, decision of 20 September 2000, p. 16.

82. Weimar deputies Mausbach and Naumann, respectively (quoted in Magen 2004: 171 and 169).

83. Deputy Mausbach, quoted in Magen (2004: 171).

84. "Wertschätzung der sozialen Kräfte der Religion und ihrer Bedeutung für das öffentliche Leben" (Deputy Mausbach, quoted in Magen 2004: 155).

85. See, for instance, Uhle (2007), who argues that even after the Constitutional Court's throwing out of the "loyalty" requirement in *Jehovah's Witnesses*, the "material" condition of being granted public corporation status was the claimant's "strengthening of the constitutional culture of the Basic Law" (p. 320). This was not a "rigid cultural condition" but followed from a "functional perspective" (p. 323) in which all religions were equal. However, he finds Islam wanting in this respect because of "fundamental difficulties" arising from shari'a law (p. 327). As plausible as it sounds, this is a distinctly marginal position among German constitutional jurists.

86. Milli Gazete, quoted in Bundesministerium des Innern (2006: 246).

87. But see Werner Schiffauer's (2010) impressive study of a "post-Islamist" second generation increasingly seeking to dominate the organization, which is said to identify with liberal constitutionalism. However, the young "post-Islamists" still control only 10 percent of the local Milli Görüs mosques (p. 327).

88. Ibrahim Cavdar (quoted in Lemmen 2002: 181).

89. Ayyub Axel Köhler, "Die strukturelle Assimilation des Islam in Deutschland" (undated, downloaded from www.islam.de/ on 25 May 2010).

90. BVerwG 6 C 2.04 *(Dachverbandsorganisation als Religionsgemeinschaft)*, p. 27.

91. Eberhard Seidel, "Milli Görüs reizt Otto Schily," *die tageszeitung,* 1 June 1999, p. 9.

92. In 2012, North-Rhine Westphalia became the first German Land to introduce creedal Islam instruction without any proviso.

93. BVerwG 6 C 2.04 *(Dachverbandsorganisation als Religionsgemeinschaft)*, decision of 23 February 2005.

94. Ibid., par. 31, 33.

95. Ibid., par. 60.

96. Ibid., par. 65.

97. Ibid., par. 77.

98. Ibid., par. 76.

99. Hessischer Verwaltungsgerichtshof 7 UE 2223/04 *(Islamischer Religionsunterricht)*, decision of 14 September 2005.

100. Ibid., par. 81.

101. Note that the IRH's Fiqh Council had issued, in 1998, the so-called camel-fatwa, according to which Muslim girls were not allowed to participate without a male "Mahram" in school retreats whose destination was more than 81 km away from the residence of the next male relative (which is the distance a camel presumably can walk in one day). See "Antrag auf Religionsunterricht abgelehnt," *Frankfurter Allgemeine Zeitung,* 20 September 2001, p. 4.

102. Hessischer Verwaltungsgerichtshof 7 UE 2223/04 *(Islamischer Religionsunterricht)*, par. 95. The IRH does not recognize the Alevites (sizeable among German Turks) and the smaller Shiite Ahmadiyya and Bahai sects as "Muslim."
103. Ibid., par. 96.
104. Ibid., par. 60.
105. Ibid., par. 66.
106. Ibid., par. 71–75.
107. MAH's self-description is quoted in ibid., par. 62.
108. Ibid., par. 66.
109. Verwaltungsgericht Berlin VG 27 A 254.01, decision of 25 October 2001.
110. Bernhard Schlink, quoted in "Atatürk als Abwehrzauber," *Frankfurter Allgemeine Zeitung*, 4 November 2006, p. 39.
111. The IFB refused the author of a comparative study of Islam instruction access to its class rooms ("Allah in der Schule," *Frankfurter Rundschau*, 11 April 2007). See also Mohr and Kiefer (2009: 15): "In Berlin, where the Islamic Federation regularly has a bad press, it was difficult to attend class, not to mention to film it."
112. "Merkwürdig und missionarisch," *Frankfurter Rundschau*, 6 July 2004.
113. "Islam in Berlin," *die tageszeitung*, 1 December 2004, p. 23.
114. The Berlin-Neukölln school director who dared facing the IFB on this and other matters received anonymous threats (*Frankfurter Allgemeine Zeitung*, 6 July 2004, p. 39).
115. "Merkwürdig und missionarisch," *Frankfurter Rundschau*, 6 July 2004.
116. Wolfgang Schäuble, "Muslime in Deutschland," *Frankfurter Allgemeine Zeitung*, 27 September 2006, p. 9.
117. Ibid.
118. Ezhar Cezairli, quoted in *die tageszeitung*, 13 March 2008, p. 6.
119. The Iranian Navid Kermani, a "secular" Muslim on the Islam Conference, quoted in "Minister Schäubles grosses Islam-Palaver," *Frankfurter Allgemeine Zeitung*, 29 April 2007.
120. Federal Minister of the Interior Wolfgang Schäuble, in Bundesministerium des Innern (2009: 3).
121. *Stand der rechtlichen Gleichstellung des Islam in Deutschland* (German Parliament: BT-Drucksache Nr. 16/2085, 29 June 2006), p. 48.
122. Interview with Wolfgang Schäuble, *Frankfurter Allgemeine Zeitung*, 22 April 2007, p. 4.
123. Schäuble, quoted in "Im Namen des deutschen islamischen Volkes?," *Frankfurter Allgemeine Zeitung*, 15 April 2007, p. 5.
124. Bundesamt für Migration und Flüchtlinge (2009: 343). Note, by contrast, that 55 percent of surveyed Muslims are member in a German association *(Verein)*.
125. This analogy was made by a "religious" Muslim on the Islam Conference (see Joppke 2009: 132, fn.17).
126. *Süddeutsche Zeitung*, 23 April 2007, p. 2.
127. An unnamed agent of the Federal Office for the Protection of the Constitution, quoted in "Am Tisch mit Islamisten und Orthodoxen," *Frankfurter Allgemeine Zeitung*, 9 March 2008, p. 14.

128. See Bassam Tibi, "Hidschra nach Europa," *Frankfurter Allgemeine Zeitung,* 18 December 2000, p. 15.
129. "Geld für Terroristen?," *Frankfurter Allgemeine Zeitung,* 28 March 2009, www .faz.net/. On the successful installation of the Muslim Brotherhood in Germany, which serves as its hub for Europe, see Lorenzo Vidino, "The Muslim Brother- hood's Conquest of Europe," *Middle East Quarterly* (Winter 2005), 25–34.
130. "Viel Selbstlob und ein Querschläger," Spiegel Online, 25 June 2009, www .spiegel.de/.
131. "Jetzt kennt man sich ein bisschen besser," *Frankfurter Allgemeine Zeitung,* 26 June 2009, www.faz.net/.
132. The very fact that organized Islam has to ask for a public corporation status that has been automatically granted to the Christian churches marks a struc- tural "legal inequality" that can never be closed by the legal process alone (Gusy 2006: 179).
133. See also Oebbecke (2008: 56), who notes that the entire "system of positive neutrality is questioned in its legitimacy if access to it is not equally open for all."

North America

1. "Shadow establishments," such as those that have existed historically in Aus- tralia and Canada, lie constitutionally somewhere between the "residual state church" of Britain and the strict nonestablishmentarianism of the United States. That is, although not formally established in the sense of conferring sanctity on the state, shadow establishments in those two countries nonethe- less were quasi-established as a result of those countries' longer-lived colo- nial status relative to Britain and enjoyed a relatively untrammeled hege- mony in each country's culture and religious affairs. See Martin (2005: 91).

4. "Reasonable Accommodation" and the Limits of Multiculturalism in Canada

1. See the account at http://en.wikipedia.org/wiki/2006_Toronto_terrorism_plot.
2. See Michelle Shephard, "The Powerful Online Voice of Jihad," *Toronto Star* online, October 18, 2009, http://www.thestar.com/news/world/article /711964--the-powerful-online-voice-of-jihad.
3. *Robertson and Rosetanni v. R.* (1963), S.C.R. 651, http://csc.lexum.umontreal .ca/en/1963/1963scr0-651/1963scr0-651.html.
4. See *R. v. Big M Drug Mart* (1985), http://scc.lexum.org/en/1985/1985scr1 -295/1985scr1-295.html.
5. *Syndicat Northcrest v. Amselem* [2004], 2 S.C.R. 551, 2004 SCC 47, http:// scc.lexum.umontreal.ca/en/2004/2004scc47/2004scc47.html.
6. *Multani v. Commission scolaire Marguerite-Bourgeoys* [2006], 1 S.C.R. 256, 2006 SCC 6, http://scc.lexum.umontreal.ca/en/2006/2006scc6/2006scc6.html.
7. Subsequent references will be to page numbers of the report, in parentheses in the text.

8. Again, however, the pollsters provide no indication of how these numbers might compare with other immigrant group members' attachments to their countries or customs of origin. Hence we have no way of knowing whether this is an unusual rate of attachment to the "old ways" or to the "old country."

9. Thanks to Loren Peabody for reminding us of the existence of this series.

10. See the statement of the Canadian Council of Muslim Women, "Initial Response to Marion Boyd's Report," http://www.ccmw.com/press/press_room_2004.html.

11. See http://www.ontla.on.ca/bills/bills-files/38_Parliament/Session2/b027ra.pdf.

12. Interestingly, this narrowing of multiculturalism to anti-racism reverses the direction taken by roughly simultaneous affirmative action programs in the United States, which started out as policies to improve the well-being of blacks but gradually came to be extended to other nonwhite minorities and to women. See Skrentny 2002.

13. "Normes de vie," Municipalité de Hérouxville, 27 January 2007, http://translate.google.com/translate?hl=en&sl=fr&u=http://municipalite.herouxville.qc.ca/normes.pdf&ei=mJkCTc_fAYH98AaP1pn3Ag&sa=X&oi=translate&ct=result&resnum=4&ved=0CDsQ7gEwAw&prev=/search%3Fq%3Dherouxville%2Bdocument%26hl%3Den%26rlz%3D1T4RNTN_en___US366%26prmd%3Div.

14. See http://news.bbc.co.uk/2/hi/6316151.stm.

15. See Gregory Crouch, "A Candid Dutch Film May Be Too Scary for Immigrants," *New York Times*, 16 March 2006, http://www.nytimes.com/2006/03/16/international/europe/16dutch.html.

16. Ingrid Peritz and Joe Friesen, "Part I: When Multiculturalism Doesn't Work," *Globe and Mail*, 1 October 2010, http://www.theglobeandmail.com/news/national/time-to-lead/multiculturalism/when-multiculturalism-doesnt-work/article1737375/.

17. "Playground Politics: Ontario Debates Religion and Schools," *Economist*, 4 October 2007, http://www.economist.com/node/9910156; see also Civil Rights in Public Education, "Quebec's New Secular School System: A Model for Ontario," http://www.cripeweb.org/Quebec<#213>s_system_1.html.

18. See Peritz and Friesen, "Part I: When Multiculturalism Doesn't Work."

19. Nelson Wyatt, "Rules Forbid Hijab, Says Quebec Soccer Federation," Thestar.com, 26 February 2007, http://www.thestar.com/News/article/185923.

20. Joan Delaney, "Quebec Seeks to Lift the Face Veil," *Epoch Times*, 23 March 2010, http://www.theepochtimes.com/n2/content/view/31925/.

21. "'Remove Full Veils' Urges Straw," BBC News Online, 6 October 2006, http://news.bbc.co.uk/2/hi/5411954.stm.

22. Martin Patriquin and Charlie Gillis, "About Face," Macleans.ca, 7 April 2010, http://www2.macleans.ca/2010/04/07/about-face/.

23. Jane Taber, "Ignatieff Backs Quebec Veil Ban," TheGlobeandMail.com, 26 March 2010, http://www.theglobeandmail.com/news/politics/ottawa-notebook/ignatieff-backs-quebec-veil-ban/article1513537/. It might be noted here that Ignatieff, who had once been expected to lead the Liberals back into the driver's seat in Canadian politics, lost his parliamentary seat in the 2011 federal election.

24. "Muslim Canadian Congress Wants Canada to Ban the Burka," 8 October 2009, http://www.muslimcanadiancongress.org/20091008.html.

25. Farzana Hassan and Tarek Fatah, "Muslims Are Not Required to Cover Up," TheGlobeandMail.com, 18 April 2007, http://www.muslimcanadiancongress.org/20070418.html.

26. Patriquin and Gillis, "About Face."

27. Steven Chase, "Passengers Must Show 'Entire Face' under Tougher Air Security Rules," TheGlobeandMail.com, 18 September 2010, http://www.theglobeandmail.com/news/politics/passengers-must-show-entire-face-under-tougher-air-security-rules/article1713073/.

28. Patriquin and Gillis, "About Face."

29. See "Non/No Bill 94 Statement," http://nonbill94.wordpress.com/2010/04/05/hello-world/#more-1.

30. *R. v. N.S.*, 2010, p. 51, http://www.scribd.com/doc/39277233/Ontario-Court-of-Appeal-Ruling-on-Wearing-Niqab-in-Court; see also Kirk Makin, "Niqab Must Be Removed if Trial Fairness Jeopardized, Court Rules," TheGlobeandMail.com, 18 October 2010, http://www.theglobeandmail.com/news/national/ontario/niqab-must-be-removed-if-trial-fairness-jeopardized-court-rules/article1754975/page1/.

31. Muslim Council of Montreal, "Muslim Community Welcomes Ruling from Ontario Court of Appeals Granting the Right to Wear Niqab," 14 October 2010, http://www.muslimcouncil.org/en/2010/10/muslim_community_welcomes_ruling_from_ontario_court_of_appeal_granting_the.html.

32. See http://muslim-canada.org/DARLQADAform2andhalf.html.

33. See Muslim Council of Montreal, "Muslim Community Disagrees with Angus Reid Poll over National Support for Niqab Ban," http://www.muslimcouncil.org/en/2010/03/muslim_community_disagrees_with_angus_reid_poll_over_national_support_for_n.html.

34. Muslim Canadian Congress, "To Fight Extremism, Muslim Leaders Must Emphasize the Seperation [*sic*] of Religion and Politics, Says Salma Siddiqui," http://www.muslimcanadiancongress.org/20070512.html.

35. See "Initial Response to Marion Boyd's Report."

36. The exposure of Ramadanian "double speak" has become a growth industry. See Berman (2003, 2010) and Fourest (2004).

5. The Dog That Didn't Bark

1. Ralph Blumenthal and Sharaf Mowjood, "Muslim Prayers and Renewal Near Ground Zero," *New York Times,* 8 December 2009, http://www.nytimes.com/2009/12/09/nyregion/09mosque.html?pagewanted=1&adxnnlx=1291219247-Jj/9PST4kUMuHLNMldEMMA.

2. Huma Imtiaz, "Sufi Shrine in Pakistan Is Hit by a Lethal Double Bombing," *New York Times,* 7 October 2010, http://www.nytimes.com/2010/10/08/world/asia/08pstan.html?ref=pakistan.

3. James C. McKinley Jr., "U.S. Judge Blocks a Ban on Islamic Law," *New York Times,* 30 November 2010, p. A22; see also "Intolerance and the Law in

Oklahoma," *New York Times*, 28 November 2010, http://www.nytimes.com /2010/11/29/opinion/29mon1.html.

4. Scott Keyes, "10th Circuit Court of Appeals Declares Oklahoma's Sharia Ban Unconstitutional," *Think Progress: Justice*, 10 January 2012, http://think progress.org/justice/2012/01/10/401693/oklahoma-sharia-ban-unconstitutional/.

5. *Fulwood v. Clemmer*, 206 F. Supp. 370—Dist. Court, Dist. of Columbia (1962), http://scholar.google.com/scholar_case?case=7340492765798140255 &hl=en&as_sdt=2&as_vis=1&oi=scholarr.

6. *O'Lone v. Estate of Shabazz*, 482 U.S. 342 (1987), http://caselaw.lp.findlaw .com/scripts/getcase.pl?court=us&vol=482&invol=342.

7. *United States v. Seeger*, 380 U.S. 163 (1965), http://supreme.justia.com/us /380/163/case.html.

8. *Employment Division v. Smith*, 494 U.S. 872 (1990), http://caselaw.lp.findlaw .com/scripts/getcase.pl?court=us&vol=494&invol=872.

9. *Cutter et al. v. Wilkinson* (2005), http://caselaw.lp.findlaw.com/scripts/get case.pl?court=us&vol=000&invol=03-9877.

10. Nina Bernstein, "Judge Rules That U.S. Has Broad Powers to Detain Nonciti- zens Indefinitely," *New York Times*, 15 June 2006, http://www.nytimes.com /2006/06/15/nyregion/15detain.html. Parts of the case are still pending as of this writing.

11. *Holder, Attorney General, et al. v. Humanitarian Law Project et al.*, http://www .supremecourt.gov/opinions/09pdf/08-1498.pdf; for a brief account, see Adam Liptak, "Court Affirms Ban on Aiding Groups Tied to Terror," *New York Times*, 21 June 2010, http://www.nytimes.com/2010/06/22/us/politics/22scotus.html ?scp=1&sq=supreme%20court%20material%20support&st=cse.

12. Ahmed Rashid, "The Times Square Bomber," *NYRB Blog*, 14 May 2010, http:// www.nybooks.com/blogs/nyrblog/2010/may/14/times-square-bomber-home -grown-hatred/?utm_medium=email&utm_source=Emailmarketingsoftware& utm_content=672677935&utm_campaign=June102010issue&utm _term=TheTimesSquareBomber.

13. See the quotations collected at http://www.sodahead.com/united-states/presi dent-bushs-quotes-on-islamso-would-u-call-him-a-terrorist/blog-307347/.

14. Gallup, "Anti-Muslim Sentiments Fairly Commonplace," 10 August 2006, http://www.gallup.com/poll/24073/antimuslim-sentiments-fairly-common place.aspx.

15. http://pluralism.org/news/view/16958. See also Panagopoulos 2006.

16. Gallup Center for Muslim Studies, "In U.S., Religious Prejudice Stronger against Muslims," 21 January 2010, http://www.gallup.com/poll/125312/reli gious-prejudice-stronger-against-muslims.aspx.

17. Pew Research Center, "Public Remains Conflicted over Islam," 24 August 2010, http://pewresearch.org/pubs/1706/poll-americans-views-of-muslims-object -to-new-york-islamic-center-islam-violence.

18. Associated Press, "Muslim Student, Oklahoma District Settle Hijab Lawsuit," 20 May 2004, http://www.firstamendmentcenter.org/news.aspx?id=13379.

19. See *Chalifoux et al. v. New Caney Independent School District*, 3 September 1997, http://lw.bna.com/lw/19970923/971763.htm.

20. See Sarah Viren, "Educators Struggle with Protecting Students' Religious Rights While Enforcing Policies Designed to Ease Safety Concerns," *Houston Chronicle,* 19 September 2006, http://www.chron.com/disp/story.mpl/front/4191316.html.

21. Oren Dorell, "Some Say Schools Giving Muslims Special Treatment," *USA Today,* 26 July 2007, http://www.usatoday.com/news/nation/2007-07-25-muslim-special-treatment-from-schools_N.htm.

22. Julie Bosman, "Brooklyn School Is Dropped as Site of Arabic Academy," *New York Times,* 5 May 2007, http://query.nytimes.com/gst/fullpage.html?res=9900E3D8113EF936A35756C0A9619C8B63; and Daniel Pipes, "A Madrassa Grows in Brooklyn," *New York Sun,* 24 April 2007, http://www.danielpipes.org/4441/a-madrasa-grows-in-brooklyn.

23. See http://caselaw.findlaw.com/us-3rd-circuit/1022700.html.

24. Many Arab immigrants were and are Christians, not Muslims; California Congressman Darrell Issa, for example, is the Christian grandson of Lebanese immigrants and bears a last name that means "Jesus" in Arabic.

25. *Muslim Americans: A National Portrait,* http://www.muslimwestfacts.com/mwf/116074/Muslim-Americans-National-Portrait.aspx; reported in Esposito 2010: 15.

26. Pew Research Center, *Muslim Americans: Middle Class and Mostly Mainstream,* 22 May 2007, http://pewresearch.org/pubs/483/muslim-americans.

27. It is notable here that al-Alwani uses the term *dar al-kufr* as opposed to *dar al-harb,* often translated as "House of War" and related to Muslim states' historical aspirations to conquer and convert neighboring non-Muslim lands.

28. "Qaradawi: Abbas Must Be Stoned if Proven Guilty," *IslamOnline.com,* 9 January 2010, http://islamonline.com/news/articles/34/Qaradawi-Abbas-must-be-stoned-if-proven-guilty.html.

29. "Israel: Cable Cites Cooperation against Hamas," *New York Times,* 21 December 2010, p. A8.

30. See Scott Shane, "US Approves Targeted Killing of Muslim Cleric," *New York Times,* 6 April 2010, http://www.nytimes.com/2010/04/07/world/middleeast/07yemen.html.

31. Inaugural Address, January 20, 2009, http://www.nytimes.com/2009/01/20/us/politics/20text-obama.html?pagewanted=all.

32. It is also worth recalling in this context that after September 11, 2001, attacks were made on Arabs, who are assumed to be Muslims though many in the United States are Christians, and Sikhs, because the latter wore religious garb mistakenly associated with Muslims. In other words, these groups were "racialized" as Muslims.

6. Conclusion

1. According to a comprehensive study commissioned by the European Parliament, about two-thirds of European "Muslims" are nonpracticing or agnostic (Dassetto, Ferrari, and Maréchal 2007: 7).

2. As, for instance, the orthodox Jewish Kiryas Joel sect; see the report on their self-segregated life near New York City, Sam Roberts, "A Village with the Numbers, Not the Image, of the Poorest Place," *New York Times,* 21 April 2011.

3. The "reasonable" proviso is in fact an extraordinarily high threshold to take in the case of religion, as it is defined as not "insist[ing] that [one's] beliefs alone are true" (Rawls quoted by Spinner-Halev 2008: 555). How can one believe in God without insisting that this belief is the only way to salvation and thus "true"?

4. See the interview with Tareq Oubrou in *Le Monde,* 15 October 2009.

5. Fouard Bahri, "Les surprenants déclarations de Tareq Oubrou," Oumma .com, 2 November 2009, http://oumma.com.

6. We owe this formulation to Rogers Brubaker, who reviewed a draft of this book and subsequently waived his anonymity.

7. Of course, Rawls's (1993) claim is that political liberalism is not just "modus vivendi" but intrinsically embraced. However, this is a conceptually daring and empirically questionable claim.

8. Werner Schiffauer's ethnographic study of the rise of a "post-Islamist" elite within the German Milli Görüs organization identifies an assimilationist logic very similar to that observed by Sahlins (1989) in the French Pyrenees, and one that works at much higher speed. This suggests optimism. However, the 3,000 "post-Islamists" estimated by Schiffauer (2010: 162) are still a tiny minority among Germany's almost 3 million Muslims.

9. For a trenchant critique of "normative secular religiosity," see Mahmood (2006: 344).

10. David Cameron, "Speech on Radicalization and Islamic Extremism," www .newstatesman.com.

11. For the rather shocking trend in Israel of ultraorthodox "Haredi" Jews no longer to stay inward-looking but imposing themselves on the secular majority, see "Israel Faces a Seismic Rift over the Role of Women," *International Herald Tribune,* 16 January 2012, pp. 1, 7.

12. European Court of Human Rights (ECtHR) (Grand Chamber), *Lautsi and Others v. Italy,* decision of 18 March 2011.

13. Ibid., 72.

14. ECtHR (2nd Section), *Case of Lautsi v. Italy,* judgment of 3 November 2009, par. 32.

15. Ibid., par. 51.

16. Ibid., par. 57.

17. Ibid., par. 55. There is an intriguing parallel here, *ex negativo,* with the U.S. Supreme Court decision *Cutter et al. v. Wilkinson* (544 U.S. 709 [2005]), which affirmed the freedom of religious exercise among prisoners because the state had so extensively curtailed their rights by incarcerating them. In circumstances in which the groups in question have little choice about being there, freedom from religion is affirmed on the one hand while free exercise is upheld on the other, and in a way that neatly echoes the differences in religious vitality in the United States and Western Europe.

18. Quoted in ECtHR (Grand Chamber), *Lautsi and Others v. Italy,* par. 15.

19. Quoted from the 2005 Italian administrative court decision, ibid., par. 15.

20. Ibid.
21. "Concurring Opinion of Judge Bonello," ibid., par. 1.4.
22. Ibid.
23. "Concurring Opinion of Judge Power," ibid.
24. See, however, Weiler's hauntingly honest and sane defense of "Christian Europe," translated from the original Italian into nine other (mostly Catholic-country) languages (Weiler 2007).
25. ECtHR (Grand Chamber), *Lautsi and Others v. Italy,* par. 47.
26. Judge Bonello, ibid., par. 2.5.
27. Judge Bonello, ibid., par. 1.2.
28. For the "Christian roots of the secular state," see Ferrari (2011).
29. ECtHR (Grand Chamber), *Lautsi and Others v. Italy,* par. 68.
30. Ibid., par. 74.
31. Judge Bonello, ibid., par. 1.2.
32. A more detailed and sustained case for a Christian identity as potentially more inclusive than a narrowly "liberal" identity is laid out in Joppke (2013a).
33. ECtHR (Grand Chamber), *Lautsi and Others v. Italy,* par. 15.
34. The quote is from a highly perceptive anonymous review of a draft of this book, to which we owe this entire observation.
35. *Lautsi* would even require the ECtHR to reconsider its own past decisions on Muslims and Islam, which have been in the spirit of militant secularism or "imperial liberalism" (Danchin 2011).
36. *Dhimmi* status entailed "deep personal indignity" (Finer 1997: 676), as dhimmi travelers had to wear a receipt of paid poll tax around their neck or wrist and otherwise could be jailed.

Court Cases

Canada

Ontario Court of Appeal. *R. v. N.S.*, 13 October 2010.
Supreme Court of Canada. *Multani v. Commission scolaire Marguerite-Bourgeoys,* 2 March 2006.
———. *Robertson and Rosetanni v. R.*, 18 October 1963.
———. *R. v. Big M Drug Mart*, 24 April 1985.
———. *Syndicat Northcrest v. Amselem*, 30 June 2004.

Council of Europe

European Court of Human Rights (ECtHR). *Affaire Ahmet Arslan et autres c. Turquie*, no. 41135/98, 23 February 2010.
———. *K.A. and A.D. v. Belgium*, 17 February 2005.
———. *Laskey, Jaggard and Brown v. The United Kingdom*, 19 February 1997.
European Court of Human Rights (ECtHR) (2nd Section). *Case of Lautsi v. Italy,* 3 November 2009.
European Court of Human Rights (ECtHR) (Grand Chamber). *Case of Lautsi and Others v. Italy*, 18 March 2011.

France

Conseil Constitutionnel. *Décision no. 2010-613 DC,* 7 October 2010 *(Loi interdisant la dissimulation du visage dans l'espace public).*
Conseil d'Etat. *Commune de Morsang-sur-Orge*, C.E., Ass., 27 October 1995.

———. *Etude relative aux possibilités juridiques d'intervention du port du voile intégral*, 30 March 2010.

———. *Mme Faiza M.*, req. no. 286798, 27 June 2008.

Germany

Bundesverfassungsgericht (Federal Constitutional Court). BVerfGE 24, 236 *(Aktion Rumpelkammer)*, 16 October 1968.

———. BVerfGE 93, 1 *(Kruzifix)*, 16 May 1995.

———. BVerfGE 102, 370 *(Körperschaftsstatus der Zeugen Jehovas)*, 20 September 2000.

———. BVerfGE, 1 BvR 618/93 (Refusal of Blood Transfusion by Members of Jehovah's Witnesses), 2 August 2001.

———. BVerfGE, 1 BvR 1783/99 (Ritual Slaughtering), 15 January 2002.

———. BVerfGE, 1 BvR 436/03 (Home Schooling), 29 April 2003.

———. BVerfGE, 2 BvR 1436/02 (Teacher's Headscarf), 24 September 2003.

———. BVerfGE, 1 BvR 1702/09 (Ritual Slaughtering and Animal Protection), 28 September 2009.

Bundesverwaltungsgericht (Federal Administrative Court, FAC). BVerwG 6 C 8/91 *(Befreiung einer Schülerin islamischen Glaubens vom koedukativen Sportunterricht)*, 25 August 1993.

———. BVerwG 99, 1 *(Schächten)*, 15 June 1995.

———. BVerwG 7 C 11.96 *(Zeugen Jehovas)*, 26 June 1997.

———. BVerwG 3 C 40.99 *(Ausnahmegenehmigung für betäubungsloses Schlachten)*, 23 November 2000.

———. BVerwG 6 C 2.04 *(Dachverbandsorganisation als Religionsgemeinschaft)*, 23 February 2005.

———. BVerwG 3 C 30.05 (Ritual Slaughtering and Animal Protection), 23 November 2006.

Oberverwaltungsgericht (Upper Administrative Court) of North-Rhine Westphalia. 19 A 1706/90 *(Befreiung vom Schwimmunterricht aus religiösen Gründen)*, 12 July 1991.

Verwaltungsgericht (Administrative Court) of Berlin. VG 27 A 254.01 *(Islamische Föderation)*, 25 October 2001.

Verwaltungsgericht (Administrative Court) of Düsseldorf. 18 K 74/05 *(Befreiung eines muslimischen Jungen von der Teilnahme am Schwimmunterricht)*, 30 May 2005.

Verwaltungsgericht (Administrative Court) of Hamburg. 11 E 1044/05 *(Ein 9jähriges Mädchen aus der islamischen Glaubensrichtung der Ahmadiyya muss am Schwimmunterricht der Schule teilnehmen)*, 14 April 2005.

Verwaltungsgerichtshof (Upper Administrative Court) of Hesse. 7 UE 2223/04 *(Islamischer Religionsunterricht)*, 14 September 2005.

United States

U.S. Court of Appeals for the Third Circuit. *Fraternal Order of Police v. City of Newark*, 3 March 1999.

U.S. District Court, District of Columbia. *Fulwood v. Clemmer*, 206 F. Supp. 370, 2 July 1962.

U.S. District Court for the Southern District of Texas. *Chalifoux et al. v. New Caney Independent School District*, 3 September 1997.

U.S. Supreme Court. *Boerne v. Flores*, 521 U.S. 507, 25 June 1997.

————. *Cutter et al. v. Wilkinson*, 544 U.S. 709, 31 May 2005.

————. *Employment Division v. Smith*, 494 U.S. 872, 17 April 1990.

————. *Holder, Attorney General, et al. v. Humanitarian Law Project et al.*, 561 U.S. __, 24 June 2010.

————. *O'Lone v. Estate of Shabazz*, 482 U.S. 342, 9 June 1987.

————. *Sherbert v. Verner*, 374 U.S. 398, 17 June 1963.

————. *United States v. Seeger*, 380 U.S. 163, 8 March 1965.

Bibliography

Abou El Fadl, Khaled. 1996. "Muslim Minorities and Self-Restraint in Liberal Democracies." *Loyola of Los Angeles Law Review* 29, 1525–1542.

———. 2000. "Striking a Balance: Islamic Legal Discourses on Muslim Minorities." Pp. 47–64 in Yvonne Yazbeck Haddad and John Esposito, eds., *Muslims on the Americanization Path?* New York: Oxford University Press.

———. 2003. "Islam and the Challenge of Democracy." *Boston Review* (April/May). http://bostonreview.net/BR28.2/abou.html.

———. 2006. *Islamic Law and Muslim Minorities.* Singapore: Majlis Ugama Islam Singapura (Muis Occasional Papers Series, Paper No. 3).

Adams, Michael. 2007. *Unlikely Utopia: The Surprising Triumph of Canadian Multiculturalism.* With Amy Langstaff. Toronto: Penguin Canada.

Alba, Richard, and Victor Nee. 2003. *Remaking the American Mainstream: Assimilation and Contemporary Immigration.* Cambridge, MA: Harvard University Press.

Albers, Hartmut. 1994. "Glaubensfreiheit und schulische Integration von Ausländerkindern." *Deutsches Verwaltungsblatt,* 1 September, 984–990.

Albrecht, Alfred. 1995. "Die Verleihung der Körperschaftsrechte an islamische Vereinigungen." *Kirche und Recht* 1, 25–30.

Allawi, Ali A. 2009. *The Crisis of Islamic Civilization.* New Haven, CT: Yale University Press.

Alwani, T. J. al-. 2003. *Towards a Fiqh for Minorities.* London: International Institute of Islamic Thought.

Amghar, Samir. 2006. "Le salafisme en Europe." *Politique étrangère* (Institut français des relations internationales) no. 1, 65–78.

Amir-Moazami, Schirin. 2009. "Islam und Geschlecht unter liberal-säkularer Regierungsführung—Die Deutsche Islam Konferenz." *Tel Aviver Jahrbuch für Geschichte,* 185–205.

An-Naim, Abdullah Ahmed. 1990. *Toward an Islamic Reformation: Civil Liberties, Human Rights, and International Law.* Syracuse, NY: Syracuse University Press.

———. 2008. *Islam and the Secular State.* Cambridge, MA: Harvard University Press.

Assemblée Nationale. 2009. *Proposition de résolution tendant à la création d'une commission d'enquête sur la pratique du port de la burqa ou du niqab sur le territoire national.* No. 1725. Paris, 19 June.

———. 2010. *Rapport d'information (sur la pratique du port du voile intégral sur le territoire national)* (rapporteur: Eric Raoult). No. 2262. Paris, 26 June.

Babès, Leila, and Tareq Oubrou. 2002. *Loi d' Allah, loi des hommes.* Paris: Albin Michel.

Bader, Veit. 2007. "The Governance of Islam in Europe." *Journal of Ethnic and Migration Studies* 33(6), 871–886.

Badevant-Gaudemet, Brigitte. 2000. "The Legal Status of Islam in France." In Silvio Ferrari and Anthony Bradney, eds., *Islam and European Legal Systems.* Aldershot, UK: Ashgate.

Bagby, Ihsan. 2006. "Isolate, Insulate, Assimilate: Attitudes of Mosque Leaders toward America." Pp. 23–42 in Stephen Prothero, ed., *A Nation of Religions: The Politics of Pluralism in Multireligious America.* Chapel Hill: University of North Carolina Press.

———. 2010. "The American Mosque in Transition: Assimilation, Acculturation, and Isolation." Pp. 120–137 in Erik Bleich, ed., *Muslims and the State in the Post-9/11 West.* New York: Routledge.

Bakalian, Anny, and Medhi Bozorgmehr, eds. 2009. *Backlash 9/11: Middle-Eastern and Muslim Americans Respond.* Berkeley: University of California Press.

Banting, Keith, and Will Kymlicka. 2010. "Canadian Multiculturalism: Global Anxieties and Local Debates." *British Journal of Canadian Studies* 23(1), 43–72.

Barry, Brian. 2001. *Culture and Equality.* Cambridge: Polity.

Bedi, Sonu. 2007. "Debate: What Is So Special about Religion? The Dilemma of Religious Exemption." *Journal of Political Philosophy* 15(2), 235–249.

Bellah, Robert N. 2005. "What Is Axial about the Axial Age?" *European Journal of Sociology* 46(1), 69–87.

Benhabib, Sheila. 2002. *The Claims of Culture.* Princeton, NJ: Princeton University Press.

Bergeaud-Blackler, Florence. 2007. "New Challenges for Islamic Ritual Slaughter: A European Perspective." *Journal of Ethnic and Migration Studies* 33(6), 965–980.

Berman, Paul. 2007. "Who's Afraid of Tariq Ramadan?" *New Republic,* 4 June.

———. 2010. *The Flight of the Intellectuals.* New York: Melville House.

Bhabha, Faisal. 2009. "Between Exclusion and Assimilation: Experimentalizing Multiculturalism." *McGill Law Journal* 54, 45–90.

Bleich, Erik. 2006. "Constructing Muslims as Ethno-Racial Outsiders in Western Europe." *Council for European Studies Newsletter* 36(1/2), 3–7.

Bloemraad, Irene. 2006. *Becoming a Citizen: Incorporating Immigrants and Refugees in the United States and Canada.* Berkeley: University of California Press.

Böckenförde, Ernst-Wolfgang. 1991. *Recht, Staat, Freiheit.* Frankfurt: Suhrkamp.

Bouchard, Gérard, and Charles Taylor. 2008. *Building for the Future: A Time for Reconciliation.* Abridged version. Montreal: Gouvernement du Québec. http://www.accommodements.qc.ca/documentation/rapports/rapport-final-abrege-en.pdf.

Bowen, John. 2007. *Why the French Don't Like Headscarves.* Princeton, NJ: Princeton University Press.

————. 2010. *Can Islam Be French?* Princeton, NJ: Princeton University Press.

————. 2011. "How the French State Justifies Controlling Muslim Bodies." *Social Research* 78(2), 325–348.

Boyd, Marion. 2004. *Dispute Resolution in Family Law: Protecting Choice, Promoting Inclusion.* Ottawa: Office of the Ontario Attorney General. http://www.attorneygeneral.jus.gov.on.ca/english/about/pubs/boyd/fullreport.pdf.

————. 2007. "Religion-Based Alternative Dispute Resolution: A Challenge to Multiculturalism." Pp. 465–474 in Keith Banting, Thomas J. Courchene, and F. Leslie Seidle, eds., *Belonging? Diversity, Recognition, and Shared Citizenship in Canada.* Montreal: Institute for Research on Public Policy.

Bruce, Steve. 2003. *Politics and Religion.* Malden, MA: Polity.

Bundesamt für Migration und Flüchtlinge. 2009. *Muslimisches Leben in Deutschland.* Berlin: Deutsche Islam Konferenz.

Bundesministerium des Innern. 2006. *Verfassungsschutzbericht 2006.* Berlin: Bundesministerium des Innern. www.verfassungsschutz.de.

————. 2008a. *Verfassungsschutzbericht 2008.* Berlin: Bundesministerium des Innern. www.verfassungsschutz.de.

————. 2008b. *Deutsche Islam Konferenz (DIK): Zwischen-Resümée der Arbeitsgruppen und des Gesprächskreises. Vorlage für die 3. Plenarsitzung der DIK.* 13 March. Berlin: Bundesministerium des Innern.

————.2009. *Deutsche Islam Konferenz (DIK): Zwischen-Resümée der Arbeitsgruppen und des Gesprächskreises. Vorlage für die 4. Plenarsitzung der DIK.* 25 June. Berlin: Bundesministerium des Innern.

Caeiro, Alexandre. 2010. "The Power of European Fatwas: The Minority Fiqh Project and the Making of an Islamic Counterpublic." *International Journal of Middle East Studies* 42, 435–449.

————. 2011. "Theorizing Islam without the State: Minority Fiqh in the West." Unpublished manuscript.

Caldwell, Christopher. 2009. *Reflections on the Revolution in Europe.* New York: Penguin.

Casanova, José. 1994. *Public Religion in the Modern World.* Chicago: University of Chicago Press.

Cesari, Jocelyne. 2004. *When Islam and Democracy Meet: Muslims in Europe and in the United States.* Basingstoke, UK: Palgrave.

————. 2005. "Mosques in French Cities: Towards the End of a Conflict?" *Journal of Ethnic and Migration Studies* 31(6), 1025–1043.

Chishti, Muzzafar A., Doris Meissner, Demetrios G. Papademetriou, Jay Peterzell, Michael J. Wishnie, and Stephen W. Yale-Loehr. 2003. *America's Challenge: Domestic Security, Civil Liberties, and National Unity after September 11.* Washington, DC: Migration Policy Institute. http://www.migrationpolicy.org /pubs/Americas_Challenges.pdf.

Cole, David. 2006. "Are We Safer?" *New York Review of Books,* 9 March, 36–39; also available at http://www.nybooks.com/articles/archives/2006/mar/09/are -we-safer/.

Conseil d'Etat. 2010. *Etude relative aux possibilités juridiques d'intervention du port du voile intégral.* 30 March. Available at the Web site of the Conseil d'Etat, www.conseil-etat.fr.

Council of the European Union. 2004. *Common Basic Principles for Immigrant Integration Policy in the European Union.* Brussels: Council of the European Union.

Crul, Maurice, and John Mollenkopf. 2012. "Challenges and Opportunities." In M. Crul and J. Mollenkopf, eds., *The Changing Face of World Cities: Young Adult Children of Immigrants in Europe and the United States.* New York: Russell Sage Foundation.

Danchin, Peter. 2011. "Islam in the Secular *Nomos* of the European Court of Human Rights." *Michigan Journal of International Law* 3, 663–747.

Dassetto, Felice, Silvio Ferrari, and Brigitte Maréchal. 2007. *Islam in the European Union.* Brussels: European Parliament. www.europarl.europa-eu/activities /expert/estudies.do?language=EN.

Davis, Derek H. 2004. "Reacting to France's Ban: Headscarves and Other Religious Attire in American Public Schools." *Journal of Church and State* 46(2), 221–235.

de Wall, Heinrich. 2008. "Verfassungsrechtliche Rahmenbedingungen eines islamischen Religionsunterrichts." In Bundesministerium des Innern (2008b), 19–27.

Drakulic, Slavenka. 1993. *The Balkan Express.* New York: Norton.

Dworkin, Ronald. 1984. "Rights as Trumps." Pp. 153–167 in Jeremy Waldron, ed., *Theories of Rights.* Oxford: Oxford University Press.

Eberle, Edward. 2004. "Free Exercise of Religion in Germany and the United States." *Tulane Law Review* 78, 1023–1087.

EKD [Zentralrat der Evangelischen Kirchen in Deutschland]. 2006. *Klarheit und gute Nachbarschaft: Christen und Muslime in Deutschland.* EKD-Texte no. 86. Hannover: EKD.

Ely, John Hart. 1980. *Democracy and Distrust.* Cambridge, MA: Harvard University Press.

Environics Research Group. 2007. "Muslims and Multiculturalism in Canada." Unpublished ms. in the authors' possession.

Esau, Alvin. 2008. "Living by Different Law: Pluralism, Freedom of Religion, and Illiberal Religious Groups." Pp. 110–139 in Richard Moon, ed., *Law and Religious Pluralism in Canada.* Vancouver: UBC Press.

Esposito, John. 2010. *The Future of Islam.* New York: Oxford University Press.

Evans, Carolyn. 2006. "The 'Islamic Scarf' in the European Court of Human Rights." *Melbourne Journal of International Law* 7(1), 52–73.

Fadel, Mohammad. 2008. "The True, the Good and the Reasonable: The Theological and Ethical Roots of Public Reason in Islamic Law." *Canadian Journal of Law and Jurisprudence* 21(1), 1–65.

Ferrari, Silvio. 2002. "Islam and the Western European Model of Church and State Relations." Pp. 6–19 in W. Shadid and P. van Koningsveld, eds., *Religious Freedom and the Neutrality of the State: The Position of Islam in the European Union*. Leuven: Peeters.

———. 2011. "The Christian Roots of the Secular State." Unpublished typescript.

Fetzer, Joel, and Christopher Soper. 2005. *Muslims and the State in Britain, France, and Germany*. New York: Cambridge University Press.

Finer, S. E. 2007. *The History of Government*, vol. 2. Oxford: Oxford University Press.

Foner, Nancy, and Richard Alba. 2008. "Immigrant Religion in the U.S. and Western Europe: Bridge or Barrier to Inclusion?" *International Migration Review* 42(2), 360–392.

Ford, Richard. 2011. *Headscarves, Hairstyles and Culture as a Civil Right: A Critique*. Paris: French-American Foundation and Sciences Po.

Fourest, Caroline. 2004. *Frère Tariq*. Paris: Grasset.

Fournier, Pascale. 2008. "In the (Canadian) Shadow of Islamic Law." Pp. 140–160 in Richard Moon, ed., *Law and Religious Pluralism in Canada*. Vancouver: UBC Press.

Garraud Rapport. 2010. *Rapport fait au nom de la commission des lois constitutionnelles, de la legislation et de l'administration générales de la République sur le projet de loi (no. 2520), interdisant la dissimulation du visage dans l'espace public*. Assemblée nationale. No. 2648. Paris, 23 June.

Gauchet, Marcel. 1985. *Le désenchantement du monde*. Paris: Gallimard.

German Parliament. 2006. *Stand der rechtlichen Gleichstellung des Islam in Deutschland*. Berlin: BT-Drucksache. No. 16/2085, 29 June.

Gibb, H. A. R. 1949. *Mohammedanism*. Oxford: Oxford University Press.

Goffman, Erving. 1963. *Stigma: Notes on the Management of Spoiled Identity*. New York: Simon and Schuster.

Goldberg, Michelle. 2006. *Kingdom Coming: The Rise of Christian Nationalism*. New York: Norton.

Goodin, Robert E., and Andrew Reeve. 1989. "Liberalism and Neutrality." In R. E. Goodin and A. Reeve, eds., *Liberal Neutrality*. New York: Routledge.

Grammond, Sébastien. 2009. "Conceptions Canadienne et Québécoise des droits fondamentaux et de la religion: Convergence ou conflit?" *Revue juridique Thémis* 43, 83–108.

Gray, John. 2000. *The Two Faces of Liberalism*. Cambridge: Polity.

Griffith, Sidney H. 2008. *The Church in the Shadow of the Mosque*. Princeton, NJ: Princeton University Press.

Gusy, Christoph. 2006. "Integration und Religion: Grundgesetz und Islam." Pp. 166–189 in Ulrike Davy and Albrecht Weber, eds., *Paradigmenwechsel in Einwanderungsfragen?* Baden-Baden: Nomos.

Gutmann, Amy. 2003. *Identity in Democracy*. Princeton, NJ: Princeton University Press.

Habermas, Jürgen. 1987. *Theory of Communicative Action,* vol. 2: *Lifeworld and System: A Critique of Functionalist Reason.* Trans. Thomas McCarthy. Boston: Beacon Press.

Habermas, Jürgen, and Jacques Derrida. 2005. "February 15, or, What Binds Europeans Together: Plea for a Common Foreign Policy, Beginning in Core Europe." Pp. 3–13 in Daniel Levy, Max Pensky, and John Torpey, eds., *Old Europe, New Europe, Core Europe: Transatlantic Relations after the Iraq War.* New York: Verso [originally in *Frankfurter Allgemeine Zeitung,* 31 May 2003].

Haut Conseil à l'Intégration. 2000. *L'Islam dans la république.* Paris.

Heilman, Samuel. 1995. "The Vision from the Madrasa and Bes Medrash: Some Parallels between Islam and Judaism." Pp. 71–95 in Martin E. Marty and R. Scott Appleby, eds., *Fundamentalisms Comprehended.* Chicago: University of Chicago Press.

Heinig, Hans Michael. 1999. "Zwischen Tradition und Transformation: Das deutsche Staatskirchenrecht auf der Schwelle zum Europäischen Religionsverfassungsrecht." *Zeitschrift für Evangelische Ethik* 43, 294–312.

———. 2008. "Ordnung der Freiheit—das Staatskirchenrecht vor neuen Herausforderungen." *Zeitschrift für evangelisches Kirchenrecht* 53, 235–254.

Heinig, Hans Michael, and Martin Morlok. 2003. "Von Schafen und Kopftüchern." *Juristenzeitung* (JZ) 15/16, 777–785.

Heinig, Hans Michael, and Christian Walter, eds. 2007. *Staatskirchenrecht oder Religionsverfassungsrecht?* Tübingen: Mohr Siebeck.

Hesse, Konrad. 1964–1965. "Freie Kirche im demokratischen Gemeinwesen." *Zeitschrift für evangelisches Kirchenrecht* 11, 337–362.

Hillgruber, Christian. 1999. "Der deutsche Kulturstaat und der muslimische Kulturimport." *Juristenzeitung* (JZ) 11, 538–547.

———. 2001. "Der Körperschaftsstatus von Religionsgemeinschaften." *Neue Zeitschrift für Verwaltungsrecht* (NVwZ), no. 12, 1347–1355.

———. 2007. "Der öffentlich-rechtliche Körperschaftsstatus nach Art. 137 Abs. 5 WRV. 213." In Heinig and Walter (2007), 213–227.

Hirschl, Ran. 2004. *Toward Juristocracy.* Cambridge, MA: Harvard University Press.

———. 2010. *Constitutional Theocracy.* Cambridge, MA: Harvard University Press.

Hofhansel, Claus. 2010. "Accommodating Islam and the Utility of National Models: The German Case." *West European Politics* 33(2), 191–207.

Human Rights Watch. 2002. "'We Are Not the Enemy': Hate Crimes against Arabs, Muslims, and Those Perceived to Be Arab or Muslim after September 11." *Human Rights Watch* 14(6) (November).

Huntington, Samuel P. 1996. *The Clash of Civilizations and the Remaking of World Order.* New York: Simon & Schuster.

Huster, Stefan. 1998. "Körperschaftsstatus unter Loyalitätsvorbehalt?" *Juristische Schulung* (JuS) no. 2, 117–121.

———. 2002. *Die ethische Neutralität des Staates.* Tübingen: Mohr.

———. 2007. "Die Bedeutung des Neutralitätsgebotes für die verfassungstheoretische und verfassungsrechtliche Einordnung des Religionsrechts." In Heinig and Walter (2007), 107–130.

International Crisis Group. 2006. *La France face à ses musulmans.* Europe Report no. 172, Brussels, 9 March.

———. 2007. *Islam and Identity in Germany.* Europe Report no. 181, Brussels, 14 March.

Janz, Norbert, and Sonja Rademacher. 1999. "Islam und Religionsfreiheit." *Neue Zeitschrift für Verwaltungsrecht* (NVwZ) no. 7, 706–713.

Jones, Peter. 2009. "Liberal Multiculturalism." Unpublished typescript.

Joppke, Christian. 2004. "The Retreat of Multiculturalism in the Liberal State: Theory and Policy." *British Journal of Sociology* 55(2), 237–257.

———. 2007a. "Beyond National Models: Civic Integration Policies for Immigrants in Western Europe." *West European Politics* 30(1), 1–22.

———. 2007b. "State Neutrality and Islamic Headscarf Laws in France and Germany." *Theory and Society* 36, 313–342.

———. 2009. *Veil: Mirror of Identity.* Cambridge: Polity.

———. 2010. *Citizenship and Immigration.* Cambridge: Polity.

———. 2013a. "A Christian Identity for the Liberal State?" *British Journal of Sociology* (forthcoming).

———. 2013b. "The Retreat Is Real—but What Is the Alternative? Multiculturalism and the Limits of 'Muscular Liberalism.'" *Constellations* (forthcoming).

Joppke, Christian, and John Torpey. 2006. "State Neutrality and Accommodating Islam in Western Europe and North America." Proposal submitted for funding to the Foundation for Population, Migration, and the Environment (Switzerland). Typescript in authors' possession.

Kandel, Johannes. 2004. "Organisierter Islam in Deutschland und gesellschaftliche Integration." *Politische Akademie der Friedrich Ebert Stiftung,* Berlin (September).

Kant, Immanuel. 1785. *Grundlegung zur Metaphysik der Sitten.* Bonn: Akademie-Ausgabe.

Kelek, Necla. 2008. *Die fremde Braut.* Köln: Kiepenheuer und Witsch.

Khan, Sheema. 2007. "The Ontario Sharia Debate: Transformational Accommodation, Multiculturalism, and Muslim Identity." Pp. 475–485 in Keith Banting, Thomas J. Courchene, and F. Leslie Seidle, eds., *Belonging? Diversity, Recognition, and Shared Citizenship in Canada.* Montreal: Institute for Research on Public Policy.

Kirchhof, Paul. 1994. "Die Kirchen und Religionsgemeinschaften als Körperschaften des öffentlichen Rechts." In Listl and Pirson (1994).

———. 2005. "Die Freiheit der Religionen und ihr unterschiedlicher Beitrag zu einem freien Gemeinwesen." *Essener Gespräche zum Thema Staat und Kirche,* vol. 39. Münster: Aschendorff Verlag.

Klausen, Jytte. 2005. *The Islamic Challenge.* New York: Oxford University Press.

Koenig, Matthias. 2007. "Europeanising the Governance of Religious Diversity." *Journal of Ethnic and Migration Studies* 33(6), 911–932.

———. 2010. "Gerichte als Arenen religiöser Anerkennungskämpfe." Pp. 144–164 in Astrid Reuter and Hans G. Kippenberg, eds., *Religionskonflikte im Verfassungsstaat.* Göttingen: Vandenhoeck & Ruprecht.

Koopmans, R., P. Statham, M. Giugni, and F. Passy. 2005. *Contested Citizenship*. Minneapolis: University of Minnesota Press.

Koopmans, Ruud, Ines Michalowski, and Stine Waibel. 2012. "Citizenship Rights for Immigrants: National Political Processes and Cross-National Convergence in Western Europe, 1980–2008." *American Journal of Sociology* 117(4), 1202–1245.

Korioth, Stefan. 1999. "Loyalität im Staatskirchenrecht?" Pp. 221–245 in W. Erbguth, F. Müller, V. Neumann, eds., *Rechtstheorie und Rechtsdogmatik im Austausch*. Berlin: Duncker und Humblot.

———. 2007. "Die Entwicklung des Staatskirchenrechts in Deutschland seit der Reformation." In Heinig and Walter (2007), 39–69.

Kukathas, Chandran (2004). "Theoretical Foundations of Multiculturalism." Unpublished typescript.

Kymlicka, Will. 1995. *Multicultural Citizenship: A Liberal Theory of Minority Rights*. Oxford: Oxford University Press.

———. 2005. "Testing the Bounds of Liberal Multiculturalism?" Paper presented to the CCMW conference on "Muslim Women's Equality Rights in the Justice System: Gender, Religion, and Pluralism," Toronto, April 9.

———. 2007. "Multicultural Odysseys." *Ethnopolitics* 6(4), 585–597.

———. 2010. "The Rise and Fall of Multiculturalism?" *International Social Science Journal* 199, 97–112.

Langenfeld, Christine. 2007. "Formale Treue zur Verfassung reicht nicht." *Frankfurter Allgemeine Zeitung*, 15 November.

Lapidus, Ira M. 1975. "The Separation of State and Religion in the Development of Early Islamic Society." *International Journal of Middle East Studies* 6, 363–385.

Laurence, Jonathan. 2010. "The French Debate on National Identity." Unpublished typescript.

———. 2012. *The Emancipation of Europe's Muslims*. Princeton, NJ: Princeton University Press.

Lavi, Shai. 2009. "Unequal Rites—Jews, Muslims and the History of Ritual Slaughter in Germany." *Tel Aviver Jahrbuch für deutsche Geschichte*, 164–184.

Leiken, Robert. 2011. *Europe's Angry Muslims*. New York: Oxford University Press.

Lemmen, Thomas. 2002. *Muslime in Deutschland*. Baden-Baden: Nomos.

Lepsius, Oliver. 2006. "Die Religionsfreiheit als Minderheitenrecht in Deutschland, Frankreich und den USA." *Leviathan* no. 3, 321–349.

Liedhegener, Antonius. 2008. "Religionsfreiheit und die neue Religionspolitik." *Zeitschrift für Politik* 55(1), 84–107.

Link, Christoph. 2002. "Der Einfluss christlicher Werte auf die deutsche Verfassungsordnung." *Akademie-Journal* 2, 58–61.

Lipset, Seymour Martin. 1990. *Continental Divide: The Values and Institutions of the United States and Canada*. New York: Routledge.

Listl, Joseph, and Dietrich Pirson, eds. 1994. *Handbuch des Staatskirchenrechts der Bundesrepublik Deutschland*. Berlin: Duncker und Humblot.

MacGarry, John, Brendan O'Leary, and Richard Simeon. 2008. "Integration or Accommodation?" Pp. 41–88 in Sujit Choudhry, ed., *Constitutional Design for Divided Societies*. Oxford: Oxford University Press.

Magen, Stefan. 2001. "Zum Verhältnis von Körperschaftsstatus und Religions-freiheit." *Neue Zeitschrift für Verwaltungsrecht* (NVwZ) no. 8, 888–891.

———. 2004. *Körperschaftsstatus und Religionsfreiheit.* Tübingen: Mohr Siebeck.

Mahmood, Saba. 2006. "Secularism, Hermeneutics, and Empire: The Politics of Islamic Reformation." *Public Culture* 18(2), 323–347.

———. 2009. "Religious Reason and Secular Affect: An Incommensurable Divide." *Critical Inquiry* 35, 836–862.

———. 2012. *Politics of Piety,* 2nd ed. Princeton, NJ: Princeton University Press.

Maier, Hans. 1994. "Staat und Kirche in der Bundesrepublik Deutschland." In Listl and Pirson (1994).

Makus, Ingrid. 2010. "Reasoning about 'Reasonable Accommodation': Charles Taylor on Negotiating Diversity in Canada and Quebec." Pp. 47–62 in Christian Lammert and Katja Sarkowsky, eds., *Travelling Concepts: Negotiating Diversity in Canada and Europe.* Wiesbaden: VS Verlag für Sozialwissenschaften.

Mancini, Susanna. 2010. "The Crucifix Rage." *European Constitutional Law Review* 6, 6–27.

March, Andrew F. 2007. "Islamic Foundations for a Social Contract in Non-Muslim Liberal Society." *American Political Science Review* 101(2), 235–252.

———. 2009. *Islam and Liberal Citizenship.* New York: Oxford University Press.

———. 2012. "Speech and the Sacred: Does the Defense of Free Speech Rest on a Mistake about Religion?" *Political Theory* 40(3), 319–346.

Martin, David. 2005. *On Secularization: Towards a Revised General Theory.* Burlington, VT: Ashgate.

Matyssek, Ulf. 2010. "Zum Problem der Trennung von Religion und Politik im Islam." In Stefan Muckel, ed., *Der Islam im öffentlichen Recht des säkularen Verfassungsstaates.* Berlin: Duncker und Humblot.

Michaels, Walter Benn. 2006. *The Trouble with Diversity.* New York: Holt.

Moghissi, Haideh, Saeed Rahnema, and Mark J. Goodman. 2009. *Diaspora by Design: Muslim Immigrants in Canada and Beyond.* Toronto: University of Toronto Press.

Mohr, Irka-Christin, and Michael Kiefer, eds. 2009. *Islamunterricht—Islamischer Religionsunterricht—Islamkunde.* Bielefeld: transcript Verlag.

Moller Okin, Susan. 1999. *Is Multiculturalism Bad for Women?* Princeton, NJ: Princeton University Press.

Moore, Kathleen M. 1995. *Al-Mughtaribūn: American Law and the Transformation of Muslim Life in the United States.* Albany, NY: SUNY Press.

Morlok, Martin. 2007. "Die korporative Religionsfreiheit und das Selbstbestimmungsrecht nach Art. 140GG/Art.137 Abs. 3 WRV einschliesslich ihrer Schranken." In Heinig and Walter (2007), 185–210.

Morlok, Martin, and Hans Michael Heinig. 1999. "Parität im Leistungsstaat—Körperschaftsstatus nur bei Staatsloyalität?" *Neue Zeitschrift für Verwaltungsrecht* 18(7), 697–705.

Muckel, Stefan. 1995. "Muslimische Gemeinschaften als Körperschaften des öffentlichen Rechts." *Die öffentliche Verwaltung* no. 8, 311–317.

———. 1999. "Religionsgesellschaften als Körperschaften des öffentlichen Rechts." *Der Staat* 38, 569–593.

———. 2001. "Körperschaftsrechte für die Zeugen Jehovas?" *Juristische Ausbildung* (JURA) no. 7, 456–462.

Nisbet, Erik C., and James Shanahan. 2004. "Restrictions on Civil Liberties, Views of Islam, & Muslim Americans." MSRG Special Report. Ithaca, NY: Cornell University Media and Society Research Group (December).

Noiriel, Gérard. 1996. *The French Melting Pot*. Minneapolis: University of Minnesota Press.

Norris, Pippa, and Ronald Inglehart. 2004. *Sacred and Secular*. New York: Cambridge University Press.

Nussbaum, Martha. 2008. *Liberty of Conscience*. New York: Basic Books.

———. 2012. *The New Religious Intolerance*. Cambridge, MA: Harvard University Press.

Oebbecke, Janbernd. 2008. "Der Islam und die Reform des Religionsverfassungsrechts." *Zeitschrift für Politik* 55(1), 49–63.

———. 2009. "Moscheebaukonflikte und der Beitrag des Rechts." In Deutsche Islamkonferenz, *Drei Jahre Deutsche Islamkonferenzen (DIK) 2006–2009*. www.deutsche-islam-konferenz.de.

Pagden, Anthony. 2008. *Worlds at War*. New York: Oxford University Press.

Panagopoulos, Costas. 2006. "The Polls: Trends—Arab and Muslim Americans and Islam in the Aftermath of 9/11." *Public Opinion Quarterly* 70(4), 608–624.

Parekh, Bhikhu. 2000. *Rethinking Multiculturalism*. Cambridge, MA: Harvard University Press.

Peters, Hans. 1954. "Die Gegenwartslage des Staatskirchenrechts." *Veröffentlichungen der Vereinigung der deutschen Staatsrechtslehrer* (VVDStRL) 11, 177–214.

Pirenne, Henri. 1970 [1939]. *Mahomet et Charlemagne*. Paris: Presses universitaires de France.

Pirson, Dietrich. 1994. "Die geschichtlichen Wurzeln des Verhältnisses von Staat und Kirche." In Listl and Pirson (1994).

Qaradawi, Yusuf al-. 1960. *The Lawful and Prohibited in Islam*. www.witness-pioneer.org/vil/Books/Q_LP/.

———. 1987. *Islamic Awakening between Rejection and Extremism*. Herndon, VA: International Institute of Islamic Thought.

———. 1998. *The Status of Women in Islam*. www.witness-pioneer.org/vil/Books/Q_WI/.

Quaritsch, Helmut. 1962. "Kirchen und Staat." *Der Staat* 1, 289–320.

Ramadan, Tariq. 2001. *Islam, the West and the Challenge of Modernity*. Leicester, UK: Islamic Foundation.

———. 2002a. *La foi, la voie et la résistance*. Lyon: Tawhid.

———. 2002b. *To Be a European Muslim*. Leicester, UK: Islamic Foundation.

———. 2004. *Western Muslims and the Future of Islam*. Oxford: Oxford University Press.

———. 2007. "Religious Allegiance and Shared Citizenship." Pp. 451–464 in Keith Banting, Thomas J. Courchene, and F. Leslie Seidle, eds., *Belonging? Diversity, Recognition, and Shared Citizenship in Canada*. Montreal: Institute for Research on Public Policy.

————. 2009. *Radical Reform*. Oxford: Oxford University Press.

Rawls, John. 1993. *Political Liberalism*. New York: Columbia University Press.

Reitz, Jeffrey G., Rupa Banerjee, Mai Phan, and Jordan Thompson. 2009. "Race, Religion, and the Social Integration of New Immigrant Minorities in Canada." *International Migration Review* 43(4), 695–726.

Resnick, Philip. 2005. *The European Roots of Canadian Identity*. Peterborough, ON: Broadview Press.

Reuter, Astrid. 2007. "Säkularität und Religionsfreiheit—ein doppeltes Dilemma." *Leviathan* no. 2, 178–192.

Roy, Oliver. 2004. *L'Islam mondialisé*. Paris: Seuil.

————. 2008. *La sainte ignorance*. Paris: Seuil.

Saggar, Shamit. 2010. "Boomerangs and Slingshots: Radical Islamism and Counter-Terrorism Strategy." Pp. 28–49 in Erik Bleich, ed., *Muslims and the State in the Post-9/11 West*. New York: Routledge.

Sahlins, Peter. 1989. *Boundaries: The Making of France and Spain in the Pyrenees*. Berkeley: University of California Press.

Sarkozy, Nicolas. 2004. *La République, les religions, l'espérance*. Paris: Cerf.

Sartori, Giovanni. 2000. *Pluralismo, multiculturalismo e estranei*. Milano: Rizzoli.

Sauvé, Jean-Marc. 2009. "Dignité humaine et juge administrative." 27 November. Available at the Web site of the Conseil d'Etat, www.conseil/etat.fr.

Scheffler, Samuel. 2007. "Immigration and the Significance of Culture." *Philosophy and Public Affairs* 35(2), 93–125.

Schiffauer, Werner. 2010. *Nach dem Islamismus: Die Islamische Gemeinschaft Milli Görüs*. Frankfurt am Main: Suhrkamp.

Schlaich, Klaus. 1972. *Neutralität als verfassungsrechtliches Prinzip*. Tübingen: Mohr Siebeck.

Scott, Joan W. 2007. *The Politics of the Veil*. Princeton, NJ: Princeton University Press.

Shachar, Ayelet. 2001. *Multicultural Jurisdictions*. New York: Cambridge University Press.

————. 2008. "Privatizing Diversity: A Cautionary Tale from Religious Arbitration in Family Law." *Theoretical Inquiries in Law* 9(2), 573–607.

Shapiro, Martin, and Alec Stone Sweet. 2002. *On Law, Politics, and Judicialization*. New York: Oxford University Press.

Skrentny, John D. 2002. *The Minority Rights Revolution*. Cambridge, MA: Belknap Press of Harvard University Press.

Smend, Rudolf. 1951. "Staat und Kirche nach dem Bonner Grundgesetz." *Zeitschrift für evangelisches Kirchenrecht* 1, 4–14.

Smith, Jane. 2009. "Islam in America." Pp. 28–42 in Jocelyne Cesari, ed., *Muslims in the West after 9/11*. London: Routledge.

Spinner-Halev, Jeff. 2008. "Liberalism and Religion: Against Congruence." *Theoretical Inquiries in Law* 9(2), 553–572.

Statham, Paul, R. Koopmans, M. Giugni, and F. Passy. 2005. "Resilient or Adaptable Islam?" *Ethnicities* 5(4), 427–459.

Stein, Janice Gross. 2006. "Living Better Multiculturally: In Canada We Seem to Get the Multi Part, but How about the Culture?" *Literary Review of Canada*, September, 3–5.

Stepan, Alfred. 2000. "Religion, Democracy, and the 'Twin Tolerations.'" *Journal of Democracy* 11(4), 37–57.

Stock, Martin. 2004. "Einige Schwierigkeiten mit islamischem Religionsunterricht." *Neue Zeitschrift für Verwaltungsrecht* no. 12, 1399–1405.

———. 2005. "Islamunterricht in öffentlichen Schulen in Nordrhein-Westfalen." *Nordrhein-Westfälische Verwaltungsblätter* 8, 285–292.

Stolzenberg, Nomi. 1993. "'He Drew a Circle That Shut Me Out': Assimilation, Indoctrination, and the Paradox of a Liberal Education." *Harvard Law Review* 106(3), 581–667.

Stone Sweet, Alec. 2000. *Governing with Judges.* New York: Oxford University Press.

Sullivan, Winnifred Fallers. 2006. *The Impossibility of Religious Freedom.* Princeton, NJ: Princeton University Press.

Taylor, Charles. 1992. *Multiculturalism and the "Politics of Recognition."* Princeton, NJ: Princeton University Press.

Tebble, Adam. 2006. "Exclusion for Democracy." *Political Theory* 34(4), 43–87.

Thüsing, Gregor. 1998. "Kirchenautonomie und Staatsloyalität." *Die öffentliche Verwaltung* no. 1, 25–29.

Tibi, Bassam. 2006. "Europeanizing Islam or the Islamization of Europe: Political Democracy vs. Cultural Difference." Pp. 204–224 in Timothy A. Byrnes and Peter J. Katzenstein, eds., *Religion in an Expanding Europe.* New York: Cambridge University Press.

———. 2009a. *Euro-Islam.* Darmstadt: Wissenschaftliche Buchgesellschaft.

———. 2009b. *Islam's Predicament with Modernity.* London: Routledge.

Tillmanns, Reiner. 1999. "Zur Verleihung des Körperschaftsstatus an Religionsgemeinschaften." *Die öffentliche Verwaltung* 52(11), 441–452.

Tocqueville, Alexis de. 1969. *Democracy in America.* Ed. J. P. Mayer and trans. George Lawrence. Garden City, NY: Anchor Books.

Torpey, John. 2010. "A (Post-)Secular Age? Religion and the Two Exceptionalisms." *Social Research* 77(1), 269–296.

Uhle, Arnd. 2007. "Die Integration des Islam in das Staatskirchenrecht der Gegenwart." In Heinig and Walter (2007), 299–338.

Veil Committee. 2008. *Comité de reflexion sur le préamble de la Constitution: Rapport au Président de la République.* Paris, December.

Vertovec, Steven, and Susanne Wessendorf, eds. 2009. *The Multiculturalism Backlash.* London: Routledge.

Waldron, Jeremy. 1989. "Legislation and Moral Neutrality." In Robert E. Goodin and Andrew Reeve, eds., *Liberal Neutrality.* New York: Routledge.

Walter, Christian. 2005. "Die Rahmenbedingungen für die Kooperation von religiösen Vereinigungen und Staat unter dem Grundgesetz." Pp. 34–40 in Beauftragte der Bundesregierung für Migration, Flüchtlinge und Integration, ed., *Islam einbürgern—Auf dem Weg zur Anerkennung muslimischer Vertretungen in Deutschland.* Berlin (November).

———. 2006. *Religionsverfassungsrecht.* Tübingen: Mohr Siebeck.

———. 2007. "Einleitung." In Heinig and Walter (2007), 1–4.

Walzer, Michael. 1984. "Liberalism and the Art of Separation." *Political Theory* 12(3), 315–330.

Weber, Hermann. 1989. "Die Verleihung der Körperschaftsrechte an Religionsge-meinschaften." *Zeitschrift für evangelisches Kirchenrecht* 34, 337–382.

Weiler, Joseph. 2007. "A Christian Europe?" *European View* 6, 143–150.

Weinrib, Lorraine. 2008. "Ontario's Sharia Law Debate: Law and Politics under the Charter." Pp. 239–263 in Richard Moon, ed., *Law and Religious Plural-ism in Canada.* Vancouver: UBC Press.

Wheatcroft, Andrew. 2003. *Infidels: The Conflict between Christendom and Islam, 638–2002.* New York: Viking.

Whitman, James Q. 2008. "Separating Church and State: The Atlantic Divide." *Historical Reflections* 34(3), 86–104.

Willems, Ulrich. 2008. "Reformbedarf und Reformfähigkeit der Religionspolitik in Deutschland." *Zeitschrift für Politik* 55(1), 64–83.

Witte, John, Jr. 2005. *Religion and the American Constitutional Experiment,* 2nd ed. Boulder, CO: Westview Press.

Yazbeck Haddad, Yvonne, and Tyler Golson. 2007. "Overhauling Islam." *Journal of Church and State* 49(3), 487–515.

Young, Iris Marion. 1990. *Justice and the Politics of Difference.* Princeton, NJ: Princeton University Press.

Zolberg, Aristide, and Long Litt Woon. 1999. "Why Islam Is Like Spanish." *Politics and Society* 27(1), 5–38.

Acknowledgments

We wish to thank the Swiss Foundation for Population, Migration, and the Environment for generously funding this project over a five-year period (three more years than originally planned) and for its patience with our repeated delays and requests for extension. Without the Foundation's support, this book would not have been written.

In addition, we would like to thank a number of people who were helpful, sometimes crucial for getting the work done. Christian Joppke acknowledges diligent assistance by Leyla Arslan in the early phase of this project. John Torpey expresses his appreciation to a series of outstanding graduate student research assistants who have done much of the legwork for the research on the North American chapters: John Boy, Loren Peabody, and Mitra Rastegar. Their own work in comparative historical sociology will soon make its mark on the field. He also thanks Bob Ratner for taking the time to read and comment—helpfully, as always—on the North American chapters.

Index